DE GAULLE AND THE FRENCH ARMY

DE GAULLE
AND THE
FRENCH ARMY

A Crisis in Civil-Military
Relations

BY EDGAR S. FURNISS, JR.

THE TWENTIETH CENTURY FUND

NEW YORK · 1964

FOREWORD

In this volume Professor Edgar S. Furniss, Jr., writing as a political scientist, inquires into French political and military behavior during and after the Algerian war, when the Fifth Republic was rocked by a clash between determined army officers and an equally determined President. It is Professor Furniss' thesis that the challenge posed by the military to President de Gaulle's political authority explains in large part the present domestic and foreign policy of the Fifth Republic.

Both in conception and in the degree to which personal judgments are expressed, this book is a more highly individual work than most books issued by the Twentieth Century Fund. It is at the same time an extension of the Fund's efforts to stimulate civil-military studies. Through such studies the Fund has sought to explore the sharing and shifting of responsibility for policy-making. To do so has seemed important in an international atmosphere made turbulent by man's precarious control over destructive weapons and by the headlong rush of new nations to sovereignty.

Mr. Furniss, a specialist in international politics and French affairs, is Mershon Professor of Political Science at Ohio State University and Director, Social Science Program of the Mershon Center for Education in National Security. The Twentieth Century Fund hopes that his book will bring new insight into a dramatic and historic confrontation.

AUGUST HECKSCHER, *Director*
The Twentieth Century Fund

41 East 70th Street, New York
December 1963

ACKNOWLEDGMENTS

De Gaulle and the French Army represents part of the author's continuing study of both French affairs and civil-military relations. Special thanks are due to August Heckscher, Director of the Twentieth Century Fund, for inviting me to submit a project for the Fund's consideration. My thanks also to the Trustees of the Fund for providing the generous assistance which enabled me to undertake the study. Included in the support were funds for an exploratory trip to France and Great Britain during the Fall of 1962.

While absolving them of any responsibility for opinions with which they would not agree or factual errors they would not have made, I should like to single out for special mention from the many French, English, and Americans with whom I talked General Pierre-M. Gallois, Jacques Vernant, and Richard B. Finn. Himself a vigorous, articulate defender of France's nuclear program, General Gallois is always prepared to discuss patiently the pros and cons of conflicting strategies and conflicting national policies. M. Vernant, Secretary General of the Center for Foreign Policy Studies, was kind enough to arrange a special meeting of members of the Center so that we might exchange views on President de Gaulle's plans for military modernization. Mr. Finn, first secretary of the American Embassy in Paris, went far beyond the dictates of duty, or courtesy to a fellow American, in helping me to obtain information and to talk with French officials.

I am grateful to Princeton University for giving me an academic year's leave of absence so that I might work on the project underwritten by the Twentieth Century Fund. The Ohio State University, particularly Lawrence J. R. Herson, Chairman of the Political Science Department, and Robert J. Nordstrom, Secretary of the Mershon Committee on Education in National Security, were most understanding in their willingness to delay for one year my appointment to their sections of the University. Ben Moore, Associate Director of the Twentieth Century Fund, devoted particular attention to my project and was helpful to me throughout. Members of the Fund's editorial staff perused my manuscript with great care and made many suggestions for its improvement. In fact, I regard the Twentieth Century Fund as the ideal employer. It has been a great pleasure, as well as intellectually rewarding, to work for the Fund.

Except where otherwise indicated, I am responsible for the translations in this book. In order to intrude as little as possible between the reader and the original material, I have deliberately chosen close renditions, even at the occasional loss of stylistic phraseology.

Although only one name appears as author, this was a joint effort. It would not have been completed, or had whatever merit it may possess, were it not for my research assistant–imaginative editor–executive secretary–indefatigable typist–wife. To Norman and Jean Furniss, our children, I dedicate this volume.

EDGAR S. FURNISS, JR.
Columbus, Ohio

CONTENTS

INTRODUCTION: *The Theme Stated*

*When all these varied modes of military intervention in politics
are examined and the "levels" to which the military press such
intervention are recognized, the phenomenon appears in its
true light — distinctive, persistent and widespread. — S. E. Finer*

THE AUTHOR'S purpose is to investigate the most recent crisis in
French civil-military relations, a crisis which arose when the army
discovered President Charles de Gaulle's intentions concerning Algeria.
The actions taken by professional officers[1] to turn De Gaulle from his
design for peace represented nothing less than an attempt to restructure
French society and French political institutions. The nature of these
actions and their effect on the army itself are examined in the first part
of this study. The challenge to himself and his regime forced De Gaulle
to exceptional measures. Throughout the crisis, however, his goal was
not simply the negative one of removing the threat: he sought — and
still seeks — to fashion the army into an effective instrument for his
statecraft. Presented in contrast to the objectives of rebellious officers,
De Gaulle's policies are the subject of the second part of this study.

Much more was involved in the French army's challenge to the Fifth
Republic than forceful expression of political preferences. By seeking
to impose on constitutional authorities a decision as to what France

---

[1] No more than anyone categorizing attitudes of a complex system does the
author seek to imply that *all* officers or even all high-ranking officers held identical
views. To the contrary, the extent to which the myth of "unity of the army," enlisted
against De Gaulle's Algerian policy, helped to produce fragmentations in the military hierarchy is explored in detail (Chapter 4).

should do with almost all its military force — specifically, to continue indefinitely the envelopment of Algeria — the army sought, in effect, to define the type of political system for the country, to revise its social and economic foundations, and to regulate its foreign relations. Defiant military leaders and their civilian supporters proclaimed and believed that their objective was legitimate. Only when the threat had progressed to its logical extreme of attempted assassination of the man who dominated the political structure did increasing numbers of officers, still without expressing any sense of outrage or humiliation over past military behavior, begin to accept as inevitable the end of an era for their foreign-based army and for France.

Following immediately on the debacle of 1940 and the rescue of France by the Anglo-American invasion force, protracted colonial combat served to reinforce traditional military views as to the decadence of the would-be peaceful society which had been left behind. This sense of alienation was particularly dangerous because of other ideas which accompanied it. The army believed it epitomized the best national virtues. It simultaneously believed that it represented the nation. It came to believe its colonial mission was vital. It accepted the proposition that military failures were the consequence of political and social defects. Therefore the army was driven to the conclusion that French society must be reshaped.

Motivation became action when the French army discovered "revolutionary war." Its theoreticians taught that tactics supposedly employed by Communist subversives could be used by the army against the "subversives" in Algeria, the rebelling FLN (Front de la Libération Nationale). However, as De Gaulle, after 1958, began his maneuvers to extricate the army from Algeria, techniques formulated to fight a revolutionary war in Algeria were gradually redirected from the external enemy to De Gaulle's French state itself. Basic to ideological teachings borrowed in corrupted form from such Communist practitioners as Mao Tse-tung was the notion that the prerequisite to successful destruction of the political system was entrenchment of the revolutionaries inside social groupings at various levels throughout the target country. No more appealing message could have been found for an army already feeling that social reformation under its guidance was the indispensable prelude to the vital task of national purification. Consequently, officers, whether or not they were convinced by the distorted, misapplied jumble of notions concerning "revolutionary war," went forth to challenge De Gaulle on the social as well as on the political plane.

Not that the political challenge was subsidiary or minimal. To the contrary, military involvement in the political process was deep and pervasive. In terms of directing personnel, the objective of most antagonists to De Gaulle was not necessarily a military or militarized state. But no trace of mitigating self-denial is to be found in this. The army wanted something more real than uniformed political leaders; it had, after all, imposed one general on France in May 1958, only to regret the consequences. What the army wanted was a policy, one simple, over-riding policy: ratification of its political-social-economic-psychological-military mission, to be pursued for an indefinite period, perhaps forever, in Algeria. To that end, officers involved the army in all parts of the policy-making process, in all ranges of force, from suggestion to overt revolt, with all sorts of civilian sympathizers, from deputies to bomb-throwing thugs. It is difficult to imagine a more thoroughly politicalized army, even though military activists, as in most insurrectionary movements, comprised a minority of the total officer corps. Even those officers who chose to remain technically within the bounds of legality did not hesitate to invoke explicitly the "unity of the army" in support of their more extremist compatriots. In their sanctimonious utterances the phrase itself became a weapon against De Gaulle. Because its challenge was not successful — although the margin was far closer than the Fifth Republic would care to acknowledge — the army tore itself to pieces in the name of unity.

"Joy through Strength" was De Gaulle's answer for himself and for his Republic. But it was not the only or exclusive answer. If De Gaulle became an obsession with the army, the President could not and did not preoccupy himself solely with the army. Nor did he, any more than others, predict all the forms military action would take. Some of his policies, therefore, may be viewed as improvisations and as extensions of initial responses, just as had been the case in many of his moves in Algeria. Military and civilian offenders, for example, were brought into a variety of courts, while De Gaulle searched, unsuccessfully, for one tribunal which would do what he wanted: exact retribution while denying defendants an opportunity to appeal to potential supporters over the President's head. The experience of Gaullists, including that with the highest French administrative tribunal, the Conseil d'Etat, ultimately impressed them with the desirability of creating one permanent court to try offenders who, in their opinion, represented a threat to the state. Thereby the authoritarian political system hoped to enlist the judicial arm in controlling antagonistic social groups.

Efforts to rehabilitate the rebellious army within French society illustrate a different pattern of Gaullist behavior. The army, as explained, posed a social challenge and was anxious to expound its views from judicial rostrums. That challenge could not be ignored. Furthermore, the end of the Algerian war returned the army to France, providing the first opportunity since 1939 to plan its place in French society. De Gaulle, however, did not meet the problem head on. Instead, he accepted the historically enshrined mystique of the Nation in Arms, in the form of a policy of continued universality of military service. This despite the incompatibility of such a conception with the post-Algerian situation of France, and the economic as well as military goals pursued by Gaullist leadership. Under auspices of the political leadership it so despised, the army was awarded the very place in society it had desired: maturing agent for the nation's young men.

In respect to military equipment and prescribed missions, Americans may well underestimate the extent to which presidential predispositions were reinforced by the urgency of inducing professional officers to accept, finally, the Fifth Republic. On many occasions De Gaulle and his subordinates told military commanders, in effect: "The Fifth Republic will provide you with an array of new weapons. Included in the national arsenal will be the most powerful of all, a nuclear striking force. Growing in both strength and size, this force will return France to its former rank as great power. The purposes for which this modern armament is being fabricated are therefore those suitable to France's impressive status. Forget the colonial past. Forget Algeria, where, by the way, you fought well and succeeded in dominating the field of battle. You can take pride in the parts you are called upon to play and in the accoutrements given you to play with. You can take pride in the country whose standing among the nations of the world you will do so much to re-establish and maintain."

Discussion of the interplay of civil-military relations in France provoked by the Algerian war would be incomplete if it ended with De Gaulle's actions to restore civilian authority over the army. Notwithstanding improvisations and inconsistencies, those actions fitted the larger perspectives of a remarkable political leader. Remarkable for the intensity of his reflection on himself, his country, and the West. Remarkable also for the persistence of purpose with which he bound the three together. Remarkable, finally, not for the sense of power which possessed him as it possesses other national leaders, but for the intimate connection he managed to maintain between goals established by his reflections and policies made possible by his successful pursuit of power. For all that commentators have seized on statements in which De Gaulle professed to see the President of the Fifth Republic as a sort of national arbiter weighing conflicting forces, surely that was a role being conceived for succeeding (lesser) figures. Little evidence exists that De Gaulle has envisaged himself as merely the helpless prisoner of events, the balancer of forces unleashed by others. When he has spoken of "living in our own time," he has meant a realistic appraisal of existing circumstance so that positive action by a "guide" might carry maximum impact in shaping men and events. No more, so Gaullist philosophy runs, the fitful spasms of strength born of the fretful weakness of the Fourth Republic. Purpose derived from clear vision must be welded to the strength created by undiluted authority so that the former might transcend even as it augmented the latter. Statecraft justified a concentration of executive power; a statesman by definition made more effective use of means at his disposal than did ordinary leaders and as a consequence increased their effectiveness.

The military-inspired threat to himself and his regime endangered De Gaulle's foreign strategy. He did not simply seek to reduce or remove that threat so that he might get on with the task he had marked out for himself. Making virtue of necessity, as he had in Algeria, the President determined to develop an army which would enhance the fortunes of France and the West as he saw them. He would do more than give the fractious child a shiny toy to keep it quiet. De Gaulle wanted — and expected — the quieted child to behave and use its toy in a certain way — De Gaulle's way. A prime example of the positive quality of negative thinking was the President's reaction to the Anglo-American "offer" of Polaris missiles made at Nassau in December 1962. Acceptance would have all but destroyed the interest De Gaulle was attempting to implant in the military for France's own *force de frappe*. But the judgment was not confined to such narrow grounds. Whether correctly or not, the President's reaction also encompassed his interpretation of Britain's and America's view of Western Europe, which in turn led to a resolve to use the opportunity for advancing the type of Western Europe deemed realistically attainable and best adapted to French interests as De Gaulle defined them.

The reader will find this a personal book: about people, their actions and their judgments, as well as about events. Military challengers were real officers, who did not hesitate to speak their minds. While De Gaulle's policies were at times deliberately ambiguous, his character and the nature of his regime made those policies also highly personal. Finally, the author has introduced, where appropriate, his own judgments as to the meaning and probable direction of events. Conclusions of three types have emerged.

One concerns the comparative study of political systems. Attempts to classify governments under such rubrics as totalitarian, authoritarian, one-party; democratic, Western; developing, emerging, neo-colonial do not advance knowledge; they stifle thought. Just as beauty is in the eye of the beholder, so is assignment to one category or another in the mind of the analyst. The label may be appropriate by definition; it may fit the example chosen ideally, and all others partially or not at all. In either event — refined or gross — the compartments can inhibit comparison even as their builders strain for real-life institutions to accord with their theoretical constructs. Where would France belong? One must ponder the darkness of pigeonholes before one answers, "in none and in all." The struggle between the French civilian government and the country's army revealed organizational structures and behavior by organized groups supposed to typify totalitarian, authoritarian, democratic, and emergent systems. Unique, the struggle had counterparts the world over. It is the unique-similar circumstances elsewhere which warrant study if one would understand the nature and direction of political processes.

The United States included, of course. Americans have pored over modern American civil-military relations with a microscope, not infrequently overlooking lessons that the experiences of other countries have to teach. In recognizing De Gaulle's close call with the French army, certain implications emerge. Let us not be too smug in assuming that the problem he confronted concerned him, his country, his era alone. No less, perhaps even more thoroughly, than France, the United States is entangled in the same double dilemma. One characteristic of the post-postwar international environment is a reduced ability of any one country to manipulate alone the outside environment to its own benefit. Another is the complexity relative to the past of the techniques required if any country is to manipulate successfully even a little bit. Against these characteristics belief persists on the part of military establishments that constraints are the "fault" of inadequate or corrupt politicians, that triumphs in foreign affairs require only inflexible will and simple, direct policies. Powerful military spokesmen, strong civilian supporters of this "Win or Lose" alternative exist in the United States and other Western countries, as well as in France.

The other part of the dilemma is also relevant to the United States. The fact that for the first time some states hold the capacity to exterminate millions of human beings in minutes makes the implacable international environment an extremely perilous one. Not national security, but national existence becomes the stake. Clearly, all national leaders must contemplate all measures which might enlarge the area of safety in such a precarious world. Yet in Western countries, including the United States, Great Britain, and France, many of the policies chosen to improve the chances for survival would in the process erode the very values for which national societies seek protection. Those willing to pay the internal price, whatever it may be, for external safety are not limited to France. Nor are French political leaders the only ones encountering difficulty in preserving even a partially "open" society from its domestic enemies.

A third set of related conclusions concerns the nature of American foreign policy toward France. Much of that policy since World War II seems to have been based on the assumption that controversy arising between the two countries was the result of temporary irrationality of French officials. Soon, we thought, there would arise in France a leader who would see things our way; then the misunderstandings would disappear. The wish being father to the thought, the United States welcomed to power "just the right man" — again and again and again. *Vide* Queuille, Pinay, Mendès-France, De Gaulle, to name but a few who, American leaders hoped, would "save" France by turning the country into a loyal supporter of American foreign policy.

Repeatedly the United States has been disappointed; either the right man departed the scene all too quickly or he showed a stubborn tendency to pursue the same policies that had led his predecessors into difficulties with Washington. The wide fluctuations in expectations concerning French official behavior have led to American policies tinged with impatience. We have not spent enough time considering the possibility that the foundations of some of our own policies are defective. There is a lag in American realization that the United States can no longer control to the same extent as just after World War II the actions of many other countries, including France. Because we prize predictability in the international environment, we are apt to espouse authoritarian political systems among our allies, without stopping to consider either the wishes of the people concerned or the greater power such a system may place behind policies we oppose.

There is little evidence that American policy makers have often considered the possibility that French predictions concerning future international configurations may be more accurate than their own. The result is that they have ignored the continuity of French policy and have instead acted in the erroneous belief that gestures toward satisfying what are regarded as temporary, irrational grievances are all that are necessary to effect a radical transformation in the statecraft of our ally. Even as American policy makers fail to give sufficient credit to French conceptions, they are prepared to contemplate too many concessions to some individual French demands. A case in point is American policy regarding nuclear military assistance, if, indeed, "on again off again gone again Finnegan" deserves to be called policy. The author has not hidden from the reader his conclusion that capitulation, even compromise, on this issue, is hopeless, since it would merely encourage contemporary French leadership to believe that continued intransigence will effect a radical transformation in *American* statecraft. The author cannot regard as anything but irresponsibly reckless a shift in official American policy which, by providing assistance either to a French or to a European-controlled nuclear force, would inevitably add to the pressures for proliferation of nuclear weapons.

PART ONE

The Political Challenge of the French Army

THE NATION

IN THE

ARMY'S SERVICE

It is necessary to offer [the army] an exalting task of education: the renaissance of the public spirit. — General Jean Valluy

THE POLITICAL challenge to President Charles de Gaulle by sections of the French army stemmed directly from the nature of the relationship between the army and the people of metropolitan (continental) France. That relationship has frequently been described as "alienation" of the military from civilian society, but the term is misleading. Even though physically separated by the series of colonial wars and disgusted by what it understood to be predominant civilian attitudes, the professional military corps did not for the most part regard itself as permanently apart, distinct, or *alien* to the social body of France. Rather were its most active elements ready, indeed eager, to re-unite the army with the Nation, whose highest virtues the army claimed to embody.

Discussions of the relations between the two abstractions *Armée-*

Nation have, of course, been going on for centuries.[1] Often at cross purposes, usually didactic, not infrequently sulphurous, this self-conscious dialogue between the people of France and their presumed protector was abruptly broken off by the circumstances of World War II, only to be resumed in 1944. Events during the four-year hiatus provided new and dangerous breeding grounds for animosity. The shockingly swift capitulation of France to the German invader led to searches for scapegoats, military and political. The defeat cut directly through the professional army and through the mind and heart of many an officer. While one segment of the army heeded De Gaulle's call to continue the struggle outside France, another segment was demobilized, or was bolstering the Nazi satellite, Vichy. Because the Allies succeeded in liberating France and winning the war by invasion of the continent, two circumstances of wartime experience assumed crucial importance for postwar relations between the military hierarchy and French society. One was the French army's colonial base and its accompanying dependence on the United States for military equipment and transport. The other was the failure to re-create a "national" army during the last stages of the war.

De Gaulle's Free French Movement built its military arm on and from a French colonial foundation, drawing to it disparate remnants of professional cadres. It was, then, the *colonial* nature of the liberating force that was salient. Without the African territories to provide a staging area and manpower, not only would the Anglo-American task of re-conquering Western Europe have been more difficult, but the French contribution to self-liberation from German rule — small as it was — would have been scarcely perceptible. Geography, manpower, and the "revolting" professional cadres (their defiance of Vichy pretenses to "legitimacy" is important, as will be related later) in turn

---

[1] For historical aspects, see especially Richard D. Challener, *The French Theory of the Nation in Arms*, New York, Columbia University Press, 1955; Raoul Girardet, *La société militaire dans la France contemporaine*, Paris, Plon, 1953; Philip C. Bankwitz, "Maxime Weygand and the Army-Nation Concept in the Modern French Army," *French Historical Studies*, Vol. II, No. 2, Fall 1961, pp. 157–189.

provided the basis for French claims to Allied matériel. De Gaulle's
followers had no weapons of their own, no supply services of their own,
few communications systems of their own. Acquisition of these indispensable ingredients of a national fighting force was claimed as a
matter of right by the self-styled leader of all the French. But there
was never enough matériel forthcoming. The British themselves were
short. Against their own estimated needs in an enterprise of unprecedented magnitude, Anglo-American leaders were never completely
convinced that it accorded with military efficiency and political wisdom
to give De Gaulle all he wanted. When liberation of France took place,
therefore, the politico-military problem confronting Gaullist leadership
was to close the gap between the colonial army and the French people
and to free the resurrected military establishment from alien, Anglo-
Saxon control. Failure to solve the first part of the problem led directly
to the struggle between postwar military leadership and President de
Gaulle on how to solve the second.

The resistance of the French people themselves was formally embodied in the FFI (French Forces of the Interior). If there were to be
a reborn *national* army, there had to be an amalgamation between the
professionalized, foreign equipped, colonially supported, external military apparatus and the amateurish, poorly supplied, unhierarchical, indigenous FFI. No one saw this better than Marshal de Lattre de
Tassigny, who escaped from a French prison in 1943 to lead the
French First Army from North Africa to Bavaria. He began his work of
unification in North Africa, with some 20,000 soldiers who had escaped
France. When the First Army paused before Alsace after its drive from
the south, he used the time to renew his efforts. "I would have liked to
have been able to put more color and warmth into this account," De
Lattre wrote later, "for it is impossible to imagine anything more animated or more colorful than the big and thrilling effort to win over
the completely vibrant and tumultuous [Resistance] force without dis-
torting it, and to lead it — with insignificant means — to transcend itself
without losing itself. It was a battle. A battle against routine, prejudice
and intransigence. A battle against shortage, anarchy and complaisance

... It was a matter of the future of our army and its unity — even more of the future of the relations between our army and the nation."[2]

De Lattre added, "it was a victory," but in truth his efforts, and those of a few others, such as Generals Leclerc and De Larminat, were, in the last analysis, failures. Although Leclerc brought no fewer than 137,000 of the FFI into his First Army,[3] he and his fellow officers could not create a new, revitalized French army. In their path stood material and psychological factors too serious to overcome. Leaders of the FFI lacked the proper credentials to be accepted by the career corps as potential senior officers. They had failed to serve the requisite time in all the grades; nor had they graduated from Saint-Cyr, or even from the Ecole Polytechnique. The type of combat they had been engaged in had not been "modern," with tanks, bombers, and the rest. Had it indeed, classically trained officers might wonder, been combat at all? Was it not, rather, undercover threats to the established order, useful perhaps when directed against the Germans, but in the nature of things also destructive of French social and economic cohesion? Was the motivation of the FFI, its inspiriting force, not predominantly ideological instead of professional, and tainted with a subversive foreign ideology at that?[4] Would not any success in bringing the external, professional army closer to the militarized section of the Resistance be heavily paid for in cancerous centers within the military establishment? Even in the euphoric flush of liberation, regular officers might be excused shudders of horror at the thought of incorporating unbroken cadres of FFI units.

The problem thus concerned, not just the fighting quality of the army, but, more fundamentally, its nature as a social system. Wholesale incorporation of the FFI would flood the officer corps with representa-

[2] Marshal de Lattre de Tassigny, *The History of the French First Army,* translated by Michael Barnes, London, George Allen and Unwin, 1952, pp. 179, 171.

[3] *Ibid.,* p. 173.

[4] Later, in Indochina, French officers learned the value of subversive war and in applying what they understood to be its principles, invoked the experience of the Resistance. See Chapter 2. In the concluding stages of World War II, however, memories were still fresh of French Communist opposition to the war until the Soviet Union itself was engaged, at which point Communist cadres began their increasingly effective role in the Resistance.

tives of classes toward which it had traditionally been most antagonistic. On the other hand, it could hardly go to the other extreme and seek support from the "best people," the civilian circles that had welcomed the armistice, Pétain, even the Germans. "The folks at Chartons[5] don't like me," wrote General Edgard de Larminat, a leader of the Free French forces and inflexible foe of Pétainist Vichy. "They are right ... The greatest fear they had during the war was in 1944–45 and arose from the existence of that horrible FFI which disturbed their tranquil life and business deals."[6] De Larminat was one of the few high-ranking officers who held the French Resistance forces in high esteem and wished to use them as the nucleus for a regenerated, purified national army. More numerous by far were those who sought reconciliation of all the professional elements which defeat, occupation, and collaboration had so deeply divided. Political leadership of the Fourth Republic carried out a purge of Vichyite military elements, especially in the navy, but De Gaulle himself had earlier helped to ensure that the purge would not be accompanied by any revolution in the social composition of the army's elite corps. It was he who, "passing over the objections of several ministers and the representatives of various committees," decreed in September 1944 the formal dissolution of FFI militias. It was also De Gaulle's decision to emphasize French, independent military contribution to final Allied victory at the expense of reconstitution of a new French army composed of Gaullist professionals on the one hand and military resistants on the other.[7]

The natural consequence of events and policies attending the final months of World War II was that separation of the Army-Nation duo became divorce, replete with recriminations from both Left and Right. "Since 1941 I know De Gaulle tried to remake France with the *élites* that betrayed her and to exclude the *canaille* that defended her ... [Our present army] is an instrument for the defense of capitalism against communism; therefore it is an army of ideological war, an army of civil

[5] De Larminat used Resistance forces to clear the enemy from the area around this city.

[6] *Chroniques irrévérencieuses*, Paris, Plon, 1962, p. 285.

[7] *The War Memoirs of Charles de Gaulle*, Vol. 3, *Salvation, 1944–1946*, New York, Simon and Schuster, 1960, pp. 44, 150–160.

war," wrote Louis de Villefosse, who had also served with the forces of Free France. He concluded that the French army, as reconstituted after the war, had no reason for existence.[8] On the other hand, De Lattre informed De Gaulle even before the war was over that "from one end of the [military] hierarchy to the other, and particularly among the officers, even at a high level, there is a general impression that the nation is ignoring and deserting them. Some even go so far as to imagine that the regular army from overseas is being sacrificed deliberately."[9]

One does not have to accept De Villefosse's interpretation in its entirety to perceive the gulf that was widening between the people of postwar France and "their" army. A common denominator among clashing social factions under the Fourth Republic was the assignment of low priority to the military technique and to asserted military virtues. "Confronted by an Army without prestige, a Navy without ships, an Air Force without production, public opinion was more responsive to those who counselled a lightening of its fiscal burden than to those who proposed a reorganization of National Defense."[10] French youths did not rush to the colors, eager to defend their country in the jungles of Indochina or the mesas of Algeria. They did not even consider garrison duty in Germany, Morocco, or Tunisia to be an attractive privilege of citizenship. They were so bold as to dispute the army's contention that military service inculcated the highest national virtues and prepared the draftees for lives of devotion to the community's welfare. "Military service is conceived [by draftees] as a period of irresponsibility . . . ," said a leader of a youth organization. "One does not serve in the army — I say very frankly — an apprenticeship in responsibility, in the responsibility that youth will have in life."[11] One general criticized his remarks in no uncertain terms, but a reader of *Figaro* thought he had been much too conservative in his statement. "Far from any affection, frustrated in those details that make life bearable, subjected to duties without interest for them, deprived of even freedom of expression,

[8] "Armée nationale ou armée de guerre civile?," *Esprit,* May 1950, p. 737.
[9] *Op. cit.,* p. 294. Note the phrase "regular army from overseas."
[10] Lt. Colonel de Fouquières, "Réarmement," *Revue de Défense Nationale,* October 1951, p. 282.
[11] François Le Meilleur, in a discussion of military service, June 22, 1962.

soldiers very quickly degenerate, some into masturbation, some into homosexuality, and some into alcohol . . . The strongest isolate themselves so as not to be contaminated, embittered by the futility of it all."[12]

The estrangement of the army from the people of metropolitan France was evident in the process of recruiting officers. Military schools were forced by a paucity of applicants to an unwelcome choice between quality and quantity. Despite some timid efforts at reform, the professional officer corps, after the war as before, drew hardly any of its complement from the workers and the farmers, the most numerous groups of French society.[13]

The military establishment was well aware of the low esteem it occupied in the eyes of the nation. Had peace prevailed, bases of accommodation, if not of mutual respect, might have been found. Unfortunately there was no peace. And as the cream of the French army was lifted from comfortable occupation tours in West Germany, from garrison service in Morocco and Tunisia, fruitlessly to fight colonial wars in Indochina (1946–1954), Suez (1956), and Algeria (1954–1962), the military naturally reacted to civilian indifference to its seemingly endless, bloody missions with a savage view of French society. The antagonists agreed on one basic matter: colonial wars were dirty wars, increasingly difficult to win decisively. But peaceful metropolitan France preferred not to be reminded of the human cost which seemed to grow without possibility of recompense. It was, then, this contrast between a nation determinedly "at peace" and its army endlessly at war which poisoned the relationship. Captain Estoup, brought to trial for participating in the so-called Generals' Revolt of April 1961, told the court, "After a separation of eight years, I had the grievous sensation of rediscovering a France that no longer knew me and that I no longer knew, a France that, instead of reproaching me for losing its patrimony, reproached me for wishing to preserve it, a nation that reproached me for making war."[14]

[12] *Figaro*, September 14, 1962.
[13] See complaint by Guy Mollet in *Figaro*, July 4, 1962.
[14] Quoted by Jacques Isorni, in *Lui qui les juge*, Paris, Flammarion, 1961, p. 120. Estoup represents the many professional officers who passed with little respite from Indochina to Algeria, the outbreak in the latter following by only a few months the truce in the former.

Little that is unique appears in the French army's list of accusations against French society. It is the same arraignment of slothful civilians at home made by fighting men through the ages. Postwar France was decadent, soft, frivolous, fun-loving, its citizens indifferent, sluggish, unwilling to change the old habits that had led to their defeat by the Nazis. French values were perverted, or non-existent. Not only did those fighting for France enjoy no prestige or respect, but the traditional ideal of the Nation as the rallying force no longer had the same appeal. "It was absolutely detestable, positively indecent that the adjective 'French' should become almost an object of mockery."[15]

Theoretically the reaction of an officer corps scorned by and scorning the society it was defending could have been deliberate separation, made all the easier by its uninterrupted preoccupation with colonial conflict.[16] Close contact with diseased France would be dangerous. Ideas, degenerate ideas, articulated by Leftist intellectuals and pandered by the popular press, would infect the army, divide its leaders, weaken its resolve, blur its sense of dedication and purpose. For all its repeated claims to represent or embody the nation, the army was not so foolish as to believe it could mirror the diversities and contradictions of French groups and still retain its fighting capability. "In reality," said a high officer willing to be franker than most of his colleagues, "whether one wishes it or not, there is an incompatibility between liberal customs and habits as we practice them and the comportment of officers . . . who to be effective must be authoritarian in their acts and in their thoughts."[17]

Isolation, insulation from contaminating civilian influences, would serve to heighten professionalism and to strengthen military competence. But, except for the Foreign Legion, with its non-French recruits,

[15] General Jean Valluy, "Le nouveau duo, Armée-Nation," *Revue des Deux Mondes,* October 15, 1962, p. 485. We shall meet the General again. Apparently aloof from military plots, yet profoundly sympathetic toward the officers driven by despair to revolt, articulate, eloquent General Valluy commanded greater attention than more passionate writings of more involved soldiers and civilians.

[16] Such is indeed the picture Jean Lartéguy presents in his novelized documentary, *The Centurions,* New York, E. P. Dutton, 1962.

[17] Quoted in *Le Monde,* May 12, 1961.

and the paratroops, who, like the United States marines, carefully cultivated a militaristic ethos, this course was not open to most units. The
reasons were simple and compelling. There was in the first place (in
spite of their mutual disregard) strong opposition to such a course from
both military and civilian leaders, opposition which, as previous pages
have suggested, rested on the historic image of the Nation in Arms. "The
army is uniquely in the service of the nation and should be closely
representative of the nation; it is the concrete and permanent mani-
festation of the capacity of the nation to survive, by arms if necessary."[18]
A strictly professionalized, career army would be nothing at all, would
deserve nothing at all. At once it would cease to be a "grand corps of
the State," an eternal "order" like Medicine or the Law.[19] Few officers
and no politicians would willingly subscribe to the notion of the army
as a branch of hired mercenaries, centurions, defending a new Rome
on the far-flung outposts of her empire.

The practical cause for rejection lay partially concealed by the vague
vaporings of would-be theoreticians groping for new formulations to
justify the tragic loss of lives and ever larger expenditures of funds in
a series of losing causes. At times, however, grand phrases could not
hide the grim bonds which tied the army, willy-nilly, to the French
people, whose anti-militaristic spirit it so resented. Testifying at the
trial of General Challe for leading the Generals' Revolt of April 1961,
Commander Louis Bouneix recollected Challe speaking many times of
"the army which draws its substance and purpose from the nation." So
impressive were Challe's affirmations that Bouneix was moved to recol-
lect "the giant Anteus, who, on being separated from the earth, loses his
force and vigor." The prosecutor immediately turned Bouneix's allusion
against him. "This Anteus to whom you refer, we recognize him, having
met him at our school desks; . . . but to recapture force and vigor he must
put his foot on the earth. This earth, it was not the earth of Algeria, it
was the earth of the Metropole."[20]

[18] Robert Chapuis, "La jeunesse et l'Armée," *Esprit*, October 1962, p. 477.
[19] Valluy, *op. cit.*
[20] *Le procès des Généraux Challe et Zeller*, Paris, Nouvelles Editions Latines,
1961, pp. 153, 154. The prosecutor was also hinting that Challe planned an invasion of metropolitan France.

The army needed the French people as a source of manpower for the task of "pacifying" Algeria. Deprived of draftees, the professional cadres alone could not come close to fulfilling the manifold aspects of a task which colonial experience, coupled with political neglect and weakness at home, had led the army to assume. Follow for a moment the progression of extra-continental entanglements. Scarcely were the institutions of the Fourth Republic in place, with the French Union, supposed repositor of a new and more equal relationship between France and its erstwhile colonies, designed as an integral part, than a revolt broke out in Madagascar in 1947. During World War II the British had occupied the island, and the restoration of French control was not easy. French civilian and military leaders, however, ignored the many forewarnings of trouble. Military reinforcements did not arrive before popular support for the uprising had become general. While Malagasy representatives in Paris condemned the French Union as "an empty formula" (hardly an extreme statement under the circumstances), French power crushed the insurrection with maximum violence and bloodshed. Leaders of the revolt were subjected to a degrading travesty of French justice, replete with forced confessions and intimidated witnesses, a dark precursor to later treatment meted out by extremist French military and civilian groups to rebellious Algerian nationalists.

Even before the army "won" its first colonial war, a much larger conflict had started in Indochina. Here the professionals were on their own; no draftees were sent. Here the military fought with more and more weapons, newer and newer equipment, in military operations which, after the Korean truce, grew to substantial proportions. The number of forces it deployed, the weakness of pro-French Vietnamese groups, the indifference of public opinion at home, the corruption of French civilian elements involved — all combined to give the army powers outside the purely military field which, in modern times, it had not before enjoyed. Always — to read its publicity releases — on the verge of decisive military victories, the army's strength was sapped by non-military factors it only dimly perceived and responsibility for which it laid, with considerable justice, at the door of quarrelling, inept, corrupt politicians at home. In the end, however, it was beaten, not just by its failure to counter successfully the guerrilla tactics of the enemy but also by a direct military confrontation at Dien Bien Phu ordered by its own leaders. Not all colonial wars, the army learned, could be won by superior arms in the hands of professionals, no matter how determined and highly trained.

But could not other types of colonial campaigns still be won? Two years after the humiliating debacle at Dien Bien Phu portions of the military "elite" were accorded a chance for revenge. French naval and air units secretly prepared with British forces to seize Suez following Nasser's assumption of control and the manifest unwillingness of the United States to lead in taking effective measures to oust him. Landing successfully and encountering little resistance, French paratroops were on the verge of a copy-book victory — programmed, decisive, bloodless. Western skills, training, and techniques — in a word, professionalism — were about to overcome boastful but backward, ignorant, and inept colonials. At this point, unbelievably, French political leadership followed the British in capitulating — to what? To bombastic threats from the East, to pressure from the West and especially from the United States, and to the cacaphonous sound and tumult of the "United" Nations. "The shortest war in history lasted 40 hours on Egyptian soil. It was won in advance by the air forces. It was lost by the politicians."[21] Officers involved in the Suez affair, and behind them the professional cadres in general, felt that both the unnecessary humiliation of French arms and the equally unnecessary rescue of Nasser would make victory in Algeria much more difficult to obtain.

By the time the Suez fiasco transpired, the army was beginning to encounter in Algeria a distillation of all its previous colonial experience. It had been duped by the politicians, betrayed by supposed allies, rejected by metropolitan France; but in North Africa the army faced a mission worthy of its talents and devotion, a mission for which it could use and justly demand unlimited numbers of troops from the nation it had left behind. For the activists, there was, as in Madagascar, a rebellion to be repressed by whatever means and with whatever vio-

21 Merry and Serge Bromberger, *Secrets of Suez*, London, Sidgwick and Jackson, 1957, p. 172.

lence might be necessary. As in Indochina, there was a large country-
side to be divided and divided yet again into military areas to be pacified piecemeal. For technicians in the art of destruction, there were new
weapons especially suited to professional action by small groups of the
army's elite. It was a colonial conflict which carried no connotation of
anachronistic battle. This was modern war, its practitioners repeatedly
explained, as modern in its conception and execution as any that might
be entrusted to Western arms: as modern, and, in the nature of things,
equally, if not more, important. While General Jacques Massu, veteran
of Indochina and leader of the Tenth Parachute Division, might sym-
bolize to some certain repressive aspects of the military operation, the
same could not be said for his fellow Saint-Cyrien, General Maurice
Challe. Chief of Staff of the Air Force, Commander of French forces in
Algeria before assignment as Commander of NATO troops in Central
Europe, Challe epitomized the renovation of the French military establishment. (For this reason he was the ideal candidate to lead an
army revolt against De Gaulle in 1961.)

At the heart of this vast and varied military venture was an experiment in social engineering. With the autonomy of decision and its expanded role in Indochina as a precedent, the army cast itself upon the
Algerian people and sought to mold them into a contented, peaceful,
prosperous society controlled by France. So weak were the institutions
of the Fourth Republic, so divided the counsels of its leaders, that the
army, in its fantastic endeavor, had come by 1958 to assume for the most
part full powers, untrammelled by civilian direction, not responsible to
political authority.[22] Of significance to an examination of the phenomenon of the army's changing relationship to French society was the
fact that Algeria served as testing ground and simultaneously as motivation and opportunity for analogous actions directed at metropolitan
society. In both cases the purpose was the same: *the Nation in the
Army's service*, a French nation restructured, purified, endowed with
new values, ready, indeed eager, to respond to the military's direction.

Toward the Moslem the French army was teacher, doctor, engineer,

[22] Military thought that served to justify this mission will be considered in the
next chapter.

advocate, judge, tutor, feeder, provider. "In the *bled* [countryside], where the mass is underdeveloped economically and culturally, the army that encompasses them, that directs them, that commands them, that nourishes them, represents parental, guardian authority. A minor has no freedom."[23] It followed that the proper, the only possible, emotional relationship between master and servant (adult and child) in this would-be totalitarian (in the literal sense of the word) social system was deep love and affection. "We accept this war because we love the population for which we are fighting . . . We sincerely believe in fraternization, but in true fraternization."[24] Ugly rumors of racism must be dispelled as irresponsible words attributable to the few bad apples that get into every large barrel, never to the professional elite. "General Salan has always been against what is vulgarly called *ratonnades*, against murder as a racist act seeking the elimination of someone of another religion or another community."[25] Jouhaud, Zeller, and of course Challe also would never speak of "rat hunts"; even as head of a large section of the Secret Army Organization in Algeria, Jouhaud, it would appear from his impassioned defenders, opposed, if he could not prevent, the mutilation of Moslem women and children by explosive plastic.[26] Sequestration in concentration-camp villages, raids of retribution on Moslem villages, retaliatory execution of hostages, summary trials and execution, "shootings while trying to escape," extraction of confessions and information by torture methods of which the Gestapo would have been envious — all these, when acknowledged at all, were motivated by love and the spirit of brotherhood. And, continued French

[23] Rabi, "Nouvelles conversations en Algérie," *Esprit*, March 1961, p. 486.

[24] Edgard Pisani, "Un officier parle," *Revue de Paris*, November 1960, p. 121.

[25] Philippe Marçais, lawyer and Algiers deputy, testifying in the trial of General Salan. *Procès de Raoul Salan*, Paris, Editions Albin Michel, 1962, p. 265.

[26] See *Procès d'Edmond Jouhaud*, Paris, Editions Albin Michel, 1962, *passim*. Raoul Salan, Edmond Jouhaud, and André Zeller, as subsequent chapters recount, were all leaders of the revolt against De Gaulle, which began in April 1961 and continued, with the activities of the Secret Army, until the end of 1962. Salan had been combined-forces commander in Algeria and recipient of France's highest military decoration, the Médaille Militaire. Jouhaud had been an air force general and chief of staff of that branch of the service. Zeller, who had retired after one tour of duty as chief of staff of the ground forces, was recalled to active service in the same capacity by De Gaulle.

military apologists, it was so understood and accepted by most Moslems; only the criminal, conspiratory, *alien* element fought on against their French protectors. An American might believe himself suddenly transported back in time to a Kafka-like version of the ante-bellum South.[27]

There remained one distracting note: the questionable place of the million and a half "whites," the "Europeans," the authentic civilian French in this supposed piece of national territory. In some respects the French residents represented to the million-man army an unwelcome intrusion, a spanner in the wheel of social reconstruction. For they formed elements which could hardly be manipulated, pulled apart and pasted back together like the Moslems. Their place in the new society was dubious. At times they were assigned the position of continuing benevolent tutor, to take over after the army had put down the rebellion and finally departed. At other times they were to form a more or less complete social system of their own, co-existing in fraternal friendship with the far larger, less progressive Moslem community. As the war went on, and particularly as the army began to see De Gaulle as its principal adversary, it became very important to dispel any malicious impressions that there was collusion between officers and Europeans against the Moslems. Although individual military leaders, such as Jouhaud, came from upper-class families in Algeria, the occupying army did not wish to think of itself as fighting to perpetuate the status and privileges of the Europeans. A distinctly radical tone entered certain military pronouncements. Large landholders (*gros colons*) should give up their exploitive habits, perhaps actually share the best land with the Moslems. Other Europeans, the overwhelming majority — shopkeepers, workers, civil servants, etc. — should accept the Moslems as their equals, entitled to the same rights, the same advantages.

"Fraternization" was the magic label attached to the Algerian dream of the military. It was in many ways analogous to the dream of voluntary integration in the American South. Because the army could not

[27] The escape from reality through invention of a mythical Moslem and an equally mythical nationalist is discussed by Jules Roy, *The War in Algeria*, New York, Grove Press, 1961, and Xavier Grall, *La génération du djebel*, Paris, Editions du CERF, 1962.

coerce the Europeans, it was indispensable for it to believe that the Europeans actually did believe in fraternization and only awaited the proper opportunity to make it a permanent reality. Hence the crucial nature of those "magical" manifestations in the Algiers Forum in May 1958, when techniques reminiscent of Nazi and fascist rallies were used nightly to rouse the mob to hysterical passion against the Fourth Republic. To maintain the illusion of racial brotherhood, recollections of the military strings that jerked the puppets and of the uniformed men that manipulated those strings had to be repressed. Later, and for the same reasons, it became important to propagate a very special definition of the Secret Army Organization (OAS). Formed by military and civilian elements in Algeria when measures of open opposition failed, the Secret Army sought to prevent at all costs the transfer of control from France to the nationalist Provisional Government of Algeria. To lend the appearance of legitimacy to its cause, the OAS pretended to represent, not just all the Europeans in Algeria, but most of the Moslems as well.[28] Marc-Jean Lauriol, who, like Philippe Marçais, was trained in the law and was a deputy from Algiers, did not shrink from quoting with approval the otherwise disliked Jean-Jacques Servan-Schreiber writing in the heartily detested and frequently confiscated *L'Express:* "There is no more OAS; there is a population."[29]

"The Algerian war separated the army — or, more precisely, what one usually calls the army, that is to say the average opinion of the officer corps — from the nation, because this nation has for fifteen years felt the repercussions of an international phenomenon called 'decolonization,' while the French officers, experiencing the same phenomenon, forged a

[28] "Represent" is, of course, a slippery word. Most of the Europeans might well have wished success to the Secret Army, but how long they were prepared to involve themselves and how many extremist measures they were prepared to support were different matters. The relation of the OAS to Europeans in Algeria and in France itself is explored further in discussion of the nature and extent of the French army's politicalization.

[29] *Procès de Raoul Salan,* p. 259. See also *Procès d'Edmond Jouhaud,* p. 256; testimony of M. Legroux, p. 309. In his plea defense attorney Perrussel said: "Who makes up the OAS? All the population, all the parties, and General Jouhaud will tell you: the OAS in Oran runs from the disabused communist to the man of the extreme right."

congeries of political and social ideas which no longer corresponded to those of the nation and separated the two more and more."[30] When De Gaulle's intention to permit the Algerian Moslems to make a choice became clear to the colonial army, the consequences were shattering. To begin with, the partially self-selected mission of the army to reconstruct the Algerian society and economy, as well as to eliminate trouble-making rebels, logically required the position that the Moslems had already embraced their French friends once and forever. "Between this presence of the army and the terror imposed by the FLN, the Moslems chose France," said General Challe in his opening statement at his trial. Like the children under tutelage that they were, further opportunities to choose could only confuse them, lead them, perhaps, into error. "When in Algeria a Moslem chooses, he chooses a chief and thereby a destiny. He doesn't understand very well — and it is the same for cultivated Moslems — that having made a choice, he is then asked to make a choice that is somewhat different."[31] General André Zeller's defense attorney put the same point, which was one of the fundamental justifications for the Generals' Revolt of April 1961, more passionately. The Army, he said, was given the role "of representing French civilization to all the inhabitants of Algeria, of being the symbol of France, and the Army was asked to make all Algerians understand the policy of France. Ah, gentlemen, for three years it was easy. By a sort of unanimous, spontaneous consent all of Algeria wished to be, proclaimed itself to be French . . . And then for political reasons (I no more than you, Mr. Prosecutor, will examine them), the road followed for three years was changed, not to say reversed, and the Army had to explain to the Algerians, first, that they were French, then that they could be, then finally that they were no longer part of a sovereign State with its own nationality."[32]

The next step in the thinking of those who opposed De Gaulle's "diabolical" policy of surrendering what had already been won was that the army-Moslem relationship involved a solemn contract. A sacred oath

---

[30] Henri Azeau, *Révolte militaire*, Paris, Plon, 1961, pp. 6, 7.
[31] *Procès des Généraux Challe et Zeller*, p. 23.
[32] *Ibid.*, p. 309.

had been given somehow, somewhere, to someone never to desert the colonial people, never to abandon them to the malefactors. ". . . Step by step the Moslem population placed all its confidence in this French army," declared General Zeller in his opening statement to the court. "In return the army in this period signed a veritable pact with the Algerian population, a pact which was tacit but sometimes also explicit. We also in this period contracted with Moslem troops and with auxiliary troops . . . " At this point came one of the most dramatic moments of the trial, as the voice of the 63-year-old former chief of staff of the ground forces faltered and he collapsed.[33]

We have now arrived at the final, crowning irony in this black-is-white fable. Algeria was what the French army said it was. But if Algeria were in the service of an all-encompassing, all-powerful military administration, it was equally true that the army became what Algeria made of it. "Oh, gentlemen," expostulated defense attorney Pascal Arrighi, pleading for General Challe, "all the Proconsuls who followed one another in Algeria were taken over, shaped by Algeria, by the African land. It is banal to say that Algiers conquered the very ones to whom it was entrusted, of whatever political complexion they might be."[34] For those driven from sullen obedience to overt revolt, and finally to clandestine subversion within the structure of the OAS, the objective was, had perforce to be, the remolding of French society in the way the French army (until interrupted by De Gaulle) had been remolding Algerian society. Only thus could the betrayal by "their" president, whom the army had installed in order that it could complete its task, be counteracted and Algeria remain a part of the sacred soil of France.

Moreover, through social action to attain political goals, that mythological ideal, the "Unity of the Army," could be preserved. Did not the army agree that it was social disease in France, translated into political ineptitude and corruption, which was at the root of military defeats? Was not the army agreed that the Army and the Nation should never be separated, that the two must come to share the same aspirations, the

[33] *Ibid.*, p. 47.
[34] *Ibid.*, p. 268.

same values, the same destiny? If the army were to continue as the embodiment of the noblest virtues of the nation — valor, dedication, self-sacrifice — must not the army seek out and cultivate those very virtues and implant them where they did not exist? The inadmissible, alternate conclusion was that the army reflected French society in all its dissonance, in all its degradation, that the army was as rotten as the sources from which it had sprung. Rather than admit to fallibility and corruption, the army must identify itself with the enduring Fatherland against ephemeral political power. "The State is for today, the Fatherland [Patrie] is for always," said defense attorney Le Corroller in denying that the specially constituted tribunal had the right to try General Salan. "Listen to the Voice of the Fatherland. Don't yield to the intolerable pressures of the State."[35] If, deluded by De Gaulle, subverted by defeatist elements, enfeebled by entrenched ideas of "radicalism,"[36] the French people did not see their duty, their glory, their destiny, then the mission of the army was clear. The army's activities in Algeria provided practical experience in social reconstruction. Now, betrayal of its mission by De Gaulle might be prevented if the effort were directed at metropolitan France itself.[37]

Military activists who would remake French society had many weapons at their disposal, in addition to the natural permeability of a Western, pluralistic social system. So long as the Algerian war continued, large numbers of French youth would fall into the hands of the army for indoctrination. Future officers would have their opinions as well as their skills sharpened by the curricula at the various service schools. Having passed through the military sieve, a million Frenchmen were potential instruments for social action. Hundreds of thousands joined veterans' organizations, in France as elsewhere powerful pressure groups for the army's cause.

Quasi-military organizations shared, or might be induced to share, the military's attitude on the need for social regeneration, by force if

---

[35] Procès de Raoul Salan, p. 33.

[36] See Valluy, op. cit., p. 486.

[37] See, for example, the statement of ex-Colonel Argoud, a leader in the Secret Army. Entitled "The Algerian Problem: French Solution," it was printed and circulated by the OAS. Extracts appear in L'Express, May 10, 1962.

necessary. In Algeria itself there were groups similar to the American National Guard — Territorial Units, formed, disbanded, re-formed, depending on whether loyal Gaullist or rebellious elements of the army were in control at the moment. In metropolitan France the army could vie with the political apparatus of the Fifth Republic for the allegiance of other security forces, such as the Republican Guard and even the police. Finally, there were the extremists to be found in any society. Individually and in groups they could be enlisted to battle the established order. At the top of the socio-economic pyramid were found remnants of some "best families," a disparate agglomeration of opponents of French democracy which had been accumulating ever since 1789 because democracy, no matter what its form, threatened their rights and privileges, as self-determination in Algeria would threaten the rights and privileges of the European minority there. At the bottom of the pyramid were outcasts, misfits, failures, psychopaths. But military activists could make instruments of purification out of even the least pure.

The end of the war in Algeria in the Spring of 1962 proved to be a contribution as well as a disaster to the subversive Secret Army. On the one hand, it was deprived of its initiating cause — a French Algeria. But at the same time there returned to France large numbers of embittered, jobless Europeans and Moslems from whom active agents might be drawn. The French government had thought that the negotiated triumph of the Provisional Government of the Algerian Republic at Evian-les-Bains on March 18, 1962 might result in an influx of some 400,000 to the Metropole. As of January 1963, the estimated number of arrivals was 700,000.[38] Most were Europeans, but there were also Moslems who had supported the French and could expect ostracism, if not worse, from any independent Algerian government. *Harkis* — Moslems who had actually joined and fought in the French army — led the exodus; including their families, 25,000 were reported to have found their way to France.[39]

Left behind to the ministrations of nationalist Algerian justice, unless

[38] *Le Monde,* January 9, 1963.
[39] *Le Monde,* November 17, 1962.

the remnants of the French forces could and would protect them, were thousands of other Moslem collaborators.[40] The Algerian government was not in a forgiving mood; never was the biblical adage "an eye for an eye, a tooth for a tooth" more swiftly followed. It has been estimated that some 10,000 Moslems were executed or assassinated between March 19 and November 1, 1962. Whatever might have been their own excesses when inside the French military system, the fate of the *harkis*, especially, assailed the conscience of the French people.[41]

Before citing examples of military, military-inspired, and military-related actions inside the social framework of metropolitan France, the nature of the military involvement should be summarized here. As has been emphasized before, not all of the French professional army desired to restructure French society, let alone actively engaged in the effort. Nor did attempts at social infusion go on at all levels, simultaneously, without progression and regression. For only the most doctrinaire was the goal consciously envisaged as a purified society. For more of the activists the purpose of social action was to provide a base for effective political control, beginning with the forcible elimination (assassination, to call things by their right names) of General-President de Gaulle. But while not all the army was dedicated to all the attacks on the social fabric of France, the logic of the interaction between the colonial force in Africa and the Fifth Republic provided a challenge of such breadth and depth as to threaten to put the Nation in the Army's service.

In drawing up its indictment of French society, the army found scapegoats for its own behavior and also for an international environment beyond its control.[42] The notorious *crise de conscience* of the military was in large part a crisis of *bad* conscience. It was made worse

[40] The Minister of Defense, Pierre Messmer, estimated that 130,000 to 140,000 Moslems had been a part of the French military effort at some time during the eight years of war. The number included quasi-military and security forces as well as regular units. *Figaro*, February 24, 1962.

[41] See *Le Monde*, November 11, 13, 25–26, December 9–10, 1962.

[42] An exception was the prolific author X. See "Pourquoi nous avons 'perdu' la guerre d'Algérie," *La Nef*, July–September 1961, pp. 19–39.

by military awareness of the mystique of Nation-Army duality and by French military schools, which effectively inculcated the art of self-conscious, reasoned, articulate discourse. The French army did not think well — on which point more later — but its thoughts reverberated throughout the military hierarchy.[43]

While the army was in Algeria, it did in fact engage itself with a society — a colonial society, to be sure, but technically and in military mythology a part of France. The special relationship of Algeria to metropolitan France provided a rationale, at the same time that military success in Algeria was providing confidence. De Gaulle's in-flexible determination to have peace in Algeria even if it meant abandoning that territory to the Moslem nationalists added incentive. To get their way military extremists were prepared to battle the President on the social front. Their objective was to undermine the foundations of political institutions, mobilize a social base for a rival military system, and then use their new strength as a lever to dictate national decisions.

"Not guilty," would remonstrate most of the French professional elite to these charges of ruthless military ambition. "It's the case of a lost soldier . . . to repeat the popular expression . . . He was the plaything of events; he was the plaything of a policy . . ."[44] So spoke Raymond Dronne, deputy and one-time administrator of Overseas France, of the man willing to accept official responsibility, while denying criminal culpability, for 148 deaths and 435 wounded in his OAS sector of Oran.[45] The robberies and murders committed by hired thugs of the OAS were but the sewer connections of the training of drafted paratroops and the cultured lectures on the Nation, the State, and the Army given to veterans' assemblies.

The rapid expansion in the membership of veterans' organizations

[43] Analogies to American officers should be obvious. In their own "crisis of conscience" following the stalemate in Korea they found the same social and political scapegoats at home. That military anguish was not more audible was due in part to a difference in military education. Unlike their French counterparts, American officers receive very limited exposure to literature or the art of systematic reasoning. The result may be seen in any comparison of French and American military writing for a non-military audience.

[44] *Procès d'Edmond Jouhaud*, p. 204.

[45] *Ibid.*, p. 132. Testimony of General Artus.

was one result of greatly enlarged military requirements to meet the all-encompassing mission. Career officers assisted the various leaders in promoting links between the groups, broadening and tightening their local affiliates, and using them as sounding-boards. These organizations were supplied with a specific assignment: "psychological action" and defense against "national subversion." They were, in other words, to introduce into metropolitan France the ideas of "revolutionary war," in which their members had been thoroughly indoctrinated while in service in Algeria, and to direct the forces of nationalism, mobilized for the maintenance of "French Algeria," against *domestic* assaults. A regional meeting in April 1959 heard the message from France's senior military figure and one-time supporter of De Gaulle, Marshal Alphonse Juin. The Marshal was still clinging, albeit with difficulty, to his thesis that the President really wanted a French Algeria and therefore any other policy was tantamount to treason. "Against the subversive plots that attack the very integrity of the country each reserve officer from now on must consider himself mobilized in his social milieu, his profession, his province to become a propagandist and a defender of the national cause."[46]

Juin's was no isolated voice in the careful orchestration. The experienced analyst of military affairs Maurice Megret warned that veterans' organizations must not arrogate to themselves the mediating function between the military and French society.[47] Later events indicated it was manipulation, not mediation which was planned. In the fall of 1959 the army helped to bring some 700 young reserve officers to Paris for a national gathering (*carrefour*), a principal purpose of which was to salute the "permanent" military mission of safeguarding French Algeria.[48] The group looked forward enthusiastically to divisional meetings of some 5,000 reserve officers in 1960.[49]

[46] Quoted by Vincent Monteil, "Corneille chez Kafka," *Cahiers de la République,* November-December 1960, p. 48.

[47] *Le Monde,* June 25, 1959.

[48] Some wished to go on to condemn De Gaulle for his "Peace of the Brave" speech of September 16, but in the end silence was chosen as the appropriate indication of contempt.

[49] Jean Planchais in *Le Monde,* September 29, 1959; Azeau, *op. cit.,* p. 65.

The government could no longer ignore what was going on. Defense Minister Pierre Guillaumat publicly complained of the "politicalization" of the National Union of Reserve Officers and succeeded in changing its leadership. The next year, however, young members formed a Center of National Defense Studies as an instrument to redirect the parent Union along the political path. In addition, they were able to effect yet another change by forcing the dismissal of the Union president as too "governmental."[50] Marshal Juin spoke at the Center's meeting in November, naturally for a French Algeria. Asked to submit his speech to government authorities in advance, he had a change of heart after first asserting, "I am not accustomed to confiding my papers to flunkeys."[51] So deeply involved in politics did the studious Center become that it prudently suspended operations for a time after the Generals' Revolt of April 1961.

Four days before he was scheduled to retire, General Raoul Salan spoke at the tenth annual meeting of the Association of Combatants of the French Union, which brought together veterans of Madagascar, Indochina, and Korea, as well as North Africa. "Europeans and Moslems must all know that the Association has only one message, only one commitment, which can be expressed in these two words — 'French Algeria.'" On his retirement Salan became president of the Association and in August 1960 was using it as a forum to threaten the Fifth Republic. "It is not the prerogative of any authority to decide on the abandonment of a portion of the territory where France exercises sovereignty. No one has this right; no one has received such a mandate from the country . . ." The blatant nature of his declaration invited the government to punish him. It did. Called on the carpet by Defense Minister Pierre Messmer, Salan was told he could not return to Algeria. More grist for Salan and his followers. In Algeria Madame Salan issued a violent criticism of the ruling, while the ex-General openly defied civilian leaders: "I have the right and even the duty to express myself as I have done."[52]

50 Azeau, *op. cit.*, p. 67.
51 *Le Monde*, November 28, 1961.
52 *L'Année Politique, 1960*, pp. 60–61, 91–92.

No public military move whatsoever developed to moderate, let alone defeat, efforts of the activists to form and use veterans' organizations for their own ends; no audible military outcry protested the definition of *subversion* as support for the government's policy of negotiation and of *legitimacy* as increasingly overt defiance and threat to political authority. One reason was that France's military schools were busily indoctrinating officer-candidates with a particular, distorted view of the relationship between military and social structures. It was a basic premise of the so-called "doctrine" of revolutionary (subversive) war that the military could enter into the very heart of a national society and restructure it; indeed, that such action was indispensable to winning a colonial war.[53]

When the society to be permeated with military sociologists (or Western Mao Tse-tungs) ceased to be Algeria, a logical, even inevitable, shift of focus made the target France itself. Although the Secret Army in Algeria and later in France did not enjoy the official support of the "regular" army, distinguished officers were always available to say kind words on behalf of fellow Saint-Cyriens so unfortunate as to be caught. The connection between the official, above-ground military training system and extremist, underground criminality was persistent and close. Said Colonel Trinquier, a leading activist, whose experience in colonial combat led him to formulate principles of revolutionary warfare in *La guerre moderne:* "Give me 100 stranglers, and I will terrorize Paris . . ."[54] Four years later Saint-Cyr was still condoning the exercise of terror and was actually helping to recruit terror's agents. It was reported that at its annual ball, all Saint-Cyr cadets who did not wear the plain black tie of the OAS were excluded.[55] In March 1962 Count Horace Savelli, head of the National Veterans Union, was arrested as the chief of one of the largest OAS networks, that located in Western France. Members of his "staff" included a major and a captain simultaneously serving as instructors at Saint-Cyr. "All preliminary military training in the schools of France has been suspended for at least a

[53] French ideas of revolutionary war and the implications of those ideas are discussed in the next chapter.
[54] Monteil, *op. cit.*, p. 51.
[55] Nevill Boyd Maunsell, "Les paras," *Time and Tide,* February 22, 1962.

month because the military instructors were recruiting plastic bombers for the OAS among the students, with astonishing success," reported Joseph Barry the same month in the *New York Post*.[56] As late as September 1962 the command at Saint-Cyr was refusing in the name of "professional defense" to oust officers revealed by police investigations to be OAS activists.[57]

The military ideal of effective social organization obviously lies imbedded in the army itself. Within the military structure the epitome of the ideal — the "idealest" ideal as it were — is the fightingest elite of the professional elite, those best prepared for whatever form the violence of war may take. In the United States it is the Marine Corps, in France the "paras" (paratroopers). Paratroop units provided the hard core of extremism in pursuit of the Algerian war. Some were found at the center of the revolt against De Gaulle's policy of ending that war. Training procedures aimed at turning recruits into unquestioning instruments in the hands of their officers and non-coms were or should have been well-known in France. Gilles Perrault, who had served in the paras in 1955, published a detailed study, *Les parachutistes*. While fictionalized, Jean Lartéguy's novel, *The Centurions*, contained realistic accounts of training methods and of measures used to combat the FLN in Algiers. *The Centurions* became a best-seller. When Algiers civilians rose against De Gaulle in the January 1960 Barricades Revolt, the loyalty of paratroop units was so suspect that help in restoring order was solicited from other military groups stationed outside the city. Suspicions were confirmed the next year by the active participation of paratroopers in the Generals' Revolt.

Although De Gaulle attempted to make the paras less conspicuous members of the military establishment, the training methods responsible for outrageous behavior were little affected. Following eye-witness reports of brutality in the fall of 1962, the Minister of the Armed Forces announced that a few officers and non-coms had been punished for what was euphemistically described as "abuse of authority."[58] Military professionals, outside as well as within the paratroop units, reacted all too

[56] March 18, 1962.
[57] *Le Monde*, September 26, 1962.
[58] *Le Monde*, October 13, 14–15, 16, 1962.

characteristically to this mild attempt at civilian judgment — they blamed the government. People, they said (meaning, of course, those in the office of Armed Forces Minister Pierre Messmer), were playing politics with the army, seeking to discredit the military through publicity given to the sanctions.[59] But the press, probing the wounds, uncovered and reported what others had already described. Systematic brutality was at the heart of a process aimed at taking young draftees, who looked forward only to their release from military captivity, and turning them into tough, conditioned automatons prepared to do the bidding of the officer or non-com who controlled them, whether that bidding was to charge into the middle of an FLN unit, march behind General Challe against the government of France, or torture captives into revealing the names of fellow conspirators. "I have seen seminary students run the magnetos [electrical instruments of torture]," wrote Jean Carta in *Esprit.* "Most certainly they do it more gently than the others."[60]

One may not wish to follow Perrault and others all the way to the conclusion that this paratroop mentality was indeed fascism, French style — same credo, same value scales, same obsession with making over "decadent" civilian society in its image. But at least the training methods showed a certain divergence from democratic ideals. As quickly as possible memories of pre-military existence of the recruits were wiped from their minds by whatever brutal contrasts the ingenuity of non-coms could devise. Once trainees were accustomed to the idea that they were completely at the mercy of their leaders, the process of depersonalization could begin. When the destruction of dignity was complete, the rebuilding process could be initiated. Ideas could be poured into the mold, including one of the most important, the superior value of military society. "You are the best, the strongest. Civilians are all pansies and all Communists." Properly refurbished, the erstwhile recruits could become teacher-torturers in their turn. " 'Certain officer instructors, who fought in Algeria and Indo-China, discuss during class sessions how one goes about turning the magneto; they give details on

[59] Louis Aigouy, *Le Monde,* October 16, 1962. This was also clearly the opinion of Pierre Branche, *L'Aurore,* October 15, 1962.

[60] Quoted in Gilles Perrault, *Les parachutistes,* Paris, Editions du Seuil, 1961, p. 181.

scenes of torture . . . They instruct us also on how to handle a loaf of plastic explosive. I wonder why.'"[61] "Ever since there was a world," commented Claude Bourdet, "there has been a law for all societies that a corps specializing in violence, if not closely watched and controlled, burgeons in cruelty and becomes, like a monster free from restraint, the persecutor and sometimes the destroyer of what it is supposed to preserve."[62]

When the OAS, no longer able to swim, like Mao Tse-tung's subversive fish, among the Algerians, jumped the Mediterranean to stir the waters of French society, it accepted recruits wherever it could find them. Such "lost soldiers" as Degueldre, Gardy, Sargent, Godot, Robin, Canal, and Vincent established connections at both ends of the social pyramid. Investigation of the attempt to murder President de Gaulle at Petit-Clamart on August 22, 1962 led to so many notables in and about Versailles that they were labelled an OAS "network" by the press. Some seven were placed under arrest. Recruits, money, fire-arms, maildrops, storage space, and refuge were supplied plentifully during the spring and summer of 1962 by respectable people elsewhere in France, particularly in the Southwest, where European refugees from Algeria were concentrated.[63] One must not be overly surprised at the lack of fastidiousness of the "best families"; the organizer of the attempted assassination, as we shall see in the following chapter, was Lieutenant Colonel Jean-Marie Bastien-Thiry, a graduate of the Ecole Polytechnique and a "brilliant officer" attached to the Ministry of Air whose family tree included many lawyers and officers. But as the courts worked their way through the list of accused, from generals through colonels to non-coms, they found that conspiratorial leaders had welcomed representatives of society's enemies, outcasts, and victims. Aberrants, alcoholics, incompetents were valuable ingredients in the Secret Army's struggle.

[61] The account of paratroop training is that of Michel Vianey, who quotes individual recruits, anonymous for obvious reasons. *L'Express*, October 18, 1962. Similar reports were written by Michel Legris in *Le Monde* and Albert Fontaine in *France Observateur*, both of the same date.

[62] *France Observateur*, October 18, 1962.

[63] See, especially, *Le Monde*, September 18, 30, November 17, 1962; and Servan-Schreiber in *L'Express*, September 20, 1962.

The evolution of the French army's attitude toward the nation was an integral part of its politicalization. Instead of healing the wounds of war, the Fourth Republic, reflecting and augmenting the flaws in France's postwar social system, had further separated the army from the nation. De Gaulle's action was even more divisive. He it was who set out systematically to remove the mission the army had finally found for itself, the mission for which the professional army corps required and was receiving masses of French youth. Instead of stilling the voices of discord — the intellectuals and the press — he posed as a rival to the army for leadership in national regeneration. The Army-Nation duo, wrote General Valluy, has become a *ménage à trois,* with the Power (the word used by all opposition elements to De Gaulle's presidency) as the third member. This Power betrayed both the Army and the Nation, but won a Pyrrhic victory in the process.[64]

A Pyrrhic victory? De Gaulle and the Fifth Republic could not ignore the challenge. It was not enough for De Gaulle to shuffle his military commanders like a deck of playing cards, placing suspects in charge of "loyal" units and *vice versa.* He had to go beyond redefining military missions to replace *the* mission which had been eliminated. He could not content himself with promising the army a panoply of new weapons, including the one with the loudest bang. All these efforts would be incomplete, quite probably they would all come to naught, if De Gaulle and his government did not make the fundamental effort of redefining the relationship between the military system and the national society of which, army mythology to the contrary, it was but one, subordinate aspect. Events, of which the outrages of the OAS were not the least, assisted the undertaking, but in a sense the endeavor could never be finally ended. And the cost paid was high; some would say too high. The social foundations on which the Fifth Republic built its military policy will be examined in the second part of this volume.

[64] *Op. cit.,* pp. 484–485.

THE POLITICAL

APPLICATIONS OF

MILITARY THOUGHT

It is clear that most of the military figures that have come to the fore since 1939 are, above all, characterized by a pitiful lack of thought and expression. — Pierre Guillain de Benouville

IT WAS a tragic day for the French army, the Fourth Republic, and De Gaulle — to say nothing of countless Algerian Moslems — when some do-it-yourself military theoreticians stumbled across the writings of Mao Tse-tung. Not troubling to analyze the specific situation which the Chinese master had confronted, French popularizers produced a distorted jumble variously labelled revolutionary war, psychological war, subversive war, guerrilla war, and their antitheses. The body of ideas which was formulated deserves to be called "doctrine" only in the sense that the principles were presented under official auspices as internally consistent guides to action in a generalized military situation.

There is much truth in Lieutenant Colonel J. Rousset's observation that all great military leaders practice psychological war just as M. Jourdain made prose — without realizing it.[1] Also, France has a long

[1] "A propos de subversion et d'insurrection," *Revue de Défense Nationale,* March 1960, p. 498.

history of attempts at colonial pacification upon which to draw. What military writers and speakers attempted to do was *modernize* as well as make explicit principles of Western warfare in Asia and Africa, to fit them to the epoch of "conflicts as much religious as political in inspiration, where the basic stake is not only the possession of such or such territory, but victory of violently opposed conceptions of the life of man in society."[2]

In the evolving stages of revolutionary war, only the final two involve military action of the overt type. Local populations are first infiltrated by trained propagandists, who, after gaining acceptance for their ideological messages, reorganize the areas for revolutionary action. On the base of mobilized groups armed with a cause, made additionally appealing by inclusion of local grievances, the leaders initiate strikes, sabotage, violence, even assassination, sometimes without any apparent direct relation to insurrectionary goals. The purpose of the upward spiral of disorder is to show that the official government has lost control and can no longer guarantee the protection of lives and property. The spectrum of popular attitudes will consequently move away from the government toward the rebels: strong supporters lose some of their enthusiasm, weak ones turn to neutrality, waverers lean toward the rebels, and rebel supporters become firmly committed. Success in these pre-military stages makes possible the organization of guerrilla bands, conducting hit-and-run raids on government forces. Finally, after the guerrillas have deprived the government of effective control over large areas, decisive military onslaughts can be launched to topple the old regime and install the revolutionists.

Analysis of subversive war was no mere academic exercise. Enthusiasts believed that they could derive from it a prescription for victory in the Algerian version of colonial combat. In other words, by fighting a subversive war itself the French army would be conducting a successful *anti*-revolutionary campaign against the FLN insurrectionists. "In Algeria, by the force of circumstances, by the 'logic of the struggle' as Lenin said, in the face of an adversary who practiced revolu-

[2] Girardet, *op. cit.*, p. 326.

tionary war learned in a good school, the army had little by little to adapt its methods of combat to the necessities of combat . . . It was the only means of opposing the adversary's arms with equivalent or superior effectiveness for the mental and moral conquest of the population, the final and real justification of the war."[3]

First, there had to be the message, the word. It did not matter whether the word were true or whether the best informed, socially privileged groups believed it, just so long as it was accepted as the truth by the bulk of the population. Primordially and indispensably the army's task was therefore psychological. Successfully implanted propaganda then made social action possible. In the phraseology which was to become notorious in French military, political, and ultimately legal circles, "parallel hierarchies" must be created, one for ideological control, the other for military action. The army must eventually dominate the population totally; from top to bottom the people must be made amenable to direction and manipulation by the French army. The requirements of psychological and social action dictated in turn the type of military organization and the definition of what constituted military action. "In this revolutionary war, it is necessary to leave to units, whatever they may be, fairly large initiative within the general direction of the command. More than in classic war it is the front that leads the fight, and success depends on the courage and other qualities of the local leaders. The command is then limited to coordination in re-inforcing military capabilities."[4] At the same time there existed a direct relation between open military action by the French army and clandestinely inspired acts of terror and violence. The "light and dark" sides must complement one another if anti-revolutionary war were to be successful. Military no less than social and psychological tactics had to be adapted to the behavior of the enemy.

As a body of thought, it is all too easy to criticize the army's views of what constituted proper anti-revolutionary action, especially as distilled into a "collection of recipes" by the " 'businessman' of colonial

[3] Thierry Maulnier, "L'Armée, l'Algérie, et la Nation," *Revue de Défense Nationale*, March 1960, p. 397.
[4] *Revue de Défense Nationale*, November 1959, "Chronique militaire," p. 1870.

war," Colonel Trinquier.[5] "If the army can and should fight the effects of subversion, it is not organized or equipped to attack its causes. *In normal times* the military cannot and should not be charged with the detection and repression of activities necessitating the use of means and methods incompatible with the spirit, the organization, and the *traditional* mission of the army," wrote Lieutenant Colonel Rousset.[6] The italicized words specify important qualifications to the indictment, since the army's claim that times were far from normal in Algeria was used to justify its most untraditional mission. Nonetheless the distinction is a valid one, between defeating nationalist forces and removing the conditions which produced those forces. "After the guerrilla and the anti-guerrilla guerrilla, what?" was avoided by using such dubious slogans as "fraternization." The army in fact thought of its task in Algeria as virtually without an end.

Nor would a thorough critique neglect the moral aspects of the prescription. "Don't they see," exclaimed Prosecutor Besson in his final indictment of Generals Challe and Zeller, "the vast movement which shakes the whole world to liberate peoples from tutelage and whose progress is irresistible? And if it is irresistible, it is because the movement is one of human dignity, which is nothing other than the reflection of the divine order."[7]

For an understanding of the political challenge posed by the army, however, one must explore the rationale and consequences of its ideas about subversive war. The French army, for one thing, was participating in a general effort by Western countries to meet postwar challenges which they had not anticipated and for which they had not been prepared. While that portion of French leadership which continued the struggle against Hitler had, like its Allies, envisaged a new relationship with colonial territories once the war was won, all the Allies, including the United States, saw in the essence of that relationship precisely the practice condemned by Besson — tutelage. Peaceful, evolutionary, and gradual movement toward independence was possible,

---

[5] Azeau, *op. cit.*, p. 50. Trinquier's study was called *Counter-guérilla*.

[6] *Op. cit.* Italics in original.

[7] *Procès des Généraux Challe et Zeller*, p. 206.

even natural, although Frenchmen continued the pedantic argument of whether the end result would be a burgeoning of African and Asian French citizens or a limited type of local autonomy as exemplified by that monument to futility, the French Union. To the revelation that colonial peoples wanted, not tutelage, not even autonomy, but freedom — and quickly — was added the discovery — equally traumatic to the French army — that Western governments were unwilling and unable to perpetuate political domination by military means. While there were isolated exceptions, increasingly recognized as temporary, to this Western retreat from non-European areas, other military forces in the anti-Soviet camp, in addition to those of France, were reluctant to abandon their historic positions outside the home territory. They recognized the need to develop new and more effective techniques to maintain control and, above all, to obtain from Western peoples a renewed commitment to the endeavor.

The Dutch in Indonesia, the British in Malaya and Kenya, even the Americans (occupiers in spite of themselves) in China and Korea, all faced native uprisings parading the banner of "liberation from foreign domination." The particular reaction of the French military to this war-induced world-wide colonial unrest was conditioned by its relatively deep and pervasive entanglement and by the absence of effective control by civilian authority. Defeated in Indochina, the army, for the sake of its self-esteem, needed to understand why. An explanation became crucial when the beaten army was not promptly rehabilitated and given new, different, and recognizably significant missions by strong, determined political leaders.

"The French army," wrote Colonel "Nemo" in reference to the Indochinese campaign, "is practically the only one to have met communism in action, in a large ground war, in a style and breadth hitherto unknown."[8] The reason it failed to win was that it was purely a professional expeditionary force. This type of army did not invoke any sense of dedication by the French nation to victory. Transported to a country whose society it did not understand, the army nevertheless succeeded

[8] "La guerre dans le milieu social," *Revue de Défense Nationale*, May 1956, p. 606.

in raising large Vietnamese forces and providing them with technical training and equipment superior to their Vietminh counterparts. But it could not, because it did not know how, supply either itself or its native *milices* with unifying ideals.[9] And, in the end, instead of echoing General Stilwell's judgment in the retreat from Burma — "I claim we took a hell of a beating" — French theorists salvaged the *amour-propre* of the military by blaming such catastrophes as Dien Bien Phu on the folks back home and on ignorance of the principles of subversive war.

Ideas concerning revolutionary war served the useful purpose of simplifying increasingly complex reality in Algeria. As the rebellion grew, the army, under the benevolent eyes of such ministers resident as Lacoste, became in effect the French state, wielding judicial and political authority as well as economic and social control. Every measure taken by this all-encompassing bureaucracy became justified by the importance and urgency of the task. Between 1954 and 1961 one million Frenchmen, nine-tenths of them in the ground forces, were sent to Algeria.[10] The period of greatest equivalence between military and civil organization in Algeria was reached just before and in the months immediately following the overthrow of the Fourth Republic. Not until October 1958 did army representatives, under direct orders from De Gaulle to Salan, reluctantly leave the Committees of Public Safety formed in May during the rebellion against the last premier of the Fourth Republic, Pierre Pflimlin.

Most in need of justification remained, of course, the army's use of torture on captives. At first denied as a base canard formulated by Communists, the accumulating evidence gradually forced the military to various explanations, of which retaliation and "need to know" were the most popular. "Torture, torture, you can't talk about anything else," Massu told Jacques Duquesne, a special reporter from the Catholic

[9] *"Milices,"* the term used by "Nemo," establishes an analogy between the puppet Viet Nam forces fighting patriotic nationalists and Vichy's quasi-military units battling the French Resistance.

[10] Official figures quoted in *Le Monde*, March 9, 1962. By the end of 1961 about 15,000 Frenchmen had been killed and another 25,000 wounded, and estimates of FLN fatalities ran as high as 140,000.

journal *La Croix*. "But I am obliged to practice it."[11] Pierre Vidal-Naquet adds: "To tell the truth, the authorities do more than compromise; they put the full weight of the State behind the tortures. Such is the case, for example, in the conflict between General Massu and General de Bollardière, which bore precisely on the question, 'Must the army be authorized to torture, or not?' All the military hierarchy — notably General Allard and General Salan — and then the civil authorities rallied to General Massu's side."[12]

Little wonder that the army could not concede that its total commitment in Algeria was in vain. To admit this would be to confess that its tenets of anti-revolutionary war contained morally corrupting elements, undermining traditional, civilized, Western, French value systems, all in the name of that worn excuse-all, expediency. The army ultimately used its "doctrines" as blinders to avoid having to look at what it was doing to Algeria and what Algeria was doing to it.[13]

The principles of revolutionary war provided not only a rationalization for Indochina and a justification for Algeria, but also embodied an attempt to dictate the role, organization, and matériel of the entire French military establishment. As applied in Algeria anti-subversive combat was a modern war — indeed, *the* modern war. "In spite of a vocabulary of 'modernization,' his [De Gaulle's] idea was as archaic as sabre charges in white gloves," wrote Jacques Soustelle in *L'Espérance trahie*.[14] General Paul Ely, an articulate advocate of French Algeria, if not of all the methods adopted to attain that end, saw the principal military problem as one of adaptation to contemporary revolutionary war in a situation in which classical warfare still hung on "like a strip of plaster or even an entire old façade on a new building." Military

[11] Quoted by Pierre Vidal-Naquet, *La raison d'état*, Paris, Editions de Minuit, 1962, p. 9.

[12] *Ibid.*, p. 28. An outspoken opponent of the army's torture tactics, General Bollardière asked to be retired. Other notable military protestors were Generals Billotte and De Larminat.

[13] An excellent statement is that of Yves Bertherat, "Lettre d'ancien combattant," *Esprit*, Ocober 1962, pp. 382–386.

[14] Paris, Editions de l'Alma, 1962, p. 78.

leaders "should first see clearly that all which has been said on this form of warfare is not theory about a far-off future. It is a reality which surrounds them. They should then understand that this enlarged, limitless warfare involves them in problems they cannot avoid."[15] Subversive war, added General Valluy, in testifying on behalf of Generals Challe and Zeller, "is not a myth. It exists . . . These engagements [by the army in Algeria] have been the honor of the army."[16]

Ideas of revolutionary war quickly began to dominate French military thought.[17] As early as 1955 Mao Tse-tung's writings, especially *Strategical Problems of Revolutionary War*, which had appeared almost twenty years earlier, were required reading at the French War College. General Chassin, Commander Hogard, Colonel Lacheroy, Colonel Rocolle, and Colonel Trinquier were only a few of the officers who repeated in print the soon-familiar themes. Hardly a month passed without an article on the subject in the *Revue de Défense Nationale*. In February 1957 a special issue on revolutionary war of the *Revue Militaire d'Information* was published by the Ministry of National Defense. It was so popular that the normal printing of 48,000 copies had to be doubled. Six months earlier the Cinquième Bureau, later to be officially disbanded by De Gaulle, had been created to coordinate psychological action in all army headquarters, not just in Algeria alone.[18]

By January 1960, when Algiers civilians rebelled against De Gaulle's policy in the Barricades Revolt, "subversive war . . . was the only doctrine, the only language used by the army."[19] Anticipating General Valluy by almost a year and a half, Minister-Delegate Paul Delouvrier used

[15] *L'Armée dans la Nation,* as quoted in *Figaro,* November 11, 1961.

[16] To which the anonymous editor of the *Procès* adds: "The authority, the bearing, the natural eloquence of General Valluy produces a sensation in the hearing." *Procès des Généraux Challe et Zeller,* p. 162.

[17] To repeat, it is possible to use revolutionary, subversive, guerrilla war and their antitheses interchangeably because the army was fighting against that type of warfare by employing its techniques.

[18] Jean Planchais, "The French Army: Not by Force Alone," *Reporter,* November 28, 1957, pp. 34–37.

[19] Merry and Serge Bromberger, Georgette Elgey, J. F. Chauvel, *Barricades et colonels,* Paris, Fayard, 1960, p. 9.

strikingly similar phraseology in his extraordinary address to the people of Algiers during the last days of the rebellion, when he announced that he, along with General Challe, was leaving the city. "For people of Metropolitan France — except for the Moslems of the Metropole — this revolutionary war is a myth. For us it is our daily life. And this daily life for the army is not usually open combat, but cunning, subterranean struggle, struggle within the population itself."[20]

The pervasion of the tenets of revolutionary war was speeded by the bandwagon psychology puffing up its popularity. As applied to Algeria, the set of ideas incorporated what most of the ground-force officers had been doing, were doing, or planned shortly to be doing. The guiding concepts, modern or not, of how to fight colonial wars were more practical than any discussions of the theoretical effects on strategy of nuclear weapons France did not possess. Such ratiocinations were also closer to reality than plans of the North Atlantic Treaty Organization for European defense, plans in which French officers participated in roles gallingly subordinate to those arrogated to themselves by the Anglo-Americans and to the execution of which France was allocating a diminishing supply of under-armed troops.

A whole set of vested interests came to be attached to the Algerian war, the prime claimant on the French national treasury and the prime rationale for steady increases in responsibility and rank of military officers. Of course General Challe did not wish to accept transfer from his position as commander in Algeria to lead NATO's forces in Central Europe.[21] Of course General Massu was indignant at being recalled to Paris just for telling a West German journalist he did not understand De Gaulle's Algerian policy and the important question was to determine when a successor to the President would arrive on the scene. And of course Massu was further disappointed when instead of receiving a perfunctory slap on the wrist from De Gaulle and then allowed to

---

[20] *Ibid.*, pp. 362–363. The book contains the text of this speech, which was not published elsewhere. Delouvrier was attempting to turn the issue of subversive warfare against its propounders. Dismantle all material and psychological barricades, he urged both Moslems and Europeans, and rally in unity to De Gaulle.

[21] *Procès des Généraux Challe et Zeller*, p. 29.

return to Algiers, the source of his autonomous power, he was re-assigned to West Germany.[22]

For old and young, "traditionalists" and "modernists," lieutenants and generals, Algeria represented something practical and tangible. So long as the war continued, so long as it was neither abandoned nor won, there would be need for all types of officers possessing all types of training and experience. While some might "represent a caste dis-appearing before technical military progress, just as medieval chivalry before the appearance of artillery," the war guaranteed against any segment of the army being entirely discarded as obsolete. For those who claimed to represent the modern army, Algerian duty provided a channel of influence within the military hierarchy that often tran-scended their official rank and prescribed responsibilities.[23]

The Algerian war was *the* mission for the army, and all other facets of French and Western defense were viewed from that perspective. Military leaders saw the FLN as an external, alien force seeking to im-plant itself on French territory. And, until the very end, they con-tended that France, not the rebels, had the deep-rooted allegiance of the overwhelming proportion of Moslems. (It was unnecessary to speak of the Europeans.) To support this claim they cited such supposedly spontaneous events as the "fraternization" of Europeans and Moslems in May 1958 and the tremendous support accorded De Gaulle in the referendum on the Constitution of the Fifth Republic later in the same year. At other times, true Moslem sentiment was forced into hiding by the terroristic tactics of the FLN, protected and provisioned in sanctuaries outside Algeria, notably in those erstwhile protectorates, Tunisia and Morocco. But behind those poverty-stricken, corrupt, scarcely sovereign states loomed the real enemy: international com-

[22] Brombergers *et al., op. cit.,* p. 174. De Gaulle got the jump on Massu by be-ginning the interview: "I am going to keep you. I won't ask you to leave the army. I am going to give you a good position."

[23] The myth that the Algerian war, as described in the credos of anti-revolution-ary action, was supported solely by officers afraid of the effect of new ideas upon them — a charge made by many critics — or solely by officers trained in the art of modern war, as apologists claimed, was well laid to rest by René Deslisle, "La crise interne du corps des officiers," *La Nef,* July-September 1961, pp. 39–51.

munism in general and the Soviet Union in particular. *Ergo,* ran the military reasoning, the battle in Algeria was not an attempt to deny independence to the legitimate, indigenous masses who were completely French in mind and heart; it was a struggle for survival against an implacable, powerful, world-girdling foe.

Fanciful? Americans should reflect on comparable opinion in the United States, which finds Communists responsible for every upsurge of nationalistic violence in Asia and Latin America. That the Soviet Union and China do, when possible, utilize national movements to involve and weaken the West lends a beguiling aura of verisimilitude to such specious generalizations. In France the tendency to look for the Communist ogre and, when found, to stop seeking other causes was nourished by the army's all but total commitment to the Algerian war, its self-intoxication with its mission, and the absence of countervailing ideas generated and forcibly implanted by determined civilian political authority. A clear identification of nationalism with communism came from Raoul Salan, vociferous expounder of revolutionary-war ideas:

> Pan arabism and its supporter pan-islamism are, in fact, consciously and unconsciously only vehicles of communism. Already communist enterprise presses vigorously on Morocco and Tunisia which find with the Soviet and other satellites necessary support for their claims on Mauritania and the oil of the Sahara . . . But there is Algeria, which remains our last chance in Africa. At any price it must remain French . . . French Algeria is the only hope that remains to us to re-establish the position of France in North Africa, safeguard our riches in the Sahara, re-create the confidence of the African states [whose elites were particularly receptive to Marxism], which will then not hesitate to link their destiny to that of France in a true community of feeling and interest in barring Soviet imperialism from the conquest of the Free World.[24]

The notion that Western military power was the indispensable ingredient in holding native nationalism within an anti-Communist alliance was reiterated in negative terms by General Valluy. Speaking in Lisbon to the Atlantic Treaty Association after France had agreed to a popular vote on self-determination for Algeria, this exponent of a

[24] *Le Monde,* October 13, 1960.

strong NATO (and defense witness for rebellious French officers) was quoted by the French Press Agency as saying that "an excess of weakness" was causing the decolonization policies of the great colonial nations. "There is not in free Europe or in Africa a single movement of retreat which is not equivalent to a gain in ground for the communist world."[25]

As they paraded before the bar of justice, the rebel generals and their defenders cited the grave threats presented to all Western nations. They depicted themselves as latter-day crusaders, defending the Faith and Europe against barbaric onslaughts. "We knew," testified Colonel Robert Thomazo, identifying himself completely with the accused Raoul Salan, "what a danger, not only for France, but for Mediterranean Europe, and for all Europe, was represented by the implantation in Algeria, under the external guidance of a supposedly 'independent' FLN government, of Asian-Soviet influence and its powerful capacities."[26] Salan himself had declared toward the end of his proferred statement and before he refused to answer any questions at all: "I do not claim exoneration for having defended, together with France south of the Mediterranean, all the free world, even amidst the indifference and blindness of this free world. I do not claim exoneration for having refused to allow communism to be installed one hour from Marseilles and Paris to be put within reach of short-range missiles."[27]

Generals Zeller and Challe also invoked the cause of Western defense to cover their rebellion against French political authority. For this purpose they made a fine combination. The former had used his position as chief of staff of the ground forces to stiffen the determination of the army to defend by whatever means might be necessary its mission in Algeria; the latter, it will be remembered, had had some unwelcome experience in NATO command. Zeller, who had broken down when speaking of the army's "pact with the Algerian population,"[28] collapsed again, and this time could not resume his statement, when

[25] *Le Monde*, June 9, 1962.
[26] *Procès de Raoul Salan,* p. 373.
[27] *Ibid.,* p. 88.
[28] See p. 29.

speaking of the importance of Algeria to France and the West. "France needs Algeria; without her [pause] France moves, on the one hand, toward a political decline in the European and Atlantic framework, toward a menace on the southern bank of the Mediterranean, toward a lack of economic progress; Algeria still wishes . . ."[29] Eight years younger than Zeller (55 as against 63), Challe did not suffer the same disability from emotion and the rigors of rebellion:

> Let us . . . create Europe instead of pretending to do so — for all the European governments are now more or less pretending, as I said when I was at Fontainebleau [NATO headquarters]. Then in ten years Algeria can be asked to choose between a nebulous Arab League and union with the United States of Europe, if we have succeeded in creating it *contrary to* or in agreement with France. Other African powers will perhaps come to us at that moment, and we shall offer our youth something to build instead of having them only reflect eternally on the memories of our grandeur. It is the whole West that will be saved. If this is not done, the end result is almost certain.[30]

Defense attorney Arrighi asserted that Challe and Zeller were engaged in a "legal" revolt within the bounds of allegiance to political authority since they were protecting France and Europe by seeking to eradicate the FLN. De Gaulle and his government, said Arrighi, had repeatedly avowed a determination to win the Algerian war and explicitly accepted the cruciality of such a policy for Western defense. He cited an address to SHAPE made on November 15, 1959 by General Jacques-Marie-Paul Allard, then inspector-general of the armed forces, and the reply of the French government to General Challe the following month: "To separate France from Algeria is to put the free world in danger."[31]

Challe's view of NATO through a telescope in Algiers accounts in part for his determination, and his alone, to conduct a purely military revolt, uncontaminated by civilian participation. It also explains a most curious episode, still somewhat shrouded in state secrecy, of the alleged entanglement of the United States in the April 1961 revolt. Testimony

[29] *Procès des Généraux Challe et Zeller*, p. 50.
[30] *Ibid.*, p. 38. Italics added.
[31] *Ibid.*, pp. 257, 258.

at the trial of Challe and Zeller brought out the fact that the generals had built their hopes for success, among other things, upon support by outside countries. Zeller mentioned specifically Portugal, South Africa, Israel, and South America, to which Challe added that he would much prefer something else — the United States.[32] Was there any ground for Challe to believe that his fondest wish might come true? Apparently the French government's suspicions after the revolt coincided with the General's anticipations. An American reporter experienced in French affairs wrote that "Foreign Minister Couve de Murville told a few favored journalists that Challe had been encouraged in his putsch by the CIA."[33] Sam White of the London *Evening Standard* asked General Gavin, "What does the American Ambassador think of the fact that the French Ministry of Foreign Affairs and the Minister himself have helped spread these rumors [of an American role in the revolt]?" Gavin refused to express an opinion, but Couve de Murville subsequently denied to the Foreign Affairs Committee of the National Assembly that he or his ministry had anything to do with the rumors. He did not, however, disclaim the existence of the rumors or that the French government placed some credence in them, an omission noted with regret by the *New York Times*.[34] It almost goes without saying that official United States sources denied any involvement whatsoever. In a more positive vein, discreet publicity was given to President Kennedy's offer to President de Gaulle of any assistance he might desire in putting down the revolt.[35]

The possibility of unauthorized, individual American approaches aside, the conclusion would seem to be that Challe's devotion to the proposition that the safety of Europe lay in Algeria had led him to an unrealistic expectation of American help. The rebels' radio voice, Radio-France, declared: "The Kennedy government cannot take a position

[32] *Ibid.*, p. 95, testimony of General Georges Héritier, chief of the combined military staff in Algiers.
[33] Joseph Barry in the *New York Post*, May 5, 1961.
[34] *L'Année Politique, 1961*, p. 435.
[35] It is not reported whether De Gaulle was more annoyed at the offer — implying weakness on his part — or at the publicity — implying ingratitude.

against the action of the Algiers generals because their essential aim is to keep Algeria French and therefore Western."[36] Challe could reason that a number of American interests would be advanced by the defeat of the FLN. The United States opposed communism. It wished to bring France back into effective NATO membership. It desired that the North Atlantic Pact mean what it said about defense of the territory of the signators. The careers of some of its military officers were involved in the doctrine of defense evolved by NATO. It wished to integrate NATO national forces insofar as military efficiency indicated the practicality of doing so. The United States, therefore, could not oppose the removal of the biggest stumbling block to attainment of all these aims — President de Gaulle. Finally, to recapture its international prestige the United States needed a dramatic success to balance the fiasco of the abortive invasion of Cuba.[37]

From formulation of the principles of revolutionary war, to passionate defense of the army's role in Algeria, to priority of that role over all other French and Western military responsibilities — the conclusion to this chain of logic was the necessity of combatting De Gaulle as long as necessary and with whatever means might be available. How long to fight, in fact, was an issue which divided the army rebels of April 1961. Although original plans called for continued occupation of all or part of Algeria until its failure to crush the revolt brought down the Fifth Republic, General Challe talked Zeller into surrendering with him as soon as it became clear that all the armed forces in Algeria would not rally to his cause.[38]

Two other generals, however, were greater believers in the practicality of revolutionary war and refused to accept Challe's plea. Instead, Salan and Jouhaud walked out of the surrender parley to organize the

[36] *Ibid.*, p. 286.

[37] Azeau elaborates the congruence of interests as Challe might have seen them; *op. cit.*, pp. 81–89.

[38] Challe thereby may have saved both their lives. In his action and in Zeller's eventual acquiescence the prosecutor found the extenuating circumstances necessary to avoid asking for the death penalty. *Procès des Généraux Challe et Zeller*, pp. 241–249.

Secret Army.[39] Salan's dedication to the West and to democracy, as he wished the court to understand it, has already been mentioned. But the tribunal's president and prosecutor were so unkind as to reveal the actions his generalized concepts led Salan to advocate by quoting a few of his directives to fellow officers in the OAS: "In a word, our action should immediately take on a more revolutionary aspect, in the practical sense of the word . . . Fear is also often the beginning of wisdom. One should not forget that, quite independently of the immediate effect, all action should try to exemplify the presence of the movement everywhere, create a climate, give the impression of force, of cohesion . . . Mission: create an insurrectional climate in the Metropole in order to paralyze the [political] power . . . Create a climate of generalized insecurity by spreading false news, false bombs, warning inhabitants or neighbors of buildings housing members of the P.C. [Communist Party], P.S.U. [United Socialists], and the UNR [Gaullist Union for the New Republic], threatening letters, anonymous telephone calls, etc. . . . We must inflame all sectors. In the type of war we make, everything is good."[40]

Salan's words provide, like Trinquier's book, a veritable recipe for revolutionary war, by a man prepared to lead the way. Air Force General and Chief of Staff Edmond Jouhaud was only a follower. He felt the need for a mere passing reference to "subversive war" as theoretical underpinning for the robberies, bombings, and assassinations he supervised in the Oran sector of the OAS.[41] In addition to seeking to escape legal responsibility by professing ignorance of the worst offenses of the OAS or by blaming them on the FLN or on government provocateurs, Jouhaud took refuge in the historic dictum that military war is hell. "The only explanation that I can give is that we were in

[39] "I wish you would tell me if you were satisfied with the arrival of General Salan [in Algiers, to join the rebellion]; if it was expected or if, on the contrary, it was a surprise to you?" asked the president of the tribunal, Maurice Patin. "I prefer not to reply, Mr. President," said Challe. *Ibid.*, p. 64. Challe's character, as revealed during the trial, would make it most unwise to attribute his answer to simple concern for his own neck.

[40] *Procès de Raoul Salan*, pp. 98, 99–100, 101, 457. "I don't believe France has ever known as abominable moments," commented Prosecutor Gavalda.

[41] *Procès d'Edmond Jouhaud*, pp. 17, 78–124.

revolt against the fate that Algeria was having to undergo; it is well understood that, beginning from the moment when one begins a revolution, one employs extra-legal procedures, one defends oneself as best one can in the struggle between life and death." And to the Prosecutor's exclamation, "What of the victims who didn't revolt, the innocent victims!": "I don't know of any war in which there were no victims."[42]

Although France had signed cease-fire agreements at Evian in March 1962 with the Provisional Algerian Government, although its two top leaders, Salan and Jouhaud, had been caught, the OAS fought on, first in Algeria, then in the Metropole, its dialecticians still mouthing the sick words of subversive war for defense of the west. ". . . It is not altogether paradoxical to suggest that for the security of the West, Algiers is at least as important as Vientiane, and North Africa at least as important as the little Laotian kingdom," Jacques Soustelle told the readers of the *National Review*.[43] Colonel Antoine Argoud's secretly printed *The Algerian Problem — French Solution,* to which reference has already been made, was distributed through military and civilian channels during the spring of 1962, shortly before the Colonel made a widely reported tour of French military units in West Germany. "As for the army," Argoud wrote, "it has put in fifteen years elaborating a doctrine of coherent, effective, revolutionary war. It has got one, but a part of the command is still far from being penetrated by it. In the face of an adversary applying with formidable effectiveness [and] with fanaticism a revolutionary technique of subversion, it [part of the command] persists most often in using anachronistic methods which are totally ineffective. It is thus not surprising that under these circumstances victory has not yet chosen our [OAS] side."[44]

"The OAS? Never heard of it," said De Gaulle in November 1961.[45] When the President made the statement — to emphasize his calm determination, of course, not to reflect any lack of knowledge — the activi-

---

[42] *Ibid.,* pp. 103, 86, 108.
[43] "De Gaulle's France on the Road to Neutralism," June 19, 1962.
[44] Extracts printed in *L'Express,* May 10, 1962.
[45] *L'Année Politique, 1961,* p. 150.

ties of the OAS had been growing for some time in metropolitan France, although they did not rival the ferocity being displayed in the principal cities of Algeria. In the same month De Gaulle spoke, Maurice Papon, Paris police chief, reported that since the beginning of the year over a thousand investigations had been made and over five hundred suspects had been arrested. Fifty-three people were specifically charged with bombings by plastic explosions.[46] Drawing up a balance sheet to demonstrate that the more the government claimed to have "dismantled," "decapitated," or "intensified the struggle against" the OAS, the bolder the outlawed group became in its acts of terrorism, L'Express cited a government report of 190 bombings in Paris and 161 in the rest of France during the first ten months of 1961.[47]

The "defense" continued to be the strange, savage rules of revolutionary war. Testifying in the trial of adjutant Robin, one of those accused of murdering a gendarme, Colonel de Sèze, himself a prisoner, first hailed the defendant's domestic virtues. His hands, it appeared, could not be covered with blood, because Robin loved his wife and children. "How, then, explain his entry into the battle that brought him here?" the Colonel asked, rhetorically. "It is natural. He followed his career. He began to fight when fifteen years old. He continued to fight for France and none other. Subversive war really exists. It goes well for those who know how to wage it. He tried it. Who could better understand him than other soldiers? *He is more than ever a true soldier.*" Did Colonel de Sèze then approve of the means (murder) employed by Robin?, the head of the tribunal, General Gardet, wanted to know. To reply was easy for De Sèze: "Entirely," he said simply.[48]

Directing the robberies, bombings, and murders in the early part of 1962 was ex-General Raoul Salan. For him, unlike Challe and Zeller, Prosecutor Gavalda could find no extenuating circumstances. "For not having saved or tried to save what was perhaps not yet lost, don't you fear — these are cruel words, but I must utter them — that when the hour comes, if it should come, God Himself, beholding your unpardon-

[46] *Ibid.*, p. 151.
[47] November 23, 1961.
[48] *Le Monde*, August 1, 1962. Italics added.

able obstinacy, will forget the promise made to the apostle Saint John, the favorite disciple, and will not deign to wipe away the tears that fall from your eyes?" Of all the summations for the state in the many trials of OAS leaders, Gavalda's was perhaps the most severe. Nonetheless, a majority of the court somehow managed to find the necessary excuses for Salan's actions to save his life, a substantial testimony to the brilliance and eloquence of his attorney, M. Tixier-Vignancour. Amidst the tumult that greeted the verdict, the defense staff shouted the *Marseillaise*.[49]

Only a few days later *L'Express* published a letter Salan had written from prison after his arrest. Addressed to "Scimitar," it called for the transfer of one hundred million francs to the person he had designated the month before to replace him. A second letter by Salan, published at the same time, but dated April 1, revealed that the man he had chosen to lead the OAS was none other than the head of the wartime Council of National Resistance and one-time Foreign Minister and Premier under the Fourth Republic, Georges Bidault.[50]

In June 1962 Salan, in response to an appeal from Jouhaud to help him escape the execution to which he had been condemned, asked the OAS *in Algeria* kindly to cease their bombings and live in "common harmony and peace" with the Provisional Government of Algeria.[51] By then, however, several changes were taking place in the terrorist apparatus. Defeated in their primary objective of preventing the transfer of authority from France to the Algerian government, leaders of the OAS began to flee Algeria for less dangerous locales in Spain, Italy, Switzerland, West Germany, Belgium, and France itself. From their scattered hideouts they proceeded to argue among themselves about the proper next steps. Additional confusion for the OAS arose as it tried to recruit for terroristic activities the thousands upon thousands of Moslems and Europeans who were fleeing to the Metropole. However good his communications might be, no prison inmate could continue to control an organization in such a state of flux. Finally, not least among

---

[49] *Procès de Raoul Salan*, pp. 480, 549.
[50] *L'Express*, May 31, 1962.
[51] *Le Monde*, June 24–25, 1962.

the changes was the explicit political coloration being given the Secret Army, as signalized by the position Georges Bidault was assuming.

Bidault's new, arrogantly named Council of National Resistance (CNR) sought to add to partisans of revolutionary war any and all groups anxious for a change in the regime. Since the Fifth Republic, as its military founders knew full well, was the personalized regime of Charles de Gaulle, a change entailed his elimination. Attacks on the head of state were therefore "continually in preparation" throughout 1962.[52] One plot called for his assassination before the July 1 referendum on the Evian agreements with the Provisional Algerian Government. "This period of democratic consultation, will it in fact take place?" asked an OAS letter. "At the moment it is impossible to say. Grave and important events are going to take place in Algiers, Oran, Paris, events which are going to modify the circumstances of what was for some years the Algerian problem and what has become the French problem."[53]

Two months later De Gaulle's entourage was assaulted near Petit-Clamart. About one hundred fifty shots were fired; twelve hit the President's car; one narrowly missed him. It was, Le Monde calculated, at least the seventh attempted assassination since December 1960.[54] It also came the closest to success, which was probably the reason the CNR boastfully and publicly embraced it. "Some patriots," it said in a widely circulated letter, "carried out Wednesday, August 22 an act of resistance, seeking to liberate France of a lying dictator who leads the country to ruin after having brought it to dishonor. The Council of National Resistance totally approves of this action."[55] In a wry twist of psychological warfare, the letter was printed on paper of the National

[52] The words are those of L'Express, May 24, 1962. The appearance of the CNR actually represented a stage in the fragmentation of the movement against De Gaulle. Although the CNR hoped to unite conspiratorial groups and provide them with a political super-structure, some OAS leaders were reluctant to submerge the identity of the Secret Army, knowing that Bidault did not command universal support among civilian activists and that military elements would not relish the conversion of the crusade into yet another battle among politicians.

[53] Quoted in Le Monde, June 16, 1962.

[54] August 24, 1962.

[55] L'Express, August 31, 1962.

Assembly, and the envelope bore the words "National Assembly" where the sender's address normally stands.[56] Not a bit discouraged by its failure, the CNR announced through its bulletin *France Presse-action* in September that "the fall of the Gaullist regime" was still its number one objective.[57] In February 1963 another plot to kill the President, this time in connection with his visit to the Ecole Militaire, was frustrated by the police, again demonstrating the persistence, if not the effectiveness, of the CNR.

Investigations following the Petit-Clamart attack on De Gaulle not only confirmed the disparate nature of the social groupings involved in the OAS-CNR, but also revealed the twisted ideological convictions spawned by revolutionary war. Captain Jean-René Souètre, one of those rounded up, had transferred from the reserve to the career air force. His part in the Barricades Revolt of January 1960 had never been made clear, but he was still in Algeria in February 1961, where he joined the *maquis* (OAS), taking three non-commissioned officers with him. Surrounded by paratroopers, he, his three sergeants, and five civilians, of whom the mayor of Saint-Bênoit-du-Sault was one, were talked into surrendering. He had the good fortune to appear before the court when boredom with the number of cases produced by the Generals' Revolt had set in, and he was sentenced to three years in an internment camp, which, it turned out, was run like a resort hotel — or like a training school for the OAS. He was married there in a large ceremony, organized by a fellow internee, former deputy Jean Dides, and witnessed by General Clément, the commander of the Ninth Military Region. A month later Souètre, together with a captain and sixteen other would-be OAS members, escaped in the confusion created in the town by an exercise most fortuitously organized by Saint-Cyr cadets. In addition to being obviously very popular with his military superiors, Souètre was assessed by them as an extremely brave man, an adventurer, an opportunist, and "an admirer of the totalitarian system."[58]

[56] See facsimile in *L'Express, ibid.*
[57] *Le Monde,* September 20, 1962.
[58] *Le Monde,* August 26–27, 1962.

Souètre's political views were no more bizarre than Colonel Bastien-Thiry's interpretation of the tenets of Christianity. This military engineer worked in the technical section of air force headquarters in Paris. The shock created by the revelation that such a high-ranking professional officer was actually the organizer of an attempt on De Gaulle's life was magnified by his words of justification. "On the moral level," he wrote, "I know that our action will be discussed. We reflected for a long time on this aspect of the question before committing ourselves to it. Like my friend [and co-defendant] De la Tocnaye, I am a practicing Catholic, and our group was formed in part by practicing Catholics like ourselves. As you know, the Church recognizes the legitimacy of what is called tyrannicide, with the reservation, naturally, that certain conditions and criteria be fulfilled. It would obviously take too long to discuss this aspect of the question. We gathered the advice of eminent ecclesiastics. This advice was that the required conditions for tyrannicide had been most abundantly fulfilled." He refused to give the names of any of the "eminent ecclesiastics," but many officials of the Church expressed dismay and indignation, and the organ of the French Assembly of Cardinals and Archbishops, without denying that tyrannicide could indeed be justified in certain situations, declared that the prerequisites for such extreme action had in no way been met in France.[59] At his trial Bastien-Thiry held to his position. "This is no place for theological quibbles," he said. "The tyranny of General de Gaulle is not that 'soft' type of tyranny to which certain fathers of the Church advise resignation in a spirit of patience and Christian mortification. It is a violent, bloody tyranny that divides and destroys, one that is responsible for the death of innumerable victims . . . This man is streaming with French blood, and he represents the shame of France."[60]

In addition to defending the Christian right of tyrannicide, Thiry's fellow officer Alain de Bougrenet de la Tocnaye treated the court to a lengthy, rambling exegesis of his political philosophy, which may well serve as a commentary on the irrationalities of revolutionary war as a system of thought. "Is it not evident that Moslem fatalism common to

[59] *Le Monde*, September 25, 1962.
[60] *Le Monde*, February 3–4, 1963.

all underdeveloped peoples still living on the tribal level prepares the way for communism? . . . Decolonization is explained by the fact that it makes easy the transactions of high finance, exacerbated by technological progress and the possession of the world that tends to fall into the hands of administrative councils as monstrous as they are irresponsible . . . We believe that General de Gaulle has for many years favored the development in France of Titoism, which by its policy of division, its Marxist and historical determinism is one of the causes of the accelerated decadence and narrow materialism that stupefy our poor country . . . Officers now must convert themselves into technicians, civil servants, or encamped policemen. This is part of the systematic plans which, by destroying noble ideals, by 'technocratizing,' makes Marxization easier . . . There is also the deliberate elimination of elites and the constant recourse to the unorganized mass indoctrinated by propaganda (press, television, radio) . . . We reject capitalism and Marxism and therefore Gaullism that leads us first to an amalgamation of the two in order then to deliver us to bolshevism." And so on and on.[61]

One can only shudder at the range of the menace revealed by De la Tocnaye: high finance, De Gaulle, the French masses, Titoists, Moslems, underdeveloped peoples — all combining to deliver the world to communism. Lacking logical coherence from the very beginning, theoretical guides on how to win a nationalist-inspired war were reduced to maunderings on the weaknesses of democracy as a political system. A group which believed it could not fight effectively without restructuring, first the enemy's, then its own social system naturally accepted as a corollary the need to restructure political institutions as well, by murder of the executive if necessary. The extent of military involvement in political action and the concept which deepened that involvement are the subjects of the following two chapters.

[61] *Le Monde*, February 3–4, 1963.

POLITIQUE

E T

POLITIQUE

The word politique *is a bit misused, for there is only one word for both policy and politics . . . The politics (policy) of General Zeller and of many in the Army is, in the best meaning of the word, what identifies the Army with the Nation but does not make of the Army the servant, the docile supporter of all the political parties which follow one another. If the Army follows political passions, it is no longer the Army of France.* — André Toulouse, pleading for General Zeller

A N EXAMINATION of the nature of the French army's involvement in politics should prudently begin by clearing away some of the tangled underbrush that obscures the subject. Participation by French and other armies in politics is no new phenomenon. As long as there have been governments concerned with defending themselves against external and internal enemies, those governments have been seeking to avoid the experience of the unfortunate Doctor Frankenstein. The French have a very long history and therefore a very long experience, unsuccessful in part, in collective self-management, of which relegation of the armed forces to the position of executors of state policy is a significant aspect. While recognizing precedents and historical antecedents, however, the author will concentrate on the contemporary configurations of the ancient problem of civil-military relations, in order, hopefully, to shed light on the nature of the Fifth Republic's political institutions and the international statecraft of President de Gaulle.

The author will also shun the argument, a specious one, that the plague, being the plague, does not acquire respectability with age, and the thing to do is eliminate it. Quite obviously military involvement in national policy-making is both necessary and desirable, given the existence of nation-states. In fact, officials of the United Nations are even now painfully discovering this requirement in their attempt to manipulate rudimentary elements of international government. There is a need for military contributions to statecraft throughout the policy-making process: the determination of national goals, the assessment of the nature of the international environment in terms of those goals, the discussion of alternative courses of action, the choice of particular policies, their arrangement in patterns of techniques, and the administration of policy. Recognition of necessity and desirability, however, provides no prescription for dosage. In military jargon, at issue is the proper "mix." Democratic and would-be democratic systems cannot avoid the difficult effort of continually defining the military component so that it remains a contributor to the policy-making, policy-executing process, not the master, dominating or usurping that process.

Western states, because of the nature of the postwar international environment, have found it exceedingly difficult to define the appropriate place for their military establishments. Military technology now makes national survival itself precarious, while hostile ingenuity adds new dimensions to both the external and the internal threat. At the same time Western governments have assumed increasing responsibilities for the welfare of their own citizenry and for that of underdeveloped countries. More and more is expected, while less and less can be taken for granted. Not unnaturally, therefore, processes for making decisions have grown more complicated. The ingredients in the "mix" are more varied, the number of individuals and groups augmented. Under these circumstances, there is no "ideal" military contribution. Nevertheless, it is evident that during the past fifteen years in all Western states at certain times and in the formulation of certain policies the military portion has been controlling. In fact, some analysts have questioned whether a Western democratic system can cope successfully with threats to its security without providing its armed forces with so great power that the system itself will be damaged, perhaps destroyed.

This chapter will be explicitly concerned with the inter-penetration of civilian and military groups involved in making and carrying out the policy of France. For all the permeability which characterized both (for civilians in France, as elsewhere, can believe in military control and military figures in civilian control), each was aware of its own separate identity and sought to limit the intrusion of the other. On the one hand, there was the professional military corps of the three services, complaining of attempted corruption by political authorities and their front men masquerading in uniform. Complaining even as it entered deeper into the political process. On the other hand, there was the civilian executive, trying to reach some rough congruence between decision-making authority and political responsibility to the electorate. Trying, even as that same executive made the task all but impossible by abdicating substantial power to the officer corps and gravely weakening the means of assessing political accountability. The emergence of civilian groups as the victors in this struggle cannot therefore be correlated with progress toward stable democracy; the second part of this book will indicate the heavy price De Gaulle and his satrapy were obliged or willing to pay to eliminate the military threat to the Fifth Republic.[1]

The military challenge to postwar civilian government in France was as direct as it was persistent. The ill-conceived actions of an increas-

[1] Thugs, thieves, murderers, and those that hired them may not legitimately find sanction for their despicable acts in the charge that elements of democracy had been destroyed under the Fifth Republic. They themselves struck the heaviest blows.

ingly politicalized army made its loudly proclaimed justification suspect
from the very beginning. Declaring that the institutions of the Fourth
Republic were feeble and fragmented, the army proceeded to weaken
them further. After ensuring the destruction of the Fourth Republic
on the grounds of its ineffectiveness, the army indicted its successor in
a manner that could hardly have been more severe. Then, when it
failed to accomplish a change in the policy of De Gaulle's republic,
army elements systematically sought to modify the bases on which national decisions rested. Again unsuccessful, military activists through
the OAS tried to demolish the Fifth Republic itself by violently removing President de Gaulle from the scene. All this, the reader is reminded,
took place in recent times in a modern Western state, demonstrating
that military intrusion into politics is not confined to so-called "backward" nations.

Although military elements assumed the functions of government in
both 1958 and 1961 in portions of Algeria, their objective for France
itself was neither a military state nor even a state militarized by the
implantation of key personnel. Their aim was more utilitarian and
more modest: a system dedicated to a particular policy, not just one
policy among many, not just one policy enjoying priority, but one
policy, first and foremost; one in the light of which all other national
policies would be determined. De Gaulle became the chosen instrument of the 1958 insurrection because the plotters believed he could
and would keep Algeria French. De Gaulle the general held very
limited appeal; De Gaulle the man was not popular. What counted
with the army was his availability, presumed capacity, and declared
intent.

Subsequent fury, bitterness, and scorn toward De Gaulle must be
read in the light of the military design. The French army had charged
the Fourth Republic with vacillation and weakness and its society with
decadence and corruption. The real accusation, however, was that both
French society and French political institutions had other goals, other
desires than winning colonial wars. It was the nature of postwar statecraft, not just an inability to formulate a policy, which crystallized the
army's hostility. The motivations of the military became clear in the

climactic revolt against Premier Pierre Pflimlin, when the army feared that Pflimlin might be able to modify, however slightly, previous French policy of giving it a free hand to "pacify" Algeria.

As with Pflimlin, so later with De Gaulle. Others might find the political system he directed weak and vacillating; what the army objected to was its strength and determination. Divisions and softness in the Fifth Republic were probed and exploited wherever possible, just as had been done under the Fourth Republic, but it was De Gaulle's consummate ability to out-maneuver the army that most aroused military anger. The army had thought it was installing an effective and willing promoter of its Algerian policy. What it got was a President who, behind a smoke-screen of public contradiction and ambiguity, sidled down the very path of "abandonment" from which the army had barred the Fourth Republic.

Military justifications for these political intrusions abound. They serve as a veritable lexicon of excuses for attempted domination by the armed forces of national decision-making processes throughout history throughout the world. Yet they have a certain naive freshness arising from supposed discovery akin to that of a child finding out for himself that two and two really do make four, that there really was a Christopher Columbus. On one justification some time has already been spent. There was, the army claimed, a distinction between the eternal Nation and the ephemeral social groups that comprised it. So was there a distinction between the eternal State, sovereign embodiment of the Nation, and passing political systems that purported to speak in its name. Of all groups comprising the Nation, of all structures speaking for the State, the Army was closest to the underlying, enduring essence of France. "The army is not only a corps that reforms itself, but an entire grouping that *transforms* itself by integrating itself into new national structures. The Army is entirely open to progress and entirely adaptable to forms of modern life. Still it is necessary that it not be made 'nihilist' by compromising the spiritual integrity of its devotion to the Country."[2]

[2] Jean Valluy, "Réflexions sur l'armée de demain," *Revue des Deux Mondes,* July 15, 1962, p. 171.

Rebuttals to this mysticism were surprisingly few, but not altogether absent. Maurice Patin, president of the tribunal trying Generals Challe and Zeller, was one who unequivocally identified the existing government with the abstract State and subordinated the Army to both. "It is not for the Army to make commitments, it is for the State," he told defense witness Colonel Pierre Buchoux, amidst "murmurs in the hall." "There is a Government, there is France, it is for them to make commitments . . . It is not for it [the army] to direct the policy of France; it is for France itself and for its government."[3] But, pointed out the army, there were three recent precedents for military judgment as to the right of a government to represent the State. De Gaulle himself had been involved in all of them. In 1940 General de Gaulle invited military officers to fight on with the Allies on the grounds that the armistice had been signed by illegitimate political authority with no right to speak for France. De Gaulle's Free France then encouraged the Resistance in its insurrectionary acts against Vichy, acts judged by the army to be not dissimilar to those carried out by the OAS under orders of Salan and Jouhaud. Finally, in 1958, De Gaulle seized power again after challenging the legitimacy of the Fourth Republic from its conception. Pleading for Jouhaud, his attorney referred to "the proposed parachute drop in Paris and the landing of parachutists in the area around Paris in full accord with General de Gaulle . . . General Challe, General Jouhaud, General Salan, and General Zeller never thought for a moment of doing what today's Chief of State had planned to execute on May 29, 1958."[4]

There is, in truth, something incongruous in the spectacle of Resistance and Free French fighters attacking their former leader and embracing their old enemies. Jacques Isorni, defense attorney in the postwar trial of Marshal Pétain, tells of a public declaration made in 1960 by Georges Bidault, one-time head of the Council of National Resistance. "Now that Isorni is here I have something to say," Bidault told the assemblage. "Henceforth, and whatever happens, I shall never say

[3] *Procès des Généraux Challe et Zeller*, p. 157.
[4] *Procès d'Edmond Jouhaud*, p. 303. See also Isorni, *op. cit.*, p. 93. The question of Vichy's "legitimacy" aside, the reader may find rather strained an analogy between De Gaulle's efforts to defeat the German subjugators of his country and efforts of French officers to destroy their own government. See below, p. 117.

another word against Pétain." To which Isorni, still seeking retribution, "risked, 'Mr. President [of the Council of Ministers], that doesn't satisfy me.' 'With Fritz on his back,' Bidault then added, 'Pétain himself saved the Empire for us.' "[5]

France experienced four political systems in the eighteen years between 1940 and 1958, if one does not count the provisional government of the liberation. The authority and legitimacy of all were questioned, contemporaneously and retrospectively. When generals join politicians in the recurrent debate, the structure of military command breaks apart, and obedience can no longer be taken for granted. What would he do, an officer was asked, if he received contradictory orders from President de Gaulle and General Massu; "I would reflect," was the answer.[6]

Each invocation of the army's right, indeed duty, to rebel against policies it judged wrong made subsequent rebellions easier. "The tragic events that have assailed France since 1940 and that have proliferated governments speaking or pretending to speak in her name have put the minds of our high [military] leaders to a hard test, for the disobedience of leaders has been successively considered as treason and as glory," Emile Toulouse, General Zeller's lawyer, declared. "I had, gentlemen, the great honor of defending many leaders before all the High Courts which have followed one another in France over the past twenty years, and whose name and composition varied with the times. The crime has always been the same — treason — but the definition varied. I pleaded, furthermore, before the Riom Court during the occupation; we defended those leaders who had faith in De Gaulle and because they had faith in De Gaulle, they disobeyed, and they were prosecuted because they disobeyed . . . And then, following the Liberation, I still defended leaders before the High Courts; they were accused of having obeyed the Marshal . . . We heard fall from the lips of a high magistrate words borrowed from the Declaration of the Rights of Man, 'insurrection is a duty.' On May 13, 1958, gentlemen, the [military] leaders disobeyed . . . They disobeyed, all the Generals. They disobeyed because their alle-

[5] Isorni, *op. cit.*, p. 51.
[6] Raoul Girardet, "Pouvoir civil et pouvoir militaire dans la France contemporaine," *Revue Française de Science Politique*, March 1960, p. 34.

giance bade them to be at the orders of what they thought to be the Nation and the Country [*Patrie*]."[7]

The purpose of positing a separation between Nation and government, of citing previous military rebellions was, of course, to lay the basis for a claim that the actions of a particular regime were illegal because the regime itself was illegitimate. M. Perrussel, taking up Toulouse's argument, went on to attack the constitutionality of De Gaulle's regime. "I have the impression," he said, "that all that's left of the Constitution we voted for with enthusiasm in 1958 is debris. I wonder if we are still under the Fifth Republic, or at least under the Fifth/2 [Fifth Republic, Second Version] . . ." Among the articles Jouhaud's lawyer contended had been violated were those establishing the institutions of the French Community, Article 66 forbidding arbitrary detention, and Article 20 confiding to the Government (the Premier and his cabinet[8]) the determination and conduct of national policy. The heart of his accusation rested, however, on Article 2 — "France is an indivisible republic" — and on Article 5 — "The President of the Republic is guarantor of the territorial integrity."[9] Far from being guilty of treason, military officers who rebelled against De Gaulle were helping to protect the sacred soil of France (in that Algeria was divided into "departments," as was France itself) against unconstitutional alienation by the usurper of political authority. "When policy and law are in contradiction," Isorni asked in his plea for General Pierre Bigot, vacillator par excellence in the Generals' Revolt of 1961, "where does duty lie?" The question was rhetorical.[10]

Although Gaullists had questioned the legitimacy of the Fourth Republic, the primary military complaint had been that political impotence was drawing the army into politics against its wishes and, perhaps, its better judgment. Since the impotence of the state forced generals to improvise, their policies could not be held against them,

[7] *Procès des Généraux Challe et Zeller*, pp. 310, 311.
[8] See note 45, p. 86.
[9] *Procès d'Edmond Jouhaud*, pp. 321–323.
[10] For the text of the plea, see Isorni, *op. cit.*, pp. 217–235.

Pierre Guillain de Benouville wrote in 1951, considerably before the Algerian war erupted.[11] Six years later an army officer was repeating: "Today there is no such thing as a clear-cut, effective, and permanent military policy in France. We would not have failed in Indochina, in Morocco, in Tunisia, and at Port Said if the government had been able to lay down a forceful and clearly shown line of conduct for us. It is not our job to serve as diplomats or to patch up the government's mistakes."[12] About the same time General André Zeller, already well known and shortly to become notorious, was advising Frenchmen to get over their fear of military coups; such adventures either took place long ago (Napoleon) or were pure vaudeville (Boulanger). In any event, he added, the greatest cause was political weakness.[13]

The army continued to be unhappy under the Fifth Republic. Some of its leaders contended that De Gaulle had misled them into believing that his policies were the same as theirs. Consequently they went astray out of ignorance. The misunderstanding arose, they persisted, because De Gaulle's aims in Algeria were shrouded in mystery, were, whether by intent or not, far too vague to be interpreted accurately. General Bigot could not understand the motivation of political leaders in Paris who kept repeating that Algeria was French and the French would never leave, but were all the while providing the FLN with cause to hope they would do precisely that. In an agony of indecision he had turned to high authority, only to meet equivocation. His direct superior, Air Force Chief of Staff General Paul Stehlin, told him: "I am not currently informed. I don't know."[14]

Equally confused were Generals Challe, Jouhaud, and Salan. General Challe thought De Gaulle's aim was to win the war in Algeria, that the dupes were the Moslem rebels, not the army. For this reason Challe failed to help the military elements that initiated the Barricades Revolt of January 1960. What he proposed to do a year later was to pacify

[11] "Les généraux devant la politique," *La Nef*, April–May 1951, pp. 133–140.
[12] "The French Officer Speaks His Mind," *Réalités* (English edition), July 1957, p. 10.
[13] "Armée et politique," *Revue de Défense Nationale*, April 1957, p. 516.
[14] Quoted in Isorni, *op. cit.*, pp. 229, 230.

Algeria "in a few weeks," and say to France, "We have made peace and return your sons to you."[15]

Stranger yet was General Jouhaud's experience. He claimed that members of Debré's cabinet approached him in November 1960 with the request that he lead a "legal" insurrection to thwart any attempt to give away French Algeria. Jouhaud received some advice from General Zeller, himself plotting to attain the same purpose: "Watch out," Zeller warned, "you are going to fall into a terrible trap." Although his civilian contacts insisted De Gaulle knew and approved of the plan, Jouhaud decided to hold out for some direct, overt sign that the President really wanted a revolt against himself to take place. (The sign was never made.)[16]

Most precise and passionate in his assault on the mysteries of De Gaulle's Algerian policy was Jean Tixier-Vignancour, Salan's able and effective defender. De Gaulle, he contended, actually favored Algerian independence as early as 1956, but of course could not get on with the job until he had recaptured power. To this end the aid of the army was indispensable, and he therefore deliberately deluded the army in 1958 and continued to do so thereafter. The President brought about the April 1961 revolt, which he then used as a pretext to assume full powers under Article 16 of the Constitution and to purge the army. The failure of the *putsch* produced the OAS, but "all the rest was prefabricated . . . to reach finally the independence of Algeria." "General de Gaulle has won," Tixier-Vignancour concluded. "The independence of Algeria will be proclaimed the first of July [1962]. It will thus have taken him four years and one month. The route was long; it was rough, but by his tenacity, by his exceptional determination, he succeeded in overcoming all obstacles."[17]

There can be no doubt, of course, that Tixier-Vignancour's ingenuity was employed to draw the tribunal's attention away from the extremes to which the army went to guard its power in Algeria. From the very

[15] *Procès des Généraux Challe et Zeller*, p. 40.
[16] *Procès d'Edmond Jouhaud*, pp. 216–232, 328–330.
[17] *Procès de Raoul Salan*, pp. 508–542; quotations, pp. 526, 542.

beginning, it was the explosiveness of the army's potential opposition which caused De Gaulle to tread warily, taking a half step backward or sideways for each one he dared take forward.

Inherent in vacillation is contradiction. Thus, the army not only claimed to be squeezed between legality and politics, but also to be caught in the political machinery. Perhaps the example most prominently featured by defense attorneys at the trials of military leaders for rebellion against the state was the Wilaya Affair. At his first press conference, held on October 23, 1958, De Gaulle startled the army by saying the Algerian nationalists had fought courageously. (What could one then think of the torture and terror used by both sides?) Let their chiefs now have the always honorable recourse to the white flag of surrender, establish contact with French commanders, and arrange a "peace of the brave." Enter General Challe two and a half years later to claim that Moslem chiefs of Wilaya IV (a nationalist military sector) had indeed attempted in March 1960 to take up De Gaulle's offer, which he had repeated in his speech of September 16, 1959 on self-determination in Algeria. The sector was a large and extremely important one, including the city of Algiers and stretching to the borders of Kabylia. The chiefs, said Challe, went to Paris, saw De Gaulle, and returned announcing that they intended to put the surrender plan into effect.[18] Moreover, the Moslems openly credited the psychological warfare of the army with their decision to turn from the FLN to France. De Gaulle and French forces were on the verge of victory in the long struggle to hold the Algerian departments. But no surrender came; the sweet taste turned bitter, all because De Gaulle continued to indicate to the Provisional Algerian Government, the "external apparatus" he professed to despise, that he would negotiate with them, not insist on separate surrenders by military leaders in the field. With De Gaulle's encouragement the "apparatus" sent representatives to Melun for political talks in the summer

[18] At this point in his recital the prosecutor warned Challe that he should weigh his words carefully; he would have to answer questions later. It should be noted that Challe himself was no longer in Algeria when the Moslem chiefs returned, having been recalled by presidential summons.

of 1960. Although the discussions were broken off without agreement, Wilaya IV leaders became so fearful of future punishment by their fellow Moslems that they gave up their plans to surrender.[19]

Challe asserted he had proof that his account was accurate, but in his summary the prosecutor pointed out that the court had waited in vain for corroboration.[20] French and Algerian leaders never did shed light on the mystery, although Robert Martel, extreme Rightist, participant in the events of May 1958 and later persistent plotter against De Gaulle, printed a detailed account in his clandestinely circulated *La voix du maquis*.[21] Challe's failure to substantiate his claims reflected his acute dilemma. While he wished all to know that in his revolt he had enjoyed the support of practically the entire professional army corps, at his trial he did not want to embroil others in his predicament by naming names. The best way out was solemn assertion. "Mr. Prosecutor, just as you don't cast doubt on my good faith, I do not doubt the good faith of officers who spoke to me as they did."[22]

While the army was at times prone to affirm an intellectual incapacity to unravel the intricacies of the Fifth Republic's attitude toward Algeria, it was simultaneously insisting that the Metropole, not the French army in Algeria, was the misinformed party. The age-old cry of the man in the field — civilian or military — was reiterated: "Those bumbling fools back home don't understand the way things are." Formed without regard for the "real" facts, government policy was misdirected and dangerous. Its authors apparently believed they were acting out of necessity, under pressure of events, whereas no such pressure, no such necessity actually existed.

Resident Ministers in Algeria, supposedly the representatives of metropolitan political authority, felt no differently from the army on this score, one reason being that they were either acceptable to the military or they did not get to Algeria in the first place. In defending Salan as a loyal officer, obedient to the government and republican by tradition,

[19] *Procès des Généraux Challe et Zeller*, pp. 30–34.
[20] *Ibid.*, p. 235.
[21] Jacques Fauvet, Jean Planchais, *La Fronde des généraux*, Paris, Arthaud, 1961, pp. 263–265.
[22] *Procès des Généraux Challe et Zeller*, p. 33.

Socialist Robert Lacoste was also defending his own conduct between 1956 and 1958. "I believe," he said, "that the policy we carried out — Salan and myself — could have been continued."[23] To Paris not the least puzzling feature of Delouvrier's emotional outburst in the last days of the Barricades Revolt was his presumption that the government lacked information on what had been going on in Algiers. "I have seen in their ["loyal soldiers' "] eyes the evidence of the crisis of conscience and the tears shed by many paratroopers, brave fighters. That's the truth, Frenchmen of the Metropole; that's the situation. It is not possible to go further in the drama, for each one knows that on the solution of his personal crisis depends disorder or chaos in Algeria or secession from the Metropole or the collapse of the regime and disorder in France. Think of the situation, men of the Metropole, whose anger also hides anguish."[24]

Even the OAS, it would appear, was victimized by the government's ignorance. It believed in "a secret pact . . . between it and the government" and only attacked when that pact was not honored.[25] All would have been well had the government only realized that, in stirring up trouble by means of police spies and *agents provocateurs*, it was producing a civil war between the people of France and the people of its Algerian departments. For the OAS was, to the OAS, the Algerian people.

If the primary characteristic of government civilian policy was its dangerous lack of accord with reality, several conclusions followed. Those who did understand the facts had the duty to bring them to the attention of the Metropole. Should those in authority in Paris persist in purblindness, leaders in Algeria must persist in their efforts to preserve a French Algeria. That was what the government wanted after all; policies to the contrary were unnecessary responses to non-existent pressures. General Challe, it will be remembered, planned to deliver a pacified Algeria to De Gaulle, presumably to the latter's relieved grati-

[23] *Procès de Raoul Salan*, p. 315.
[24] Quoted in Brombergers *et al., op. cit.,* p. 362.
[25] Testimony of Jean-Marie Le Pen, then deputy to the French National Assembly. *Procès de Raoul Salan*, p. 270.

tude at having been awakened from nightmares of his own devising. Perhaps, thought Jouhaud, he could accomplish what General Challe had failed to do if he added a political element to the military movement Challe had headed. Then the Metropole might finally comprehend.[26] The OAS sought only to keep the peace in Algeria by taking the place of the French army as it withdrew under illogical orders from Paris.

The OAS, too, would make Algeria French. Had not De Gaulle promised to consult *all* opinion in Algeria? How could such consultation take place if the field were left to the alien, Communist-supported FLN? Since the OAS was equivalent to the population of Algeria, any real assessment of popular will would record an overwhelming victory for France. The Algerian departments would be won despite De Gaulle's unnecessarily dangerous and confusing second referendum.[27]

Assertions concerning the shortcomings of governmental policy all tended, it can be seen, toward the same conclusion. The army and its supporters had better qualifications to define the policy of France than did the political authorities in Paris. Maintenance of a French Algeria more accurately reflected existing power relations, for the rebellion had been crushed and rebel forces driven outside the territory to take refuge in neighboring states. The one objective of the army was consistent with the national interest of France. It would be painful to surrender territory in defeat, but it would be criminal folly to do so when definitive military triumph had taken place. Was it not Michel Debré himself who had said in 1959, "In our national preoccupations Algeria has an absolute priority . . . It is by our indisputable presence, our uncontested authority that we guarantee the security of the Western Mediterranean and thereby our own security . . . What a tragedy it would be for us, for Europe, for the West if the whole Mediterranean became a frontier between two hostile worlds." The investiture address of the new Premier, made in January 1959, contained, in the military view, a valid and realizable definition of French aims. When the policy of the Fifth Re-

[26] *Procès d'Edmond Jouhaud*, pp. 34–36.

[27] The first being that on the Constitution of the Fifth Republic. *Procès de Raoul Salan*, pp. 85, 113, 134, 269, 519.

public began to oscillate crazily and then to veer in other directions, the army fought to preserve its free hand in Algeria, the free hand accorded it by the Fourth Republic, the free hand it had reasserted against Pflimlin in May 1958, the free hand it thought for a time De Gaulle had given it for an indefinite period. Last, but far from least, the unity of the army depended on metropolitan recognition of the sacred inviolability of the military mission in Algeria.

Thus all forms of influence, intimidation, intrusion on the political process were warranted, especially as the civilian elements in that process represented illegitimate authority seeking to act illegally against the interests of the Nation they did not represent.

Four variables exist in the relationship of the military to the French policy-making process. One concerns the *time* of military involvement. A second has to do with the *portion* of the policy-making process affected by the army's determination to go its own way in Algeria. A third is the amount of *force* (pressure) exerted upon the political system. A fourth relates to the *extent* of military involvement in attempts to make, maintain, or reformulate official policy. Since treatment of the same events from the perspective of each variable would involve far too much repetition, primary emphasis will be placed on the portion of the policy-making process affected by efforts to keep Algeria French.

It is possible to review the time variable with brevity. The previous chapters and this one have already indicated how the French army became embroiled after the end of World War II in a series of colonial conflicts — Madagascar, Indochina, Suez, and Algeria. Each of the first three encounters left its mark on the army, with the result that intensification of the Algerian war found French military elements determined so to structure their relationship to metropolitan social and governmental institutions that the war could be conducted on their terms, toward the end they wished to reach. Ideas, old and new, as well as borrowed, about the meaning of Nation, Government, Army combined with thoughts on the nature of the struggle in Algeria to lengthen the time span of military intrusion into politics, as well as to deepen its intensity. De Gaulle found the army the greatest of his obstacles in his slow maneuvering toward a settlement. No sooner had the President begun to loosen the army's grip on Algeria than four distinguished generals openly challenged his authority. The end of this rebellion marked the beginning, under military auspices, of the OAS. Surviving the successful transfer of sovereignty to the Algerian government, the OAS jumped the Mediterranean to carry on its nefarious program in France itself. The mere existence of the clandestine OAS–CNR apparatus in France and neighboring countries does not indicate more than bitterness and, perhaps, nostalgia. Investigations of the activities of various OAS networks, including the repeated attempts to assassinate De Gaulle, however, do show continued military participation, if not leadership, in desperate efforts to change the direction of national policy by changing its directors.

Since 1956 military involvement in politics has been continuous, extensive, and tenacious. Even in 1963 there are many in the army who are reluctant to admit that the Algerian page has been turned, still more who are unprepared to help lay the foundations of a new civil-military relationship in which the civilian element, legitimate embodiment of freely expressed popular will, would be paramount. One reason for its tenacity has been the pervasiveness of the army's intrusion. Dictating for a time the *execution* of policy in Algeria, the army sought to use its position to ensure the *formulation* of congruent directives from Paris. From end to beginning to end, all parts of the decision-making process were therefore affected.

Under the Fourth Republic the army began to take a hand in establishing the lines national policy must follow before responsible political authorities had a chance to act. On February 6, 1956 newly invested Premier Guy Mollet went to Algiers to install personally his choice for Resident Minister, General Georges Catroux. As he stood at the war memorial, rioting crowds pelted him and his party with rotten eggs, fruits, and vegetables. Military and guard units stood by passively; Algiers police notably failed to restrain the demonstrations (which they may have had a part in encouraging in the first place). The Premier, who had had the temerity to use in his investiture address the taboo words "Algerian personality," as well as the sanctioned "indissoluble union between Algeria and metropolitan France," read the message loud and clear. Catroux was withdrawn. Mollet's fellow Socialist Robert Lacoste became Resident Minister. Thousands of French troops were rushed to Algeria in support of the army's rapidly expanding mission. The process of military envelopment had begun.

Two years later the leaders of the swollen expeditionary force were pre-empting the policy-making process more directly. After the fall of the government of Félix Gaillard in April 1958, Generals Jouhaud and Salan were called to Paris by René Pleven, who had been asked by President René Coty to form a government. Warned by Lacoste of Pleven's presumed intentions to seek an Algerian settlement, the generals informed him they could not accept any policy involving negotiations with the rebels. At Pleven's request, they proceeded to draft a memorandum on the requirements of national policy as seen by the army.[28] But Pleven failed to win legislative commitment to "his" policy, and he abandoned his effort to solve the crisis.

It was Pflimlin, already compromised in military eyes by suggestions that the possibilities of a negotiated settlement should be explored, who was next approached by Coty. Without waiting this time for any request, the army repeated its familiar demands "and invited the government to follow this policy without deviating from it one iota."[29] On May 7, six days before the military insurrection, a telegram to this effect was drafted by General Salan in the presence of Generals Jouhaud, Allard, and Dulac, and addressed to General Ely for transmittal to Pflimlin. A copy was given to Resident Minister Lacoste, who indicated his complete approval. On May 11 Pflimlin sent delegates to Algiers to treat with the French military leaders as though they represented substantial, independent power, as indeed they did. The delegates read to an audience which included Generals Jouhaud, Allard, Dulac, Salan, and Admiral Auboyneau the investiture address Pflimlin was proposing to deliver in the National Assembly. Not only were the parts pertaining to Algeria declared to be unacceptable, but Salan invited the emissaries to tell Pflimlin he should withdraw in favor of De Gaulle.[30]

[28] *Procès d'Edmond Jouhaud,* pp. 18, 19; *Procès de Raoul Salan,* p. 78.
[29] Azeau, *op. cit.,* p. 24.
[30] *Procès de Raoul Salan,* pp. 78, 188, testimony of Salan and Allard respectively.

At his base in Colombey-les-Deux-Eglises, General de Gaulle was, of course, kept well informed of the progress of the uprising against the Fourth Republic, although the nature and extent of his initiatives will for some time, if not forever, remain obscure. He was certainly aware that he had not been the unanimous first choice of the military revolutionists to take power in France. It behooved him to deal warily with the explosive force — a politicized military — which had so quickly restored to him the authority he had abandoned a dozen years earlier. Scarcely had the National Assembly, faced with the unpalatable prospect of civil war, invested him as Premier, than De Gaulle went to Algiers to tell the successful destroyers of the Fourth Republic, "I have understood you. I know what happened here. I see what you wanted to do. I see that the road you have opened in Algeria is the road of renewal and brotherhood."[31] Hearing the General in the superheated atmosphere of the Algiers Forum, the army might be pardoned the belief that it had finally prescribed in advance the one road civilian policy could henceforth follow "without deviating one iota."

The counterpart to its efforts to predetermine what single policy would emerge from the political process was the army's practice of interpreting, even reconstructing, decisions taken by the government so that they would mean what supporters of French Algeria wanted them to mean. Favorable pieces were taken out of context and construed to be the whole policy. Negative elements, qualifications, nuances, were ignored. The army tuned in on one wave-length only, accepting messages along that one channel, deliberately deafening itself to any "discordant" tones. De Gaulle's statement of September 16, 1959 defining self-determination was "interpreted" by Jacques Massu as propaganda aimed at a hostile foreign audience, particularly the deliberating bodies of the United Nations. When De Gaulle added secession and autonomy as alternatives to "complete Francization," Massu responded with a restatement of *the* one military objective: "building a French Algeria."[32]

[31] De Gaulle became Premier on June 1, 1958; he spoke in the Algiers Forum June 4.

[32] Fauvet, Planchais, *op. cit.*, p. 24.

Edmond Michelet, member of Debré's government, explained Gaullist tactics: "It was necessary . . . to convince the army that it does not end the [Algerian] adventure beaten, quite the contrary, that its acts of pacification will have contributed to the humane and honorable solution of an unprecedented conflict."[33] De Gaulle himself made several trips to Algeria to attempt to explain this difference between military means and national ends. Early in 1961, for example, he told a group of officers at Blida, "Although the military effort that we have accomplished is not ended, it is well on the way; that's the least one can say. Not only will there be no military defeat for France, there will undoubtedly be a military success for the French Army in Algeria."[34] The army, however, did not need to be told that it was winning in Algeria; it knew that already. Still less did it want to be told that it had won and could now go home. It could not tolerate being told that the purpose of winning was a negotiated peace with the FLN, however "humane and honorable." Militarism was, like Gaullism, a "passionate adventure" with a grand and permanent design.

In presenting De Gaulle's statecraft through his own words, André Passeron[35] quite properly points out that a problem "of some importance" arose as soon as De Gaulle assumed office in 1958. " 'What does the Army think? What does the Army wish? What is the Army going to do?' Its presumed intentions have as much weight as its actions; its abstentions are as consequential as its interventions. It is the arbiter of every situation, and this conceded importance made it — often incorrectly — the occult, imposing, all-powerful, and secret element that dominates the life of the Fifth Republic."[36] This oft-repeated concept of the "suspensory veto," like the proverbial club in the closet, needed only to exist. "It appears we are playing politics too much," said Massu at the long trial of those involved in the Barricades Revolt. "As if it were possible not to do so. After all General de Gaulle made me a prefect."[37]

[33] *Le Gaullisme, passionnante aventure,* Paris, Fayard, 1962, p. 142.
[34] Quoted by André Passeron, *De Gaulle parle,* Paris, Plon, 1962, p. 272.
[35] Political journalist for *Le Monde,* assigned to the Elysée and Hotel Matignon (President and Government respectively).
[36] *Ibid.,* p. 349. Note the use of the present tense.
[37] Quoted by Fauvet, Planchais, *op. cit.,* p. 25.

General Massu, a realist himself, was convinced that for another realist like De Gaulle reminders of the importance and authority of the
army would surely suffice to end any thoughts of moving away from a
French Algeria policy. For this reason he expressed himself openly and
did not participate in undercover plots, thereby ultimately escaping an
appearance in the dock of one of the many tribunals.[38] After his recall
to Paris to explain one of his "open expressions," his fellow officers
sought to force his return by demonstrating that "Massu's" army, and
only his army, controlled the destiny of the protracted Barricades Revolt.[39] In 1961, it will be remembered, General Challe planned to follow
the same procedure by sitting with "his" army in Algeria until De
Gaulle recognized where the balance of power lay.[40]

The line between influence merely by reason of existence and positive
intimidation proved difficult for army officers to draw, even if they had
so desired. During the Barricades Revolt military pressure on De Gaulle
certainly deserves to be called intimidation; furthermore, it won from
the President some (though temporary) concessions. All this, it must be
stressed, while civilians, not military personnel, were the ones officially
declared by Paris to be defying its authority. Generals Salan and Jouhaud wrote De Gaulle to demand that an end be put to fratricidal conflict by reaffirming the army as the guarantor of a French Algeria.
Marshal Juin told the President that if he ordered the army to fire on
those manning the barricades, Juin would publicly oppose him. General
Jacques de Guillebon, when he was asked to consider replacing Guillaumat as Minister of the Armed Forces, dictated as preconditions for
his acceptance: no firing on "patriots" (i.e., the Algiers rebels), Massu's
return to Algiers, a guarantee to the army that Algeria would not be
"abandoned," and five years "of full power to reform the army."[41]

In Algiers during this week of January 1960 army officers were
desperately trying to use the Barricades Revolt against De Gaulle.
When the President began to show signs of impatience, they adopted

[38] Brombergers *et al.*, *op. cit.*, pp. 11, 12.
[39] *Ibid.*, p. 214.
[40] Testimony of Colonel Goubard, *Procès des Généraux Challe et Zeller*, p. 107.
[41] Brombergers *et al.*, *op. cit.*, pp. 285–286, 294, 297.

the device of the threatening manifesto. The number of officers involved was small, but they were "Massu's men," influential advisors to General Challe; and they were confident that the views they expressed were those of the entire professional officer corps in Algeria. Their initial, proposed declaration could hardly have been more blunt. "This population," it ran, "no longer has confidence in the word of France and, since September 15 [1959] in that of the Chief of State." Despite the position that General de Gaulle was recognized as holding "on the international plane," metropolitan France must be treated to a renewed public demonstration by the Moslems of their determination to remain French.[42] General Challe and Resident Minister Delouvrier both refused to approve this effort to transform a localized revolt of Europeans into a massive demonstration against French policy. Instead, the Resident Minister made an emotional appeal to the metropolitan French to understand Algerian reality and called on the Moslems to show their support for De Gaulle as an individual. Returning to the attack, Colonels Argoud, Broizat, and Jacquelot next made an attempt to head off or at least change the nature of an address De Gaulle was preparing to deliver to the nation. At their invitation three leaders of the Barricades Revolt, Joseph Ortiz, Pierre Lagaillarde, and Victor Sapin-Lignières, helped them draft a second pronunciamento which they hoped (futilely) Delouvrier would sign. The Resident Minister was asked to hail the action of the people of Algiers (the rebellion) as contributing "greatly to saving French Algeria," and both Delouvrier and Challe were urged to commit themselves "irrevocably to do everything necessary to keep Algeria a French province."[43]

But the game of barricades had gone on too long. De Gaulle would not be turned from his public call to order. Above all, the bulk of the army was not yet ready to progress from tactics of pressure and intimidation to outright revolt. Military activities did, however, force some statements from the government which prolonged the ambiguity of its objectives in Algeria. On January 26 Premier Debré was authorized by the President to speak publicly to "all those who, *on this French land,*

[42] *Ibid.*, pp. 354–358 for text.
[43] *Ibid.*, p. 387.

are French, will remain so . . ." In his televised address of January 29, which the colonels could neither stop nor postpone, De Gaulle combined a demand that civilians and military men both return to a respect for constitutional authority with some seemingly important concessions. At the proper time, he said, he would make known his own preference for the future status of Algeria. Who could doubt, the President asked, that France and De Gaulle would be delighted if the Moslems, when consulted, chose the solution "which would be the most French?" The army would guarantee the "complete and sincere freedom" of this consultation. In short the army was being invited to contemplate a future parallel to the 1958 referendum on the Constitution. Again De Gaulle himself would campaign, and the army would vote the Moslems.[44]

A distinctive feature of the Fifth Republic was its bifurcated executive, which presented another opportunity for military intrusion. The independent identity and constitutional prerogatives of the Government, as distinct from those assigned to the President, offered two sources of possible leverage on official policy.[45] Debré's Council of Ministers could be used to bring pressure to bear on De Gaulle, or, even better, the hierarchy of authority might be reversed. Was it not true, as defense lawyers later pointed out, that the Government was charged by the Constitution with responsibility for making policy? Debré might actually welcome support to such an end, since he was supposed to be personally a continuing advocate of a French Algeria. Thus, during the Barricades Revolt parliamentarians from Algiers waited on the Premier to inform him that because De Gaulle no longer enjoyed their confidence, they wanted his cabinet to make a public, definite commitment to a French Algeria.[46]

Military activists had a more realistic sense of where the power lay. Regardless of what Debré might wish, they recognized that it was De Gaulle who actually made the decisions for the executive. Jouhaud cited in his statement before the military tribunal the words of General

[44] Text in *ibid.*, pp. 392–397.

[45] In French constitutional terminology "Government" refers only to the Premier and his cabinet; the author uses "government" to include both President and Government, i.e., executive.

[46] Brombergers *et al.*, *op. cit.*, p. 314.

André Petit, at one time the Premier's military aide and subsequently sentenced to seven years in prison for his indirect part in the April revolt. "I have seen Michel Debré; he thinks as you do; he thinks as I do; but he does not dare to say so."[47] Army officers therefore directed their energies toward persuading the Government to change De Gaulle's position or toward at least neutralizing the President by exploiting divisions within Debré's cabinet.

During the Barricades Revolt the President gave his permission for Premier Debré and Minister of the Armed Forces Guillaumat to go to Algiers to find out what was going on. When they arrived, military leaders put on a heavy drama for Debré's benefit. They began by telling him that they would listen to what he had to say only after he had heard the opinions of high-ranking officers. No fewer than five generals — Crépin, Dudognon, Coste, Gracieux, and Martin — spoke, and then it was the colonels' turn. Most had jointly prepared their little speeches, whose flavor is indicated by the words of Colonel Argoud, then Massu's chief of staff, later a leader in the OAS: "The army," he asserted, "is at one with the population of Algiers in resisting a policy of abandonment. Let the government renounce this policy." The playlet had an almost farcical ending. Colonel Georges de Boissieu, refusing Debré's profferred hand, said he would leave the room ahead of Debré; otherwise he would be obliged to pitch the Premier out.[48]

Debré had scarcely returned to Paris when rumors arose that disagreement between him and De Gaulle might lead to his resignation.[49] However, despite his policy preferences, despite his fear of a military coup in France itself, Debré retained the premiership and became increasingly effective as executor and articulator of his President's policy. At Salan's trial he not only appeared voluntarily to beat back Tixier-Vignancour's attempts to link him to a plot to kill Salan; he also used the occasion to defend the measures which had led to the negotiated independence of Algeria.[50]

[47] *Procès d'Edmond Jouhaud*, p. 33.
[48] During this production by his supposed subordinates General Challe stayed discreetly with Delouvrier in the wings. Brombergers *et al.*, *op. cit.*, pp. 282–287.
[49] *L'Année Politique, 1960*, p. 8.
[50] *Procès de Raoul Salan*, pp. 275–300.

Debré's position had been made no steadier by the obvious divisions existing inside his cabinet. His military aide, General Petit, was an open supporter of the army's goal of a French Algeria. When the Barricades Revolt broke out, "the ministers were divided into three opinions," reported Soustelle, who was then serving as Minister for the Sahara.[51] "One [faction], represented by Malraux, Buron, Sudreau threw fire on the flames, demanding an immediate and brutal repression of the uprising."[52] "Others, like Cornut-Gentille and myself," continued Soustelle, "opposed unleashing a bloody repression of Frenchmen who, above all, wanted to remain French"; others "still suspending judgment" awaited the results of Debré's trip to Algiers.[53] Divided within himself was Minister of the Armed Forces Guillaumat. He understood and sympathized with the army's policy in Algeria. On the other hand, he had faithfully juggled military commands at De Gaulle's order to attain the President's objectives in Algeria. Thus, he was of little use to either side; military and civilian leaders dealt directly with one another by-passing Guillaumat. "I have become useless," he is reported as saying.[54] He also had become dispensable. Messmer assumed his office shortly after the end of the Barricades Revolt, and Guillaumat was thrown upstairs to be a simple Minister Delegate.

Ministers were easier to oust than generals. Jouhaud could tell De Gaulle, "General, I'm very sorry, but I am in total disagreement with you,"[55] and wangle a shift from Chief of Staff to Inspector General of the Air Force. Other officers were shuttled around according to the assessed state of their infection, and Jacques Massu (as of this writing) escaped cashiering. Soustelle, on the other hand, recognized that his and Cornut-Gentille's ministerial responsibilities were rapidly drawing to a close.

An important part in the struggle to determine the Government's policy was played by the personal entourage of the President. Its mem-

[51] Op. cit., pp. 141–146.
[52] L'Année Politique adds Couve de Murville and Joxe to the "hawks," op. cit., p. 9.
[53] Triboulet is listed with the "doves" by L'Année Politique.
[54] Brombergers et al., op. cit., p. 299.
[55] Procès d'Edmond Jouhaud, p. 24.

bers did not embody any particular political or partisan point of view nor did they represent any substantive policy or competence. Loyalty plus efficiency in transmitting loyalty into action were the criteria for their selection and retention. To swing the Government behind De Gaulle in 1960 they marshalled the full prestige of the office and the man. "The Republic, the regime, even the life of General de Gaulle are menaced . . . He must be protected. No other question is involved. It is now no longer possible to postulate crises of conscience. At all cost we must not allow ourselves to be made hysterical by the military. All we can and should do is unite around him."[56]

In addition to providing De Gaulle with clues as to which military units and officers were of doubtful loyalty, the Barricades Revolt hardened the executive branch of the Fifth Republic for the more severe test to come. A special session of the legislature in early February 1960 granted the government's request for special powers for the "maintenance of order, safeguard of the State, and pacification and administration of Algeria." Participants in the Algiers rebellion and suspected supporters were immediately rounded up for trial. In the same month the sixth shake-up of Debré's cabinet since its formation thirteen months earlier ejected Soustelle and Cornut-Gentille, added three new members, and changed the responsibilities of several others. By the time the generals rebelled in April 1961, there was no longer any doubt that De Gaulle was in firm control of the executive branch in its formulation of France's policy toward Algeria.[57] It was the fault of the President himself that the executive was then deprived of any organized, effective political and economic support to mobilize against General Challe and his cohorts.[58]

[56] Brombergers et al., op. cit., pp. 298–299.

[57] Any division that may still have existed within Debré's cabinet was never reported to the public. However, Salan's OAS was later said to have continued to benefit from contacts within the government. At his trial Captain Ferrandi asserted that an anonymous minister kept the OAS informed of cabinet proceedings. L'Express, May 31, 1962.

[58] The absence of such support was demonstrated by Debré's pathetic appeal, asking the people of Paris to submerge in a sea of humanity any hostile paratroopers landing at the surrounding airports. De Gaulle's concept of executive responsibility is discussed in Chapter 5.

De Gaulle had never cared much for politicians or for the factions they claimed to represent. His Constitution of the Fifth Republic permitted non-political figures to be selected as cabinet ministers and compelled deputies to resign their seats when named to the Government. The Constitution also made it much more difficult to bring down a premier than had been the case under the Fourth Republic. Effective barriers were thereby raised to political-military allies seeking to use legislative groupings for influence, control, or dictation of presidential policy on Algeria.

The extent of support within the parliament for the maintenance of a French Algeria is, under the circumstances, difficult to measure precisely. In 1960 two motions were introduced to free Deputy Pierre Lagaillarde, jailed for helping lead the Barricades Revolt. Jean-Marie Le Pen, an Independent, sought to make his motion attractive to his fellow deputies by arguing his case on the constitutional principle of parliamentary immunity. Although he was defeated 268–165, leaders of the Gaullist UNR (Union for the New Republic) thought it prudent not to invoke party discipline in the vote, and Le Pen's colleagues in the Independent Party followed him 77–4, with 40 abstentions. A second attempt to secure Lagaillarde's release, made late in the year, came even closer; this time the vote was 219–201. Besides 30 members of the group known as Unity of the Republic (i.e., Algeria is a French province), 8 MRP (Mouvement Républicain Populaire), 26 UNR, 95 Independent, and 13 Entente Démocratique deputies supported Le Pen. But although Le Pen lost his second battle, he won the war. Lagaillarde was released from captivity by the court and promptly fled. In a sense he thereby forfeited his parliamentary immunity, which was promptly lifted 424–21.[59]

The voting pattern of these motions indicated that there were those who would defend the legislature against the executive and who would oppose De Gaulle even at the cost of siding with French-Algeria extremists. On the other hand, there were obviously many sympathizers with Lagaillarde who saw no reason in the end to fight further for a parliamentary immunity he no longer needed.

[59] *L'Année Politique, 1960*, pp. 59–60, 118–119, 126.

During 1959 and 1960 the difficulties of the deputies in interpreting De Gaulle's Algerian policy were reflected in a considerable confusion in votes on such matters as military budgets and credits for Algeria. Partisans and opponents of military conquest of Algeria might find themselves on the same side, either by voting in principle against the government or by supporting measures in the belief they would help attain the contradictory ends of victory or negotiated peace. By 1961 the picture was clearer; the army had become convinced that De Gaulle intended to abandon Algeria. During the Assembly's budgetary debates in November of that year several speakers openly argued the cause of the OAS. Again in the vanguard, Le Pen declared that for the first time deputies "have been able, without arousing protests, to affirm the legitimacy of the OAS and declare that the overwhelming majority of Algerian Frenchmen were behind it."[60] One hundred thirty-eight voted against the government (on its proposed credits to Algeria), the largest blocs being the solid Unity of the Republic and 58 Independents. Only 34 of the 120 Independents supported Debré.

The next day, November 7, a clearer test arose, when Jean Valentin intervened in the debate on the military budget to propose a reduction in the length of military service from twenty-eight to eighteen months, compensating for the consequent loss of manpower by calling up men "residing in the Algerian departments." The proposal was immediately labelled "the OAS amendment," since Salan had suggested just such a course of action in a letter addressed to all the deputies.[61] Had the amendment been voted, it would, of course, have produced a more united, predictable army, one equipped and ready to fight all opponents of a French Algeria. To Messmer's statement that a reduction in service would be a crime and he could no longer remain as Minister of the Armed Forces if it were approved, Alain de Lacoste Lareymondie, an Independent, responded, "So much the better." In the end, however, only 80 supported Valentin; of these, 4 belonged to the MRP, 25 to the

[60] *L'Année Politique, 1961,* p. 143.

[61] In a pirated broadcast over the Algiers radio he had coupled the idea with his own "draft" of Europeans. Also, General Challe the year before had ostentatiously "freed" conscripts as part of his attempt to mobilize the army against De Gaulle.

Independents, 1 to the UNR, 16 to no group; 34 from the Unity of the Republic — all that voted — made up the balance.[62]

The last hurrah was occasioned by a motion of censorship introduced against the Pompidou government by the Unity of the Republic in June 1962. The seventh formal effort to bring down a premier of the Fifth Republic was provoked by the Evian agreements for an independent Algeria. In addition to the 38 members of the French Algeria group, 60 of 124 Independents, 1 MRP, and 14 who belonged to no group voted for censure, the total of 113 being far short of the required absolute majority. During the debate Socialist Francis Leenhart said, to loud protests from Unity of the Republic deputies, "Whatever the tricks used in drafting the motion, it has but one concern, the Algerian problem, and one aim, support for the propaganda and the action of the OAS." In his defense of the motion the vocal Le Pen expressed alarm for the fate of the army "forced to lower its flags and retreat." He inveighed against the military tribunal established to replace the one which had failed to sentence Salan to death and requested the government to influence the President toward a general amnesty of military and civilians convicted of attacks against the security of the state.

Georges Pompidou's harsh defense of his government annoyed many of his listeners. He described the OAS as "created by soldiers lost to France and to themselves, animated by authentic partisans of totalitarian regions" and called the vote a tabulation of those opposing peace. His words caused the Independents — the group most divided by De Gaulle's policy — to demand a break in the session, following which the group's president, Bertrand Motte, told the Premier his eloquence had decided him to support the motion of censure. Motte's comment evoked applause from the MRP, but the vote of only Jean-Marie Domenach.[63]

Assembly votes indicated the struggles going on within the various political parties. The perturbation increased the further one moved toward the right of the political spectrum. Only the Communists were united in their ideological reconciliation of hostility toward De Gaulle with support for peace in Algeria. The Socialist Party had to cope with the followers of Lacoste and Max Lejeune, partisans of French Algeria,

[62] *L'Année Politique, 1961*, pp. 143–145.
[63] *Le Monde*, June 7, 1962.

who had joined with others of the "Left" in subscribing to a manifesto
in June 1960, which said: "The only solution we believe conforms to the
requirements of reality, democracy, and peace is the maintenance of
Algeria in the French Republic."[64] Split right down the middle were the
Independents. After the debate on the censure motion cited above, *Le
Monde's* political reporter Pierre Viansson-Ponté summarized the
group's situation: "In scarcely three months the Independents have
thrown out their secretary-general [Duchet] for his extremism, and a
fifth of their representatives at the Palais-Bourbon [National Assembly]
choose to be called 'deputies of the OAS,' a third to support Debré's
government. Tuesday half of the group voted censure of Pompidou's
ministry, and of the orators it sent to the speaker's stand almost all
appeared so virulent that, in contrast, the deputies from Algeria, however passionate, distressed, or agonized, appeared almost deliberative
and resigned." The reporter found as "principal reason" for both the
violence and fragmentation of the Independents the persistence within
France of Right-wing affinity for secret plots and subversive movements against democratic institutions.[65]

The UNR was able during this period to present in public a more
united front only because its own schism had taken place earlier. Formed
in 1958 to support De Gaulle, though denied his official imprimatur,
its deputies included many who believed that loyalty to De Gaulle
meant loyalty to French Algeria. When the incompatability of the two
became apparent, some of its members split away, either to the Unity
of the Republic or to non-affiliation with any Assembly bloc. The remainder of the UNR was left with loyalty to De Gaulle as its sole credo
and program. Without him, it would have broken into the many factions that its disparate social and economic views comprised, just as
the earlier Gaullist movement, the RPF (Rassemblement du Peuple
Français), had divided when its leader withdrew (temporarily) to
brood and plan at Colombey-les-Deux-Eglises. As a "government party,"
purged of its Algerian dissidents, it had power and influence inside the
legislature, if not with the executive.

Certain individual representatives were shown or alleged to have a

[64] *L'Année Politique, 1960*, p. 61.
[65] *Le Monde*, June 8, 1962.

particularly close affinity to the OAS. André Noël, a member of the first legislature of the Fourth Republic, belonged to the MRP until he was arrested in the aftermath of the Generals' Revolt and languished some weeks in a detention camp. Upon his release he became editor of a "newsletter," which he circulated clandestinely and which on occasion the Ministry of the Interior ceremoniously banned.[66] In 1961 Algerian deputy Marc Lauriol had his parliamentary immunity removed after he was accused of plotting against the security of the State.[67] In August 1962 Senator Claude Dumont was being unsuccessfully sought for trial as reputed member of an OAS band in Algeria led by Colonel Jean Gardes. Also accused were his secretary and two other Algerian deputies, Marçais and Marcellin.[68] One-time parliamentary supporters of Pierre Poujade, Robert Pesquet and Marcel Bouyer, were said to be members of OAS networks in metropolitan France; Bouyer was reputed to belong to the notorious "Resurrection-Country" group, distinguished by the participation in its activities of Lieutenants Godot and Bernard and Adjutant Robin.[69]

It was only to be expected that Algerian deputies should sympathize with and support military and civilian organizations attempting to fight De Gaulle's policy. Poujadists came to the same position from the opposite end. They were as opposed to the Fifth Republic as they had been to the Fourth, and some of them were therefore willing to help along any movement seeking to destroy the regime. They provided another link in the chain that bound together secret plotters, OAS groups, direct activists in other causes, military extremists, and the political Right.

The capstone of the overt-clandestine agglomeration of opponents confronting President de Gaulle became Georges Bidault. Despite his proclaimed leadership of the CNR and his flight from France, it was not easy to remove his parliamentary immunity. His supporters followed his example in sweeping together issues involving Western defense, European unity, and the French nuclear force to cover the OAS-

---

[66] *Le Monde*, October 19, 1962.
[67] *Le Monde*, October 8–9, 1961.
[68] *Le Monde*, August 14, December 10–11, 1962.
[69] *Le Monde*, June 8, July 10, 1962.

CNR determination to assassinate the President. In July 1962 an *ad hoc* committee of the National Assembly recommended 9 to 3 to lift Bidault's immunity, but only after it had decided 8–7 that his relations with the OAS had not been proved. In the subsequent vote of the full Assembly the proposal, while obtaining a plurality, failed to receive a majority. Against the 241 "ayes" stood 72 "nays" (of which 47 came from Independents), and 169 abstainers and absentees. In this latter category were 55 of 57 members of Bidault's own MRP, 18 members of the UNR, and 24 Independents.[70]

Political groups were both a part of the formal political system and of the environment which surrounded it. That environment can be thought of as a proliferation outward of a series of concentric circles. At the core were the armed forces themselves. Immediately beyond lay mobilized, quasi-military forces. Of these the Territorial Units of Algeria, the Security Guard, and the police were the most significant. One circle beyond were para-military groups, for example, armed, Right-wing movements. Farther outward were direct-action organizations — overt defiers of state authority like some farm groups and Poujade's union of small shopkeepers. On the outer fringe may be located organizations of workers, employers, teachers, and the like. As has been suggested in discussing the army's attempt to place the nation in its service, military elements, working outward from the center, tried to convert to their cause as many of these groups as possible. If the environment within which the political system operated could be changed, the policy produced by that system would be correspondingly altered or the system itself risked being undermined. Understanding this only too well, the Fifth Republic strove to hold the loyalty of military and security groups, even though it spurned assistance from political parties and union movements. De Gaulle appealed directly to the undifferentiated *Françaises, Français* themselves.

Sometimes the victory in the struggle belonged clearly to the military proponents of a French Algeria, as with the veterans' organizations (once an officer always an officer) and the Territorial Units (once a

---

[70] *Le Monde*, July 6–7, 1962.

French Algerian always a French Algerian). For Algeria, separated from the Metropole and enveloped by the army, the issue was therefore long in doubt, despite advantages gained by the Gaullists through the failure of the Barricades Revolt of 1960 and the Generals' Revolt of the following year. The aim of the OAS was to neutralize forces supposedly under the control of metropolitan authorities, such as the police and the regular army, by persuading them not to act against their fellow Algerians or fellow officers. With forces of law and order standing helplessly or benevolently by, the OAS could then convince the Provisional Algerian Government that the Paris regime of De Gaulle could not make good on any negotiated pledge to hand over Algeria. The territory would either remain French, or the OAS itself would negotiate a compromise arrangement with the Moslem nationalists.

For a time it appeared that the OAS might succeed in its policy of rule or ruin. It flaunted its control over Algiers and Oran and demonstrated considerable strength in other cities. That it ultimately failed was due to the fact that Europeans would not stay for an indefinite period under its orders and the police and army units could not be induced or forced to abandon neutrality for positive action in behalf of the OAS. With increasing belief that there were several ways to lose, but none to win, the Europeans, who had been willing to help the OAS with money, weapons, and hiding places, began to contemplate exodus to France or even temporary arrangements with the nationalists as alternatives to destructive violence to the bitter end. They were moved further toward accepting the independence of Algeria by a limited but crucial process of "infiltration" of the army and police by elements responsive to French government directions. Military leaders loyal to De Gaulle, such as Generals Katz and Ginestet, held the army to its duty in Algerian stations. In desperation the OAS turned to direct attacks on "traitorous" military personnel. Between September 1961 and June 1962, 76 were murdered, fourteen of whom were officers. General Ginestet, commander of the French troops at Oran, became the fifteenth that same month.[71] But cowardly attacks with plastic bombs and firearms did not serve the purpose of converting the army.

[71] *Le Monde,* June 16, 26, 1962.

Especially discouraging to the OAS was its failure with the police. Adroit action by metropolitan France changed the position of the police from benevolent neutrality, if not outright collaboration with the Secret Army, toward impartial enforcement of the law. Summoned as a witness at Salan's trial, Debré admitted the job had been neither easy nor tidy. "In the nature of things the organization of the police in Algeria rests fundamentally on the local recruitment of Algerian French, and, when events began to heat up, it was very clear that the ordinary police and especially those in the large towns, were not capable — that's the least I can say — of obeying the orders of the government, of the General Delegate,[72] and the commanding general. Thus it was necessary to send politicians from the Metropole" to replace or be added to local forces. Inevitably "there was a certain disorder," until the structure of authority from Paris had been clearly established. Tixier-Vignancour's account of what happened was somewhat different. Blaming the violence of which the OAS was accused on these metropolitan *barbouzes* (police spies), he labelled them "bandits, torturers, and common criminals."[73]

So notorious did the *barbouzes* become that the satirical journal *Canard Enchainé* jokingly claimed that it was embarrassed to repeat an infamous rumor, to wit: Colonel Trinquier and M. Poujade were both police spies in the pay of the Minister of the Interior. No humorist, the colonel challenged the editor to a duel, whereupon the latter, claiming the offended party's right to choose the weapons because Trinquier's second had called on him in ordinary street clothes, selected popguns.[74] It must have been cold comfort to the loyal members of the OAS to witness the fate of an authentic *barbouze*. One policeman inserted as a spy into the Secret Army carried simulation too far and risked dismissal from the force for his "excess of zeal" in participating in a plastic bombing.[75]

The changing relationship of the regular or "above-ground" officers to their "lost" brethren in Algeria illustrates a portion of the spectrum of army involvement in opposition to the policy of De Gaulle, a policy

[72] The change in title from Resident Minister reflects the Evian agreements for Algerian independence.

[73] *Procès de Raoul Salan*, pp. 299, 536.

[74] *New York Times, Le Monde*, July 26, 1962.

[75] *Le Monde*, November 22, 1962.

which, again it should be emphasized, was endorsed by the National Assembly and ultimately by the people of France through a popular referendum. The preceding pages have illustrated the range of military opposition. At one end lay neutrality toward De Gaulle's policy. Since the army was, after all, supposedly an instrument of national statecraft, the political result of such neutrality was a positive failure to support and carry out decisions taken by the responsible authorities of the Fifth Republic. The army, it has been stressed, had its own aims in Algeria. When they coincided with De Gaulle's (or previously with the Fourth Republic's), well and good. When they did not, the army was clearly reluctant to obey what it regarded as aberrant directives.

As the gap between military and political aims grew, neutrality took on another meaning. Now it featured notable hesitancy in suppressing opposition manifested by civilian and quasi-military groups to official policy. Non-commitment was the least friendly attitude assumed by the military toward the barricades erected by Ortiz and Lagaillarde. The reason was more than a belief that an obvious hands-off position would prevent bloodshed; the predominant attitude was hope that the defiance in Algeria would place De Gaulle again on the path toward a French Algeria. "In his unstable situation," the Brombergers wrote of the French commander, General Challe, "stability could very much resemble immobility." Military opinion branded Colonel Debrosse as little less than a criminal for involving his unit in an exchange of fire while he was seeking to carry out orders to disperse the crowds. By contrast, the behavior of Colonel Broizat, future participant in Challe's own revolt, was defended, although his deliberate delay in executing the same command contributed to the violence of the melee, if it did not actually help to inspire it.[76]

Even neutrality was a difficult position for the supposed executors of national policy to maintain. Sympathy for the rebels of the Barricades led units closest to them into active assistance. "Cordons" nominally "sealing off" the barricaded areas were opened so that friends could bring in food, supplies, and firearms. Ortiz, Lagaillarde, and Sapin-

[76] Brombergers et al., op. cit., pp. 305, 184–185, 227–239.

Lignières were informed, and sometimes actually consulted, before the "loyal" army carried out instructions from Paris it decided could no longer be ignored or changed. Military officers even went so far as to construct a communications system for Lagaillarde so that he could parley more conveniently with those ordered to suppress his insurrection.

Assistance in its more direct forms blended into downright collaboration. Lagaillarde turned away an entire paratroop unit that wanted to join him. His reasoning, in which military spokesmen had given him confidence, was that an order to forces surrounding his barricade to fire on those inside would produce instead such active civil-military fraternization that the whole army would indeed abandon its passivity — but for his, not De Gaulle's, benefit.[77]

Another short step carried military interference in policy from collaboration with the rebels to promotion of opposition where none had previously existed or where it had remained dormant. When "the great mute" (the army) began to speak, in the latter days of the Fourth Republic, it found many voices to say the same thing: Algeria must remain French, no matter who attempted to make policy leading in any other direction. Mobilization of reserve officers in the Metropole had as its Algerian counterpart organization of civilian groups. Military figures like Ely and Juin publicly pretended that De Gaulle really wanted the same thing they did, although he could not express himself very clearly. When that justification wore threadbare, army leaders continued to inspire agitation against the President's policy among carefully constructed groups of veterans and reserve officers.

It was the contention of his defense attorneys that Challe had conducted a purely military (and legal) rebellion, rejecting proffered offers of assistance by civilian groups.[78] To Jacques Isorni this restraint was unfortunate and provided one reason for the failure of the revolt,[79] while Salan felt that rectification of the error through his Secret Army would win him victory over De Gaulle. Actually the two attitudes to-

---

[77] *Ibid., passim*, especially pp. 222, 251.
[78] *Procès des Généraux Challe et Zeller*, p. 109.
[79] *Op. cit.*, p. 124.

ward civilian supporters only exemplified different concepts of leadership, the next stage of military involvement. The president of the tribunal inquired whether the directorate established by Challe with his fellow generals was not in fact an act of government. Challe was disposed to quibble over terminology, calling his formation a Higher Council of Algeria, but admitted that it had taken "certain measures" of government. Reverting to the point in his summation, Prosecutor Besson observed that this "purely military" revolt sought to arouse the Algerian Europeans by pronunciamento, mobilized the Territorial Units, which had been disbanded after the Barricades affair, opened the jails to people convicted of crimes against the State, and used connections with the OAS to give orders to cooperating civilian elements.[80]

In simple terms, Challe's military junta was the forerunner of Salan's and Jouhaud's Secret Army, similar in the leadership it provided to civilian as well as military elements. When it came Jouhaud's turn to explain his acts, he was naturally reluctant to accept more than nominal responsibility for bombings and murders. He operated on a far loftier plane, far above the sewers his followers frequented. The former chief of staff of the Air Force seemed to think this separation might make his conduct smell better to the court. "I ran things from a very high position by reason of my duties; an army general does not discharge responsibilities of this type by selecting people to kill or murder. I had political contacts with political men, with union presidents, with agricultural leaders, etc., with professional organizations that represented a political element, and I didn't concern myself with these questions of action."[81] As its death sentence showed, the court was not convinced of Jouhaud's logic.

At the upper end of the spectrum of involvement stood situations in which the army did more than assist, foment, cooperate, or lead the opposition — it *was* that opposition. The army tried to bar Pflimlin from assuming office as Premier. General Jacques Massu viewed "his" Algerian army as political make-weight. The units surrounding the barricades had their arms pointed both ways. While they fraternized with

[80] *Procès des Généraux Challe et Zeller,* pp. 58, 218.
[81] *Procès d'Edmond Jouhaud,* p. 111.

the civilians, their leaders were trying to pressure De Gaulle and Debré into redefining official policy and renewing the grant of full powers to the army. Although the defense contended Challe had joined a plot already under way, controlled it, and succeeded in ending it with remarkably little violence, the prosecution was not convinced. "Is it possible for Challe to pretend he was just a simple passenger on this famous moving train onto which he climbed? He had in truth become at once the stationmaster and engineer or, alternatively, he has shown total ignorance of what was going on." His intimate advisors had wider horizons. "If it's necessary," said Colonel Gardes, "we'll overturn the government, for we shall not stop." "We shall have a government of our own in the Metropole," declared General Zeller. "First, it will be composed of military men, but we shall leave the way open later for a government of politicians."[82]

One cannot establish with precision the hierarchy of responsibility within Secret Army networks scattered throughout France. It is clear, however, that military elements have comprised a substantial portion of the leadership. They and their civilian counterparts recruit sympathizers where they can be found and, before entrusting them with such major responsibilities as attempting to murder the President, frequently test their dedication by ordering them to commit lesser crimes, like *les hold-ups*.

The upper limit of political action — conspiracies to overthrow the Fifth Republic — took two forms. The collapse of the regime was first sought by rendering it powerless. Challe and his fellow generals at the very least tried to show that De Gaulle's writ did not run anywhere in Algeria. Their protestations to the contrary notwithstanding, plans envisaged continued separation of the territory from the Metropole if De Gaulle failed to mend his ways. This was certainly included in the evolving goals of the OAS. Continued secession would in all probability have brought down the Republic. In metropolitan France itself transplanted OAS networks attempted to deprive De Gaulle of effective control over such large areas that the people would bring about the end

[82] *Procès des Généraux Challe et Zeller*, pp. 230, 229, 101.

of the system by believing and acting as though that system had no control over events anywhere.

Finally there was direct insurrection against the regime. Threats of force gave way to shows of force, which in turn were followed by use of force. At one time the President may have planned his position in the executive branch to be that of arbiter among contending points of view. However, as national problems pressed for solution, it became clear that one word and one word alone counted. After that there was nothing (the tired pleasantry of the empty cab from which the Premier emerged), and after that there was nothing (brouhahas in the Assembly resembled echoings in an empty rain barrel), and after that there was nothing (loyal yes-men needed no parties), and after that there was the People, with whom the Solitary Eminence communed from time to time. "A civil war against one single man, and France at the mercy of a killer!" exclaimed Paul Reynaud after the failure of the assassination attempt at Petit-Clamart.[83]

Military involvement in all aspects of political action and resort by the military to upper ranges of force do not in any way imply either participation or use of force by all the army. Fragmentation of France's armed forces was one of the unhappy consequences of their politicalization. The meaning and extent of that fragmentation will be explored in the next chapter.

[83] *L'Express,* August 30, 1962.

CHAPTER 4

MILITARY UNITY—

A CONCEPT FOR

POLITICAL ACTION

Those who said "no" to us bluntly can be counted on ten fingers, and, moreover, when I mentioned this number to General Zeller, he told me I was exaggerating. — General Maurice Challe

GENERAL CHALLE divided military opinion into supporters, fence-sitters, and the very small minority who actually opposed the revolt he led. His companion in the box, General Zeller, divided it between the best, "those whom you now see imprisoned, elite officers [who] represent the intellectual elite of the Army," and the rest.[1] In reply to questioning by the tribunal's president about the attitude of particular officers, Challe, as has been indicated, felt he could cite evidence to support his contention only by betraying his friends. In the end he contented himself with what was described in the proceedings as an "ironic look" and an expression of scepticism at the president's conclusion that "a good part of the army" resisted him. The president did not press

[1] *Procès des Généraux Challe et Zeller*, p. 68.

the matter and, in fact, made specific allusion to the general's forbearance.[2]

Both the accused and the accuser were seeking to enlist the myth of a united army to bolster their respective positions. Challe and Zeller hoped for extenuation of their offense against the security of the state. De Gaulle's representatives, by claiming that the army opposed or at least did not support the revolt, hoped to minimize before the public the seriousness of the challenge to the Fifth Republic. They also hoped to avoid sharpening that challenge by attacking a principle held sacred by the army.

Invocation of the concept of military unity by the army in its efforts to direct the Fifth Republic's Algerian policy ended in disaster. It was a device that had not been necessary in the destruction of the Fourth Republic, when common opposition to Pflimlin was real and needed only the recognized spokesmen readily available in General Salan and the army's chosen political instrument, General de Gaulle. Pflimlin's government discovered that the military units in metropolitan France and West Germany were not prepared to use force or even demonstrations of force to bar the insurrection from the mainland. At best, they might assume a position of hostile non-belligerency toward the regime, as seemed to be the attitude of naval leaders. Most units, it was feared, only awaited some sign that the rebels would succeed before they helped to pull down the rickety political structure. The invasion of Corsica, publicized plans for paratroop drops around Paris, and De Gaulle's announcement that he was beginning the process of forming a government therefore provided sufficient motivation for the Fourth Republic to commit suicide.

Things were not so simple when the Algerian satraps turned against the king they had made. Because De Gaulle's regime was stronger and resisted, even derided, suggestions it take its own life, an army which had not retired from politics was forced to intrude more deeply. The concept of military unity represented an indispensable support to attempts to control the decision-making process. Reciprocally, its manipu-

[2] *Ibid.*, pp. 58, 64.

lation by military activists dragged the army deeper and deeper into the political quagmire until it became lost in the black madness of the OAS. Since the concept was no more than an expedient myth, its enlistment in the cause of a French Algeria produced new cleavages within the military organization, even as the struggle with De Gaulle plastered over some old cracks in the façade.

Military unity is obviously a sometime thing, an evanescent creation of circumstance, time, and place. Like all large, complex social structures, the military establishment of a nation is characterized by internal rifts. Tensions exist between branches of the armed forces, within each branch, and are deeply imbedded in each military section. Disputes range from the petty to the professional, from desires for personal gratification to designs for changes in military doctrine. Yet out of these conditions of incipient disintegration enough cohesion must somehow be attained to perform, however fallibly, the functions for which the system was created. Because the purposes of the military establishment are potentially crucial to national survival, the elements of cohesion must be ever at hand, if not always in operation. The central congeries of cementing factors bears such titles as "unity of the army," meaning particularly the sanctity of hierarchical organization from top to bottom, the bonds of command and obedience that tie tight military men one to all the others, while defining for each his relative position and thereby his degree of authority and responsibility. In this way authenticity is given to orders and predictability to response. Without both authenticity and predictability, military leaders would hesitate, and have historically hesitated, to commit the force nominally at their disposal. While one must recognize in the military establishment, as in other social systems, an informal set of relationships, these exist because the legitimatized, sanctioned set exists; the informal helps to ensure the viability of the system by providing supplementary guides to behavior.

The degree to which a military establishment is functioning effectively is the degree to which the concept of military unity can be left abstract. Specific assertions of unity are in reality appeals to end fragmentation; they are indications that formal and informal definitions of inter-relationships are no longer accepted, that the range and persistence of division threaten to cause the breakdown or even the disappearance of the system itself.

Such was the case with the French armed forces. What happens when an army defines the enemy in general as the very set of political institutions of the country which it is supposed to serve, and the enemy in particular as the man ratified by the electorate as director of those institutions? What meanings, positive and negative, does "unity of the army" then assume?[3]

Contained in the idea of unity was the minimal principle that the military would not fight the military. While Paris regarded Challe's immobility during the Barricades Revolt of 1960 as evidence of disobedience to civilian direction, the army's view was that Challe was preserving the unity of the army by postponing as long as possible the importation of troops from the rest of Algeria to reduce the barricades. Since the twin battlements erected by Ortiz and Lagaillarde were "surrounded" by sympathetic units, manifestly rejecting the notion of force, an assault might well have resulted in soldiers pointing weapons at soldiers. At least it would have placed on public display the disparate attitudes and loyalties held by various officers. A year later General Challe did not feel it necessary to obtain commitments from all Algerian commanders before launching his revolt. He felt confident that reluctance of professional officers to fight each other would keep those who did not approve of his action from obeying any governmental orders to march against him.

A second connotation imparted to military unity through its use as a political weapon was that the military would not judge the military, figuratively or actually. There were few Gambiezes and Aillerets (stigmatized as "political generals") who would aid the prosecution of fellow officers by calling things by their correct names. "He [Challe] wanted to sit beside me [for a discussion taking place during the revolt]. I told him I would not have a rebel officer sit at my side."[4] Much

---

[3] As pointed out in the last chapter, the French military challenge, while unique by definition, contained elements observable in other countries, including some that like to pretend that military aloofness from politics is a hallowed tradition.

[4] General Fernand-Charles-Louis Gambiez, *Procès des Généraux Challe et Zeller*, p. 80.

more typical were "attempts to understand." "It's a question of the re-action of human beings placed at the peak of exasperation."[5]

Not infrequently actions of the accused were vigorously defended by displays of camaraderie. At the end of his testimony Colonel (and deputy) Robert Thomazo turned and faced Raoul Salan. "My general," he said, "you were victorious on May 13 [1958]; they took your victory away. They took from all the army its victory, its long, bloody, painful sacrifices. They killed the soul of the army. If it still lives, it is owing to men like yourself and like those who followed you. My general, what-ever the judgment of men, we know that the judgment of History will recognize in you the magnificent chief that we have served."[6] Gestures as well as words of fellowship were present. Naval lieutenant Pierre-Jean-Marie Guillaume, summoned as a defense witness, saluted Challe and Zeller after his testimony. So did Colonel Pierre-Julien-Paul Gou-bard, supposedly a witness for the prosecution.[7]

Responsibilities related to punishment of rebellious officers, includ-ing service on military tribunals themselves, were avoided whenever possible. General Demetz, military governor of Paris, refused to attend ceremonies connected with his office, considering these incompatible with his attitude of sympathy for officers languishing in jails under his jurisdiction.[8] General Partiot, commander at Versailles, requested re-tirement rather than designate an execution squad for officers con-demned to death in military trials, most particularly a squad to shoot Jouhaud, who had been his friend at Saint-Cyr.[9] Soon afterward Air Force General Hugo quit as commander of the region which included Paris when it fell to him to sign the necessary orders for the execution of OAS leaders, including the same Jouhaud.[10]

Amidst the trials of Secret Army members the reverberating voice of Jacques Massu was heard demanding, not just an end to prosecutions,

[5] General de Montsabert, testifying for Jouhaud. *Procès d'Edmond Jouhaud,* p. 242.

[6] *Procès de Raoul Salan,* p. 375.

[7] *Procès des Généraux Challe et Zeller,* pp. 187, 111.

[8] *Le Monde,* November 16, 25–26, 1962.

[9] *Le Monde,* April 29, 1962.

[10] *Le Monde,* June 8, 1962.

but an amnesty for those already convicted. Widely regarded as a barometer of military feeling, the General declared that "the army corps is suffering from a sickness born of the conflict between honor and discipline . . . The remedies? Clarification of the situation in Algeria and also an amnesty benefiting the 'sick ones' who have been interned or condemned."[11]

Finally, unity of the army meant resistance to "political penetration," the maintenance of an artificial esprit against contamination from non-military elements. All social groups maintain their sense of identity by favorable contrasts between members and outsiders, and "morale" derived from an inculcated sense of superiority is clearly a significant factor in performance by military units. With regard to the Fifth Republic, however, repeated emphasis on separation and superiority became a device to frustrate civilian direction. More, it became a method of fortifying the army for extrusion into the political institutions established by De Gaulle.

At De Gaulle's door was laid the basic responsibility for cleavages within the army. Admitting to the court that the Generals' Revolt had "aggravated" the condition, General Valluy immediately added it "had been accomplished some time before."[12] The policy of De Gaulle, Jouhaud's attorney claimed, drove 1,800 officers from the army between January 1960 and November 1961.[13] And within each officer who remained, commented General Valluy, ran a personal division, a personal conflict. Notwithstanding the catastrophic consequences of the President's Algerian policy, however, from that division had come unity — unity against De Gaulle. "I cannot prevent myself from being in my heart with you," Valluy concluded, as he turned toward Generals Challe and Zeller.[14] "The hostility of the army [toward De Gaulle] has become unanimous, except for the bureaucrats," wrote Isorni.[15] Less partial

[11] *Le Monde*, September 19, 26, 1962; *L'Express*, September 27, 1962. There is some disparity between reports of what Massu said and official quotations, possibly arising from the continued desire of the government to protect its "favorite rebel" as a source of information.

[12] *Procès des Généraux Challe et Zeller*, p. 161.

[13] *Procès d'Edmond Jouhaud*, p. 323.

[14] *Loc. cit.*

[15] *Op. cit.*, p. 130.

observers agreed with Valluy and Isorni that the failure of the *putsch* of April 1961 and the trials which preceded and followed it had indeed produced military cohesion of a sort.[16]

Demand for amnesty, it may now be seen, was a "heads-I-win, tails-you-lose" proposition. No amnesty — stronger unity against De Gaulle; amnesty — confirmation of that unity binding members of the "white" army with those "lost" ones belonging to the "black" army. But which was which? It was frequently difficult to tell. A resident of Clermont-Ferrand reported, "I am never in the presence of an unknown officer without asking myself right off if he is one of the 'good ones' or of the others, and I always wait for him to begin by exonerating himself."[17] As a group, however, officers had no wish to absolve themselves from the charge of forming a solid resistance to De Gaulle's objectives in Algeria. One poor soldier found this out the hard way. After forming an anti-OAS committee in his company, he began to circulate tracts condemning activities "dishonoring the army." He also wrote the military tribunal an open letter demanding the death penalty for Salan. Court-martialed for "political activity," he pleaded that he was only following Minister of the Armed Forces Messmer's order requesting all military personnel to combat the Secret Army. To the charge that he had not cleared his tracts and letters through military channels, his answer was that "the political attitude of most of my superiors didn't permit me to do so." Four months in prison.[18]

In order to arrive at a full understanding of the concept of military unity, certain negative aspects must be added to its definition. Unity of the army, as events demonstrated, did not in practice mean respect for the hierarchy of command within the branches of the armed forces nor within the units comprising those branches. During both the Barricades Revolt of 1960 and the Generals' Revolt of 1961 the right of command became problematical. While Ortiz and Lagaillarde magnified their defiance of Paris under the benevolent eyes of military units in 1960, "General Gracieux [head of the Tenth Paratroop Division] . . . assumed

[16] Azeau, *op. cit.*, pp. 108, 262; Fauvet, Planchais, *op. cit.*, p. 248 ff., for example.
[17] *Le Monde*, March 2, 1962.
[18] *Le Monde*, August 1, 1962.

military power only nominally. He commanded on condition that he was in agreement with his subordinates." Gracieux himself recognized only too well that he had been neutralized as an agent of the government. Even so, he was better off than General Crépin, who arrived in Algiers the day before the revolt to replace Massu. "His isolation is striking. The officers of the Combined Staff stop talking when he enters a room, leave offices in which he hunts for desk space . . . He can obtain neither the key to his own office, which remains Massu's, nor the allegiance of the Staff."[19] During the April 1961 revolt it was Gambiez who was immobilized. While his position was supposedly that of commander-in-chief, while his courage and loyalty were both above question, "he had only been in Algiers since February 16. He had not been able to put trustworthy men in all positions; he still did not personally know all his subordinates, and he did not know on whom to rely."[20]

The breakdown of the command structure of course led to uncertainty as to whether orders would be followed. "To learn if the army is going to obey," Minister Delegate Delouvrier said in his hour of public anguish, "it is necessary to ask, one by one, each of its officers, each of its men."[21] A year later confusion became compounded. Some officers, like Colonel Gouraud, invited orders from the rebels, so that they might join the revolt. Some, like Colonel Roca, followed orders in whichever direction they led, remaining loyal while General Simon was on the scene but joining the revolt when Simon, rather than change his instructions under Challe's pressure, fled to Paris. Still others, like General Ginestet, used the absence of their superior as an excuse *not* to follow conflicting orders emanating from Algiers.[22]

Because "orders" became detached from the military hierarchy, they inevitably were retrospectively defined as those particular instructions which were obeyed. Some officers found it better to wait and assess the tolerances of the situation rather than to risk having their impotence

19 Brombergers et al., op cit., pp. 267, 185, 321.
20 Fauvet, Planchais, op. cit., pp. 97–98.
21 Brombergers et al., op. cit., p. 361.
22 Fauvet, Planchais, op. cit., pp. 124, 130, 131, 169, 171, 174, 235.

publicly exposed. Such was the attitude which led to the delicate maneuvering during the Barricades Revolt. In circumstances still more chaotic, officers preferred to "state a position" if forced to that point, and leave the interpretation of their statements to others. "At six P.M. he [General Autrand] called his officers together. 'The hour is about to strike,' he told them. 'You know what my choice is, but I leave you free to make yours.' What did he mean by that? ... If the occasion arose, each one would be free to follow him in a march on Algiers or to remain in Philippeville [General Autrand's base]."[23]

If unity of the army did not entail adherence of each unit to the hierarchy of command and the imperatives of legitimatized orders, still less did it prescribe lateral cooperation among units in the fulfillment of assigned missions. Even "loyal" troops who were brought from the country to replace or stiffen those encircling the barricades could not be counted on to support the government. Some officers quickly assumed the same sympathetic attitude toward the rebels held by colonels surrounding Challe. Some paratroopers fraternized with the military fraternizers around the barricades.

In 1961 a paratroop unit moved toward Algiers to join Challe's revolt. The troops were halted and their leader was asked the nature of his mission: "'I have my mission. You are obstructing it.' 'You shall not pass.' 'I shall pass. Will you fire?' 'I will not fire, but you shall not pass.' At which point the paratroopers went through the road block. Who would prevent them? The paratroopers enjoyed formidable prestige, reinforced in this particular instance by the prestige of the Foreign Legion. *They are accustomed to attach only limited value to orders given them by officers and non-coms who don't belong to their branch of service.*"[24]

The unpredictability of cooperation among groups hurt the rebels as well as the government. In 1960, while some imported formations were corrupted by the troops they met in Algiers, others were inspired by the same accidental encounter to remain overtly loyal. Still angered by

[23] *Ibid.*, p. 127.
[24] Fauvet, Planchais, *op. cit.*, p. 106. Italics added.

the deliberate withholding of military support in the shooting affray with Algiers civilians, officers of the security forces and mobile guards appealed to the newcomers in the name of unity, but in the opposite cause. "Are we here to be murdered by Algiers fascists?" they asked.[25]

Colonel Jean Gardy was confident that he could rally to Challe all the units of the Foreign Legion by appealing to them not to abandon the Algerians they had sworn to protect. Loss of Algeria, he warned, would mean the disappearance of the Legion itself. Notwithstanding his eloquence and his logic, he failed. "Gardy was in reality only a sometime legionnaire. He did not have the prestige of men who had held commands in the Legion throughout their careers and were imbued with its spirit."[26]

To General Challe the meanest cut of all was that unity of the army did not mean that officers, graduates of Saint-Cyr though they might be (and usually were), could give orders to draftees in the ranks and have them obeyed. The General could think of only one reason for this shocking breakdown of military discipline, which deprived his revolt of its chances for quick success. "Communist cells had been developed among the troops; it seems that it was they above all that had bewitched the draftees."[27] This explanation was no more in harmony with reality than Challe's equating of the Algerian nationalist movement with communism. Draftees had reacted against the revolt quite spontaneously. They feared separation from their metropolitan homeland and had no desire to be caught on alien territory which threatened to become a battleground. They were hopeful that France could, by negotiations, produce real peace in Algeria. As between rebellious officers and De Gaulle, they had every reason to choose their President.

Loyalist leaders emerged among the draftees without regard to rank or length of service. They delicately assayed the opinion of fellow soldiers and explored the attitude of their non-coms and officers. As soon as they could, they exchanged information with loyalists in other companies and reassured Moslems about them who were following

---

[25] Brombergers *et al.*, *op. cit.*, p. 277.
[26] Fauvet, Planchais, *op. cit.*, p. 134. Gardy had been Inspector of the Legion.
[27] *Procès des Généraux Challe et Zeller*, p. 43.

FLN orders to remain quiet. While Challe and his cohorts were still drumming up support, blocs of loyalist draftees, having discovered their own potential power, were applying pressure on wavering officers. One form of influence was a reminder that enlisted men held indispensable, though lowly, jobs in transport, communications, and supply. Officers might declare themselves for Challe, but without agreement by their men, they could not travel to see him, talk to him by telephone, or even be certain they would be served their lonely meals. Where passive demonstrations were not enough, the men took positive steps. Officers ordering conscripts to march were themselves invited to march to their offices and stay there. Officers foolhardy enough to attempt to inflict physical punishment on disobedient draftees were on occasion beaten up, as, in fact, were some who merely persisted in expressing defiance of De Gaulle.

Frequent breaks in the command structure had already taken place before the President moved to take advantage of the loyalty of the draftees. In his speech of April 20 the Chief of State said, "I forbid all Frenchmen, all soldiers to carry out any of their [the rebel officers'] orders. The argument that it might be necessary in some locales to accept their command because of operational or administrative obligations can fool no one." Air Force General Michel Fourquet later reinforced the theme: "Your duty is clear. You cannot give in to the threats made you . . . This is what for the moment your attitude should be: no order you receive from the insurgent command should be executed. Preserve discipline in your units. Your officers, by and large, are rejecting the situation in which they have been placed. You have only to question them. They cannot fail to reply to you. *If they have ceased being faithful to the Government and to France, they have by the same token ceased to be your leaders. In that event follow the orders of the most senior of your officers who have remained loyal.*"[28]

Thus civilian leadership made legal, often retroactively, passive disobedience, positive insubordination, even acts of violence. Soldiers listening to their President on transistor radios felt the encouragement

[28] Fauvet, Planchais, *op. cit.*, p. 23. Italics added.

of firm instructions from home. Non-coms, caught between pro-government enlisted men and wavering or rebellious officers, were relieved at orders to join the troops in opposing the professional corps. When the revolting generals got around to issuing a pronunciamento "releasing" the draftees from military service, it was too late.[29]

Finally, it should be obvious from the above that unity of the army did not mean uniform respect for the over-riding responsibility and authority of the political system. To the contrary, disobedience within the ranks of officers had been consistently motivated by the desire to disregard, flout, undermine civilian leadership and its recognized agents. Government officials were under no illusions on this score. Guillaumat knew in 1960 that he had no real hold over the army; in 1961 the control of Messmer, his successor as Minister of the Armed Forces, was, to say the least, tenuous. Resident Minister Jean Morin was held prisoner in Algiers by the rebellious generals, along with Robert Buron, a member of Debré's cabinet, and other loyal representatives of the government. When De Gaulle sent Louis Joxe and General Jean Olié to Algeria in an effort to provide a focus of allegiance to which military units could rally, they were intercepted and sequestered.

Joxe was no problem, being a civilian, but Olié presented a threat even greater than had Gambiez: "We can't of course have two commanders in chief in Algeria," Challe declared. But, argued the president of the tribunal trying Challe and Zeller, Olié was not just "commander of Algeria; he was the Chief of the French Army, wasn't he?" In answer Challe tried to hide behind the superior authority conveyed by one-time positions within the military hierarchy. "I know General Olié well, since he was formerly under my orders when he commanded the Constantine region." Once a subordinate, always a subordinate in the unity of the army against the President of the Republic.[30]

---

[29] For the draftees' revolt against the Generals' Revolt, see Christian Hebert, "Quatre journées d'avril en Algérie," "L'Etat d'esprit du contingent," both in *La Nef*, July–September 1961, pp. 112–123, 123–129 respectively; Azeau, *op. cit.*, pp. 168–199; Fauvet, Planchais, *op. cit.*, pp. 143–149, 182, 218, 219, 230, 240.

[30] *Procès des Généraux Challe et Zeller*, p. 61. When the tribunal's president repeated his question, Challe admitted he was correct.

Army officers professed to hold military unity as a sacred principle; yet their grotesque definitions distorted it beyond recognition. Their use of the concept between 1958 and 1962 so fragmented the military establishment that its effectiveness as an instrument to defend the security of France against external enemies was destroyed. Worse, by identifying the threat to the Nation with the political institutions of the Fifth Republic, the army actually became an accomplice to the country's foreign foes. The onus for this tragedy cannot be laid at De Gaulle's doorstep; to do so would be to support the claim of the President's military opponents that they alone were the proper judges of the legitimacy of civilian authority. The army's manipulation of the principle of military unity was an irresponsible, desperate technique adopted to forward the destructive aims of its activists. Irresponsible because the basic value inherent in the concept was greatly impaired. Desperate because the activists could not have been so blind as to be unaware of the consequences of their actions. Indeed, the conclusion is inescapable that they did know, but calculated the price as reasonable if they could direct the course of French statecraft in Algeria.

The military extremists were encouraged by knowledge that there did exist military unity of a sort: the overwhelming proportion of the officer corps, inside and outside Algeria, supported the proposition that Algeria should remain French, although they were in some disagreement as to what "remaining French" ought to mean in the future. Therefore, they saw nothing incongruous, let alone dangerous, in the vast economic, social, and political responsibilities which would continue to devolve upon the army. Few protested publicly at the outrages, including terror and torture, which French units perpetrated in the envelopment of Algeria. Equally few failed to share outrage against De Gaulle, as the President moved to deprive the army, not just of victory, but of its broad, deep, and long-lasting power over French territory.

Behind some forms of political pressure, therefore, a military consensus did exist. But when direct action took the form of rebellion and assassination, military politicians by appealing to unity produced only division. The formal organizational structure ceased to provide clues to the actual hierarchy of power and influence within the army. In the scale of who could command how many to do what, colonels at times outranked generals; lieutenants instructed majors; and privates emerged on the top of the heap. The informal structure, paralleling the formal one, became so problematical that officers relied on it at their peril. What emerged was an army out of the Middle Ages, a changing patchwork of feudal fiefs. Each fief was held by personal loyalties, which could always be revoked; limited, temporary cooperation among fiefs was negotiated on the same principle.

The substitution of loyalty to an individual chief for obedience to the impersonal authority of the state was no new phenomenon in France or in military organization generally. Students of military affairs unwittingly assisted apologists for the army by reminding them of useful historical precedents. Again it turned out to be — surprise! — De Gaulle's fault. He had, so they said, challenged existing, legitimate political and military authority in 1940. He had built an army on the basis of personal loyalty. In place of unquestioning obedience he planted seeds of doubt, hesitation, introspection. For the spiritual, professional ideal of service he had substituted temporal, political ideas. The supposed advocate of a modern career army was in reality an anachronistic chieftain seeking to direct his own army toward his own goals.

To old patterns of obedience the army's frustrating conflict in Indochina, it was conceded, had added still more qualifications. In the war against Ho Chi-Minh, questioning the right of leaders to lead, commanders to command became a habit.[31] Devotion to France acquired a limited definition. While De Gaulle could not be blamed for Indochina, he could be and was charged with the ultimate degradation of the army in Algeria. Again General Valluy graphically expressed the hostile position. "Our army has become a body whose living parts are sluggish, malfunctioning, or shriveled. Informing has been established every-

---

[31] See above, Chapter 1. Political corruption at home, inability to repress the Viet Minh in the field led combat officers, exposed to the unending rigors of guerrilla combat, to find in themselves and their immediate cohorts the only associations worthy of allegiance.

where. Respect for titles or insignias of command becomes gradually
blurred, and alliances with yesterday's enemy, local combinations, in-
cessant changes do not help matters."[32]

In the mouths of military apologists the precedent of 1940 for behavior twenty years later has a disagreeably oily, self-serving sound.
To be sure, De Gaulle did issue personal appeals after France's defeat,
which some of the professional army followed (though not as many as
later mythology would have it). But there is, as a few generals like
De Larminat and Billotte have pointed out, a distinguishable difference
between calls for help to continue the struggle against an invading,
external enemy and similar cries when the enemy is the President of the
Republic, presiding over a constitution duly ratified by the French
people.

Other factors besides the iniquitous De Gaulle were also certainly at
work. The nature of warfare in Indochina and in Algeria placed a high
premium on individual initiative by local unit commanders, often very
junior officers, and the presence of officers with special skills and training. Teachings about the contingencies of atomic warfare were simultaneously stressing the same need for decentralization of responsibility
and specialization. Moreover, dolorous events undergone by France had
led to the creation of several armies which were far from overlapping.
The pre-war army split into at least three wartime organizations —
Vichyite, Gaullist, and Resistance. Postwar years superimposed Indochinese, German, and North African armies even before the great
rendezvous in Algeria.

Into these divisive forces politicalized officers willfully introduced the
explosive ingredients of changeable loyalties, impermanent affiliations,
questionable legitimacy. There was no necessary reason why the ad-
mittedly searing experiences of World War II and succeeding conflicts
should have caused such a degree of organizational dislocation and

[32] *Le Monde,* August 1, 1962; editorial in Saint-Cyr journal attributed to General Valluy. Among those discussing the so-called "precedent" of 1940 are: articles
in a special issue of *Esprit,* May 1950, entitled *Armée française?*; Vincent Monteil, *Les officiers,* Paris, Editions du Seuil, 1958, pp. 162–164; Georges Lescuyer,
"Les militaires et la politique," II, *Revue Politique et Parlementaire,* June 1962, pp.
78–81.

moral corruption. The experiences of France were not unique; they were shared, in part, by other Western armies. But the determination of a large group of officers to go to any lengths to obtain the type of decision in Algeria they wanted, plus the shocking quiescence of their fellow professionals, combined to blow apart the French military establishment. "This questioning costs me as much as you," the tribunal's president told Jouhaud at his trial. "These assassins [of the OAS] will be guilty of passive obedience, of military obedience. You arrived at the highest posts of the army, and you know that the army lives only by its organization, by its discipline, that everything reaches down from grade to grade and that beginning at the moment when a five-star general commands certain acts, those acts in the eyes of everyone become legitimate."[33]

By forcing new issues on the army, military activists actually served to alleviate certain of the older divisions mentioned above. They thereby lessened even as they added to De Gaulle's task of forging a powerful French army. The stigma of the navy's attachment to Vichy was covered over, if not erased, by its minimal involvement in attempts to usurp the responsibilities of the Fifth Republic. Challe's leadership of the April revolt illustrated the connections that existed between the Algerian army and the bits and pieces of what might be called the European army. Activists, although placing highest priority on manning the African ramparts against the Soviet menace, also stressed the common mission of all the military segments in fighting Communist aggression. Finally, although the obsession with dicta concerning revolutionary war caused a lag in training in the complexities of modern military technology, it still built a tattered ideological tent large enough to shelter, after a fashion, different generations and different educational experiences.[34]

[33] *Procès d'Edmond Jouhaud*, p. 118.

[34] Persistence of pre-war cleavages within military ranks is stressed by, among others, John Tremaine, "The Army in Modern France," *History Today*, November 1961, pp. 733–743; Jean Planchais, "Quelle est cette armée?" *La Nef*, July–September 1961, pp. 57–64; Eugène Carrias, *Pensée militaire française*, Paris, Presses Universitaires de France, 1960, pp. 350 ff. The effect of political action by the army on old divisions is discussed by François Gromier, "Une conception archaïque," *Cahiers de la République*, November-December 1960, pp. 15–31.

The main result of politicalization of the French army, however, was to superimpose a bevy of new divisions on the old ones. First, the officer corps was scattered along the entire gamut of involvement in pressures upon the institutions of the Fifth Republic. As has been shown, each engagement with De Gaulle left clusters of officers strewn in various postures over the battlefield. Although general sympathy and identification with the standard-bearers of the insurrections certainly encouraged activists, many officers withheld any permanent and irreversible commitment to participate directly themselves. General Marcel Lennuyeux, for example, when informed by one of his officers, Colonel Alain de Boisseau, that he wanted to get into Challe's revolt, replied in effect: "Blessings on you, son. Go to it."[35] But the attitude of the General himself was "wait and see." If the revolt were doomed, his own career would be safe; if it rolled on toward ultimate success, as had the uprising of 1958, there was always time to jump aboard. Within the wait-and-see attitude itself there were, of course, many gradations.

The decision of Salan and Jouhaud to convert Challe's overt revolt into a continuing, clandestine conflict, increasingly focussed on the person of the President, produced further separations inside the officer corps. The distance between the few skulking through the back alleys of bomb-throwing politics and the many sitting respectably in camps or offices can, however, be over-estimated. For, again, the many identified themselves with the few and therefore were sympathetic. Large numbers of professional officers did not stop there; they provided aid and comfort by defending accused assassins in court and even called for grants of amnesty for those convicted. As each OAS network in metropolitan France was dug out by police, it is a striking fact that military personnel were discovered as central inspirators. Official investigations have, moreover, revealed that each abortive attempt to kill De Gaulle was organized and directed by officers. In contrast, there emerged only very weak and limited protest by military leaders against the criminal assaults on the head of the state.

At the white end of the legality-illegality spectrum did stand a few officers ready to echo General de Larminat's statement, after the failure

---

[35] *Procès des Généraux Challe et Zeller*, p. 145.

of the April revolt, that he awaited word of the suicide of the military conspirators, such a course being the only one compatible with honor.[36] Or General Pierre Billotte's demand, when the military tribunal had failed to sentence Salan to death, that "an abrupt and total break should be made with the men of May 13, their friends, and their friends' friends, who still lie in wait within the structure of the government." Billotte suffered retaliation for his outspoken views: army officers helped civilian officials to persuade De Gaulle to cancel Billotte's mission as Resident Minister in Algeria during the critical transition period between the cease-fire and the advent of formal independence.[37]

It proved easier to separate draftees from their officers, as the Generals' Revolt of 1961 had done, than to put the two back together again. By their actions draftees had shown that rejection of orders and breaches of discipline were not luxuries restricted to professional graduates of Saint-Cyr. The shock they administered to the officers was profound. In many units things could never be the same again, once limits had been placed on authority and discipline. Even when the personnel was changed, each side had to reach tentatively toward the other over the chasm that had opened between them.

Instead of placing blame where it belonged, the army found that a handy instrument with which to rebuild internal cohesion was renewed criticisms of decadent, Leftist society and, naturally, of De Gaulle for his open encouragement of the conscripts. Military opinion argued that respect for the army's ideals and organization could only be re-instilled in the troops if the army were given an even larger role in training the nation's youth. At the same time, sections which had enjoyed some success in training automatons responsive to any and all commands found justification for even greater severity. Thus the way was cleared for fresh abuses of human dignity, as well as for a fundamental re-examination of the nature of France's manpower requirements. Such a re-examination was certainly long overdue. It had been delayed by the succession of colonial wars, by the incoherence of the Fourth Republic, and by

[36] *L'Année Politique, 1961*, p. 56.
[37] *L'Express*, May 31, 1962.

the continual military assaults on the Fifth. In this respect, also, military activists performed a substantial, if unpremeditated, service to De Gaulle.

The ground forces, navy, and air force revealed different attitudes toward political action, the determining factor being the nature of their respective relationships to Algeria. Least involved in the conflict, and least politicized, was the navy, as Challe discovered to his sorrow. Although Challe and Jouhaud held high positions in the air force, that branch escaped thorough contamination. Individual officers did participate in the 1961 revolt, but many pilots brought their planes back to France to get them out of the generals' reach. In contrast to the other two services, the ground forces, by fighting De Gaulle, were fighting to preserve their prestige, their vested interests, and, many thought, their very reason for existence. If colonial warfare ended, officers feared, the emphasis on nuclear confrontations would require a thorough shake-up in the organizational structure of the army. The service as a whole would no longer enjoy a near monopoly of national attention, and some of its units might even receive lower priority than sections of the air force or the navy.

Within the branches of the armed forces certain units had manifestly thrown in their lot with the rebels. With a liberal definition one might contend that paratroop units remained loyal during the Barricades Revolt, thanks to paratrooper Lagaillarde's refusal to accept their services. Not so the Territorial Units (which are roughly analogous to the American National Guard), portions of which ended up half in, half out of Lagaillarde's barricade. Challe understandably had high hopes in 1961 that the Territorials could replace the conscript companies he planned to release.

Embittered by the failure of the Algiers barricade-builders to inspire a general revolt against De Gaulle, Guy Forzy, Lagaillarde's emissary, cried out to the officers with whom he was negotiating surrender terms: "You are sacrificing us to the unity of the army, in spite of all that has been told us. You won't preserve this unity any more than you'll preserve French Algeria. Our gesture hasn't been for nothing . . . You won't save yourselves. [Colonels] Gardes and Broizat have already gone. That's only the beginning. You will all go."[38] Logical and prophetic words. The leader of the next Algiers insurrection was the same general who had sought to settle the first by appeasement. To his own "purely military" venture Challe attracted paratroop units and elements of the Foreign Legion. The presiding judge at his subsequent trial found it "curious" that Challe's patriotic movement to protect the sacred soil of France should be based on units composed of foreigners.[39] The commitment of the Legion to Algeria was all but total; there was nowhere else to go. The same was true of the *harkis,* Moslem troops fighting for France.

Paratroopers, legionnaires, and *harkis,* therefore, presented a special problem to De Gaulle in the wake of the Algerian settlement. They epitomized the general attachment of the army to the nation's colonial past. From that attachment had come the politicalization of the armed forces, which had ultimately focussed on issues of military unity and division. De Gaulle's success in returning the military to its proper role as instrument, not determiner, of statecraft depended less on forging new bonds to tie the army together than in convincing its disparate sections that their respective missions, as envisaged by the President, were worthy of their dedication.

[38] Brombergers *et al., op. cit.,* p. 438.
[39] *Procès des Généraux Challe et Zeller,* p. 53.

PART TWO

Toward a New Ordering of French
Civil-Military Relations

C H A P T E R 5

EXECUTIVE POWER
UNDER THE
FIFTH REPUBLIC

His [De Gaulle's] power is one of the feeblest ever known, his regime one of the most precarious. — L'Express, November 23, 1961

Everyone knows that our people have appointed a president, chief of State, guide for France, keystone of our institutions . . . — Charles de Gaulle, October 19, 1962

THE CONCLUSION of the Evian agreements with the Provisional Algerian Government in March 1962 gave De Gaulle an opportunity to take the measures he thought necessary to strengthen his regime. He could now move further toward the type of political system he had quite probably envisaged for a long time as best suited to France. Experience with the operation of the Constitution of 1958 provided indications of desirable changes, as did developments in France's domestic and international position. Finally, as the President realized only too well, stronger executive power was a prerequisite to recapturing control of an army generally reluctant to "turn the Algerian page."

Discussing the referendum on Algerian independence which was to take place on July 1, 1962, the President, in June, forecast his basic aim and method. "Above all, women and men of France," he told them, "everyone has seen that the loyal confidence which you as a body have bestowed upon me has spurred and sustained me day after day and that this direct agreement between the people and the one who has the responsibility for leading them has become, in modern times, essential to the Republic. To maintain, in this domain, what has just been tested — such must be our conclusion once the Algerian question has been settled . . . Women and men of France, we shall by the same means [universal suffrage], at the proper time, have to make sure that, in the future and above and beyond men that pass, the Republic may remain strong, well-ordered, and continuous."

The "proper time" for an announcement that yet another referendum would be held, in this instance to approve the direct election of the President, was deemed to be September 1962, when the legislature was not in session.[1] The method by which De Gaulle proposed to modify the Constitution was, to say the least, of doubtful legality. In fact, the Constitutional Council declared it invalid, although the Council of Ministers loyally upheld the President the next day.

Unable to reach the President on his Olympian heights, frustrated deputies mustered the absolute majority necessary to censure his premier, Georges Pompidou, as soon as the regular autumn session of the National Assembly began. On the eve of the referendum the four great democratic groupings of the Fourth Republic — Independents, MRP, Radicals, and Socialists — even agreed to a common program of action, the first point of which was "application of the Constitution as concerns the balance of powers, and the initiation of legislative government."[2]

Fundamentally at stake, however, was neither a constitutional issue nor, in fact, the substantive question of whether the president should be elected by direct popular vote or by a crowd of some eighty thousand "notables." As in previous referenda and elections since 1958, the issue was De Gaulle himself. As Jean-Marie Domenach forcefully

[1] The date selected was October 28.
[2] *Le Monde*, October 28–29, 1962.

pointed out, violation of French constitutions was nothing new; some of those rushing to rescue the Fifth Republic had helped to evade the terms of the Fourth and had explicitly approved the alienation of national territory (Algeria), supposedly guaranteed by the Constitution for which they were belatedly concerned. "What good is it," he asked, "to enlist in a coalition men who have nothing in common but the memory of defeats they have survived?"[3]

De Gaulle's appeal to the voters was, if anything, even more vigorously and personally presented than in the past. "Each 'yes' by each Frenchwoman and Frenchman which will be given me will be for me the direct proof of their confidence and of their encouragement . . . It is thus your replies which will on October 28 tell me if I can and if I should pursue my task in the service of France." The implication that he would leave if the proposed amendment were not accepted De Gaulle made crystal clear just before the balloting. "If your response is 'no,' as all the old parties want, in order to re-establish their disastrous regime, as all the seditious wish, in order to launch into subversion, or even if the majority of 'yeses' is feeble, weak, precarious, it is very evident that my task will be immediately and irrevocably ended. For what could I then do without the wholehearted confidence of the Nation?"

Thus De Gaulle drew out his threat of resigning if he did not get his own way, just as he had done four years earlier, when he was helping to push over the Fourth Republic. The old political formations this time, however, reacted differently; instead of capitulating, as they had in 1958, they challenged him to carry out his threat. If the President, as he said, had planned all along to change the method of election, why had he not indicated this when his tailored constitution was being drafted? What rationale was there in his claim that direct election would ensure stability in the unhappy event plotters succeeded in assassinating him? Admitting that under any circumstances the sudden loss of this leader of a highly personalized regime would produce considerable confusion throughout France, was it not reasonable to believe that the very indirection of the original method of selecting a successor would contribute some semblance of calm?

[3] *Le Monde,* October 4, 1962.

Only an absolute majority, his followers had hinted, would satisfy De Gaulle. Opponents were hopeful that voters unwilling to return to old party figures would still vote "no" in an impersonal referendum, or at least would abstain. In many respects they were not disappointed. Less than 47 percent of the total electorate voted affirmatively. In fourteen of ninety departments the President received less than half the total ballots cast. Everywhere his support fell off. The percentage of abstentions — 22.75 — was greater than in 1958, though less than in the two previous referenda. However, abstentions did not tell the full story. Of those who cast their ballots, 61.75 percent voted for direct election of the President, and less than 39 percent against it.

Were there, then, in reality "no victors, no vanquished," as *Le Monde* claimed?[4] De Gaulle, who has as acute a sense of the theatrical as any Western politician, prolonged the period of popular uncertainty over whether he would stay or resign as President. But after an extra day's seclusion at his home in Colombey-les-Deux-Eglises, he returned to Paris prepared for the next step in his struggle to shape governmental institutions and personnel to his taste. Seasoned antagonists should by this time have gauged the temper of the man. Campaign oratory was one thing; reality was another. Had not almost two of three voters followed his direction? What other Frenchman could command such support? De Gaulle had no intention of withdrawing, as he had at the end of 1945, to wait, perhaps in vain, for a spontaneous recall.

Now that the presidency was more than ever his own, De Gaulle could proceed to shore up the battered prestige of the other half of the executive, the Government. Premier Debré, it was reported, had in the Spring opposed De Gaulle's intended strategy. After the referendum had ratified the Algerian settlement, the Premier thought the National Assembly should be dissolved, new elections held, and subsequent stress laid on the "parliamentary" aspects of French democracy. Debré's plan would certainly have improved the position of the Government and his own ministry; it would also have led to greater legislative autonomy vis-à-vis the presidency. This of course was not at all

4 October 30, 1962.

what De Gaulle had in mind. It was not the Assembly which was dissolved, but Debré. "After such an accomplishment," De Gaulle told his faithful first servant after the Evian agreements were concluded, "I think, as you do, that it is in the interest of the public service that you now have the freedom to undertake at the appropriate moment and in new circumstances another aspect of your career."[5] The immediate aspect of Debré's career envisaged by the President was apparently not a place in the executive branch.[6] For when Debré was beaten in the November elections (apparently by a fusion of Left and extreme-Right opposition), he was advised by De Gaulle to learn something about the world by travel abroad. Debré profited by the advice to the extent of getting himself elected to the National Assembly as a representative of the French island of Réunion, in the Indian Ocean.

To replace Michel Debré De Gaulle called on a long-time associate, Georges Pompidou. The change was significant in a number of respects. Debré had had a prominent political career before 1958, Pompidou none. Debré had had substantial responsibility in drafting the Constitution of 1958, Pompidou none. Debré had, by all reports, differed with De Gaulle on important matters of policy, including Algeria; Pompidou's views were almost completely unknown. Debré was a lawyer; Pompidou for eight years had been associated with the House of Rothschild. Although Debré's several cabinets had contained a heavy admixture of "technicians" and Pompidou appointed a number of politicians to his, the Government was for the first time headed by one who might justly be called an anti-politician. "Under Michel Debré," wrote the *New York Times*, "there was a semblance of duality in the French executive power. With M. Pompidou, even the semblance disappears."[7]

The perspicacity of the *Times'* judgment was demonstrated in the way De Gaulle treated what had now become to all intents and purposes *his* Government. Hardly had the National Assembly (on April 27) invested Pompidou by an unimpressive plurality (259 to 128) than the President

[5] Passeron, *op. cit.*, pp. 145–147.

[6] There were the usual rumors that De Gaulle was grooming Debré to be his successor. Since the presidency was neither hereditary nor appointive, however, it would be a difficult, even if desired, task.

[7] April 16, 1962.

caused a cabinet crisis. His condemnation of European "unification" provoked the resignation of all five Catholic MRP members. An "outburst of bad humor among people who engage in politics," De Gaulle caustically labelled the action of such prominent leaders as Pierre Pflimlin, last Premier of the Fourth Republic, and Maurice Schumann, long-time party secretary and spokesman on foreign affairs. Pompidou filled the breach by moving up a number of Gaullists and abolishing three positions in his cabinet. Further resignations were avoided only by the refusal of the Independent members to follow the demand of their party. The separation of the Government from the historic political formations became even wider.

Conversely, the identification of the Government with the President was emphasized when De Gaulle refused to accept Pompidou's resignation after the National Assembly had passed a motion of censure. As most observers had expected, the President dismissed the Assembly and called for new elections in November. In the interim the Premier remained in office, not just as caretaker, but as though he headed a sanctioned cabinet empowered to take any and all decisions falling within its purview. When the new Assembly convened, Pompidou put in an appearance as past and present Premier, introducing a government with only three new faces, although there had been some juggling of ministerial assignments. In 1963 three lonely, sometime Independents and one former Radical relieved the monotony of the long list of non-politicians and Gaullist UNR members. Never had the Fifth Republic looked less like the Fourth.[8]

Hand in hand with strengthened ties between Government and President went revisions in the organization of national defense. Ever since World War II French regimes had wrestled with components of the problem. Augmented authority for the Premier implied, if it did not

---

[8] Some Frenchmen professed differently. See, for example, Jacques Fauvet's column in Le Monde, October 10, 1962, in which he wrote, "It is not exact to say that we are returning to the Fourth Republic. We are already there, and because of the failure of the Fifth." The habit of historical retrogression dies hard in France. The Fourth Republic was said to be the Third; doubtless the Third was called the Second, as Bonapartists were labelled Orleanists, and all likened to the Ancien Régime.

actually entail, a congruent loss in position of ministers charged with supervising the armed forces. Within the cabinet itself ministries for the three services conflicted with attempted centralization under one civilian head. Some attempted to draw distinctions between the broad requirements of national defense and the narrower needs of the armed forces, in order to separate cabinet responsibilities. Officials, confronting crisis after crisis, all beyond the country's capacity to solve successfully, desperately turned to committees and secretariats, large and small, for planning and advice. The category of problems was not dissimilar to an American or a British list, but the weakness of the Fourth Republic and the growing defiance of the army added purely French ingredients of incoherence.

While the Algerian war was on, its exigencies dictated the formal structure of national defense as it did so much of the Fifth Republic's operation. The Constitution of 1958 and the ordinance of January 7, 1959 provided the basis for a system entailing heavy responsibilities for the Premier. There was to be a Superior Council of Defense and a Defense Committee, over both of which the President formally presided, but the operating body was supposedly the Restricted (smaller) Defense Committee, which could be activated by the Premier. The Superior Council was designed to be a planning group, the full Defense Committee an instrument for general decision, while the smaller Defense Committee was to take action "on the military direction of defense." Debré added to the effectiveness of his office by creating a General Staff for National Defense to coordinate the activities of the various ministries working both in the wide area implied by the title and in the actual direction of the armed forces. While De Gaulle defined the broad lines of policy, Debré was its executor, and power was centralized in the Government to that end. His military chief of staff had the duty of passing on instructions to the various field commanders, particularly in Algeria. By contrast, therefore, both the Minister of the Armed Forces and the Chief of Staff of the Armed Forces were relatively low in the administrative hierarchy. In both military and civilian respects, their roles could be construed as advice, coordination, and administration.

With the end of the Algerian war, the need for a direct line of authority from President through Premier to military leaders ceased to be as urgent. At the same time, the pressing need to brighten the future for an army mourning the loss of Algeria made it desirable that national defense committees already appearing on the administrative charts be given more to do. The Generals' Revolt and the complicity of whole military units were removing any lingering impression that "national defense" could somehow be kept separate from military policy. Moreover, both the experience in Algeria and the requirements of modernization, in which planes, missiles, and nuclear warheads would occupy a central position, pointed up the need for coordinated civil direction as counterpart to unified missions for combined forces of the three services. Therefore, decisions of the cabinet in July 1962 undertook to simplify the structure of national defense and to reduce somewhat the range of authority exercised by the Premier.

One decree replaced the cumbersome General Staff of National Defense with a General Secretariat. Unlike its predecessor, the Secretariat was not to transmit orders, but to assist the Premier in coordinating activities of the ministries concerned. It was also, as its name implies, to prepare studies for consideration by its parent body, the Committee of Defense. Decisions of the latter were, in turn, to pass through the Secretariat for definition of executory responsibility. To assist the Secretariat in its planning and initiating roles, there were attached to it both the Institute of Advanced Studies of National Defense and the Committee of Scientific Action for Defense. The Institute and Committee were to receive suggestions for military research and training from the Secretariat, as well as initiate studies on their own responsibility. De Gaulle selected Air Force General Michel Fourquet to be the first Secretary-General of the Secretariat. Before 1960 Fourquet had received principally staff assignments, including NATO's Standing Group in Washington. He had also served as military aide to Premier, then President de Gaulle. Named to command an air unit in Algeria toward the end of 1960, Fourquet's loyalty to the President prevented the rebellious generals in April 1961 from commandeering enough aircraft to drop troops on the Metropole.

Another decree changed, at least in nuance, the relative responsibilities of the President and the Premier. Article 21 of the Constitution
stated that the Premier "is responsible for National Defense," and the
Ordinance of January 7, 1959 established that "defense policy is determined by the Council of Ministers," although, as has been pointed out,
the President formally presided over the various defense committees.
In July 1962 the powers of the committees, and hence the channel open
to the President for formal decision in the matter of national defense,
appeared to be substantially broadened, as compared with those of the
Premier. "General defense policy," stated the new ordinance, "is determined by the Council of Ministers. The councils or committees of defense, called and presided over by the President of the Republic, supervise the over-all direction of national defense, and, if necessary, the
conduct of war . . . The prime minister supervises the execution of the
decisions of the government . . ."[9]

One must beware of deducing actual procedures from administrative
regulations. As with the Fifth Republic itself, tests and experience, to
say nothing of the individuals involved, would determine relative responsibilities. However, taken together with the replacement of Debré
by Pompidou and the double victory of De Gaulle — in referendum and
Assembly elections — the ordinance would seem to bring the President
closer to the cabinet as a collectivity in the civil-military determination
of policies for national defense.[10]

The same set of decrees conferred on the Minister of the Armed
Forces some of the responsibility formerly assigned to the Premier. The
Minister (who was Pierre Messmer) "is responsible for the execution of
military policy and assumes, in conformity with the general directions
of the prime minister, the missions . . . governing the general organization of defense. He translates into orders and instructions directives set
forth by the prime minister." He is "responsible for the security of the
military means of defense."[11] Under the Minister of the Armed Forces

[9] Article quoted by Le Monde, July 20, 1962.
[10] The reinforced powers of presidential decision are stressed by Louis Dullin,
"L'Armée de nos enfants," II, Revue Politique et Parlementaire, November 1962,
p. 84.
[11] Ibid.

were placed a ministerial delegate for armament, an administrative secretary general, and the Committee of General Staffs of the three services. Separated from this Committee and directly responsible to the Minister was the Chief of Staff of the Armed Forces, who was charged with coordinating military preparations for defense, initiating their application, and overseeing their execution. He was also to supervise advanced combined-forces education.[12]

To the position of Chief of Staff of the Armed Forces, President de Gaulle brought General Charles Ailleret. Like General Fourquet a graduate of the Ecole Polytechnique, Ailleret had acquired the title "atomic general" by supervising the preparations for the first French nuclear explosion, accomplished in March 1960. He defied General Challe in April 1961, informing Paris that he continued to operate his command at Bône normally. After the failure of the revolt, he was made commander of combined French forces in Algeria and given the delicate task of re-organizing the French Algerian army and keeping it aloof from the erupting OAS. At General Salan's trial Ailleret was one of the few unequivocal supporters of De Gaulle. Although both defense and prosecution sought his testimony, General Ailleret refused to accord the accused any military rank (referring to him simply as "Salan") and described his Secret Army as a bunch of paid terrorists.[13]

Finally, adjustments were needed in the structure of national defense to reflect the increasingly important place of nuclear technology in programs for military modernization. Announcement was made in June 1962 that Minister of the Armed Forces Messmer and the Minister of State for Scientific Research and Atomic and Space Questions, Gaston Palewski, had joined in the formation of a directing committee composed of both administrators and technicians. Administrative representatives were to establish nuclear military requirements, while the technicians were to reconcile them with the needs of the Commissariat for Atomic Energy. It was readily apparent that Palewski, long-standing advisor to President de Gaulle, could exert great influence on general

---

[12] The revised organization of national defense is discussed in *Le Monde*, July 12, 13 and 14, 1962. The last issue includes a chart.

[13] *Procès de Raoul Salan,* pp. 121, 111.

military policy. His equally significant responsibility in French economic development will be discussed in a later chapter.

"Reconstruction or Tinkering?" was the title of a column by *Le
Monde's* military commentator Tony Albord, appearing the month after
the decrees revising the executive organization for national defense.
"Can we claim," he wrote, "that it will be enough to extol tomorrows,
to announce law-programs, to create or transform combat units and give
them new and powerful material in order that a moral and intellectual
balance may be restored within the army and in order that finally
France might accomplish what it has been attempting for almost thirty
years: a rational and effective military system?"[14] Executive reorganization was certainly an indispensable prerequisite to control, let alone
improvement, of the armed forces.

Strengthening of the Fifth Republic as a personalized instrument in
De Gaulle's hands resulted in still further weakening of the National
Assembly and the traditional political groupings that inhabited it. Ever
since the institutions of the Fifth Republic began to operate with
Debré's investiture as Premier in January 1959, the Assembly had
looked for ways to recapture some of the control it had enjoyed over
the executive during the lives of the Third and Fourth Republics. When
annoyance reached a boiling point, motions of censure were introduced,
but until 1962 these uniformly failed to secure the requisite absolute
majority. Some of De Gaulle's opponents hesitated to disrupt the government in the midst of the seemingly perpetual Algerian crisis; others
preferred abstention to keeping public company with inveterate political foes; and all were uncomfortably aware that censure would only
produce another election, which might retire them to private life, with
no early chance to slip into the Senate, as some of their colleagues had
done after having been blown down by the Gaullist windstorm of 1958.

With the passage of time, however, legislative behavior reverted to
a pattern familiar to French political historians. (In this respect Jacques
Fauvet's analogy to the Fourth Republic is correct.) Pompidou's failure
to win an absolute majority for his investiture — 259 as compared to

[14] *Le Monde,* August 27, 1962.

276 — was reminiscent of feeble endorsement given previous premiers. Once more a negative majority was gathering, awaiting only the proper moment to strike against the government. Deputies had tired of the sterile game of minority motions of censure; the new Premier looked like an easier target, particularly in view of his original difficulties in holding together his cabinet. However, the approaching conclusion of the Algerian war meant that time was running out to attack the recently installed Government. With the independence of the erstwhile French territory, some 68 deputies would lose their mandate. With each passing month, they feared, Pompidou might consolidate his position under De Gaulle's protective wing.

Spurred by conviction, frustration, boredom, and spite, the National Assembly launched its assault. The first salvo, fired by the Algeria-firsters, was weakly supported. Pompidou himself provided ammunition for the second round. "I am astonished," he declared, "that I have committed so many crimes in so little time." He then proceeded to alienate delegates who, he felt, were recent and opportunistic converts to European unity. "Since when this proud passion for Europe?" he asked. "Where are the scars of wounds received in the battles for the C.E.C.A. [Coal-Steel Community], the C.E.D. [European Defense Community], and the European assemblies?" For "true believers" he vouchsafed respect; "to the others I now say: cut the comedy!"[15]

Assembly opponents quickly seized the rare opportunity openly handed them. After byzantine maneuvers which would have done credit to the Fourth Republic, a "manifesto" was drafted opposing De Gaulle's European policy. Made deliberately vague to bridge the gap between the strongly "European" MRP and the Independents, who showed signs of incipient Gaullism, the draft failed to mention either Great Britain or a national nuclear force. The manifesto form was also chosen for strategic reasons: the unpopularity of the Government could be demonstrated without running the risk of a censure motion, which fewer would support and which, if successful, would only lead to the dissolution of the Assembly. It took more negotiation before those who

[15] *Le Monde,* June 7, 1962.

signed the manifesto, 293 in number, could agree on how and when to present their dramatic defiance. Finally, the motion was read toward the end of the debate, and the "Europeans" noisily left the hall after listening to Foreign Minister Couve de Murville defend De Gaulle's policy.[16]

Pompidou was still not impressed. His "debating style" did not mellow. "It is the Government," he told the deputies, "that has taken the initiative in this debate. It has chosen the form in conformity with the Constitution and the rules [of the Assembly] . . . The Government will carry on with its task. The Assembly showed its confidence less than two months ago, and I am convinced it is going to do the same today."[17]

De Gaulle and Pompidou then opened a counter-attack. Into the bill for supplementary credits, primarily for social measures, the Government inserted a request for more funds to support its nuclear plant at Pierrelatte. The bill was made an issue of confidence; the Premier demanded a single vote on the entire measure; the President warned that if the executive did not get its way, the Assembly would be dissolved and new elections held, in which he would campaign actively.

Who were these "Europeans"; how much would they pay to win? De Gaulle and his supporters thought they knew the answers already — they were a hodgepodge of deputies whose ideas conflicted, and they would not be willing to pay much. The Gaullists were right. Although artistic draftsmen produced a censure motion supporting an "atomic industry," opposing an "exclusively national striking force," and advocating a "community solution," the Democratic Center, the Independents, and the MRP all divided on whether or not to vote against the Government. Ultimately only 206 did so.[18]

Viewed against this background, the "success" of the Assembly in finally censuring Pompidou in October takes on a more dubious aura. Was it, in fact, a victory at all for the opposition groups? De Gaulle had

[16] There was some attrition, however. Pflimlin, Maurice Schumann, and Reynaud were among the more than half-dozen signers who stayed behind.

[17] Le Monde, June 15, 1962.

[18] This compared with 207 who had opposed the nuclear striking force in the long battle taking place in October and November 1960. Le Monde, June 29, July 1–14, 18, 1962; L'Express, July 12, 1962.

proved himself a better strategist than Debré in opposing the latter's suggestion that elections be held in late April and early May. By July the President had forced his legislative enemies into a weak position; by October he was presented with the opportunity to link the elections to his referendum and deal the traditional parties a severe blow.

De Gaulle's view of parties ("factions") — straight out of the eighteenth century — was no secret. The last portion of the third volume of his memoirs is replete with complaints about "politicians." He reports his adieu to his ministers on January 19, 1946 in these words: "The exclusive regime of parties has reappeared. I disapprove of it. But aside from establishing by force a dictatorship, which I do not desire and which would certainly end in disaster, I have not the means of preventing this experiment. I must therefore withdraw."[19] That De Gaulle's own Rally of the French People became not one but two parties in the legislature of the Fourth Republic only increased his doubts as to both the durability and the desirability of parties. They were interruptions in the dialogue "between the citizens and the power."[20] If only, he said in 1960, the French could be more like the English. "Sure of yourselves, almost without seeming so, you operate in freedom a regime both solid and stable," he told the British Parliament. "So strong are tradition, loyalty, and the rules of the game in your political affairs that your government naturally possesses cohesion and continuity." In contrast, "every move [of the French Government] arouses the diverse teams of surliness, grouching, and complaint [*hargne, grogne, rogne*]. Hence the contrast between the stirring of the surface and the reasoned calm of the French depths."[21]

One must be clear on several points. French parties were weak and in many respects ineffective representatives of electoral opinion. Their persistent proclivity for internecine combat did make them poor vehicles for reaching any semblance of national consensus. But these qualities reflected the preferences of the French themselves. Manipulations

---

[19] *Salvation*, translated by Richard Howard, New York, Simon and Schuster, 1960, p. 325.

[20] Michelet, *op. cit.*, pp. 151–152.

[21] Speech of July 1961.

of the electoral system, adjustments in relations between executive and legislative branches, the appearance of the most ominous domestic and international crises produced neither cohesion among the parties nor, indeed, coherence in their individual definition of issues for resolution by French voters.

Furthermore, De Gaulle himself was not the least responsible for the sorry plight of the traditional parties. Despising them and their leaders as weak, he helped to make them more so. Challenging the Fourth Republic as impotent, he helped, through the massive and obdurate RPF, to ensure that it remained so. Seeking to destroy the regime, he encouraged those of his supporters who entered government coalitions to subvert it from within. As he surveyed the wreckage his actions had helped bring about, he could exclaim, "See what the factions have done!" When he rebuilt to his own design, he could argue that France's safety forbade any return to the old way of doing things. "There are some countries, especially our own, which are at every instant in danger of sudden death," he told the same press conference at which he excluded Britain from the Common Market and gave the back of his hand to Anglo-American proposals regarding Polaris submarines. Conditions, he added, "exclude the old system of unstable, uncertain, inconstant parties."

Battle with political formations was a rewarding duty for De Gaulle. In the elections of November 1962 he crushed the opposition. Unswerving loyalty to his every wish became ratified as the only sure road to the Assembly. The Assembly itself was purified, humbled, rendered even less important than its predecessor, which at least had dared to rise against the President's premier.

Apathy and indecision had characterized the electorate in the latest contest. On the first round the percentage of abstentions was larger than in any general legislative election since 1881 and almost as large as in the October 1946 constitutional referendum — 31.25 and 31.4 respectively. When the choice became clearer on the second round, abstention dropped, but, at 27.9 percent, it was still high for France. Not only its close association with De Gaulle, but this relatively apathetic mood of the voters aided the anti-party party, the Union for the

New Republic. In the first balloting the UNR won a significant victory, rising from 17.5 percent of the vote in 1958 to 31.9. The fate of the other groups showed that the UNR had won over the Center-Right, not the Center-Left, if the Catholic MRP (perhaps unfairly) is assigned to the first category. From Communists to Radicals losses were an insignificant .07 percent; from MRP to extreme Right, 14.36. The augury for the final selection proved accurate. Independents found themselves with 1.6 percent of the vote, the MRP with 5.3.

Overwhelmed in the balloting were members of the extreme Right. "If one wished for a condemnation of activism and even of integrationist [French Algerian union] theses by the electorate, it is found in this unanimity without the least extenuating circumstance, the least exception to the rule. It is only in those very rare cases where partisans of French Algeria, like M. Jean Valentin, author of the famous 'Salan amendment' to reduce the length of required military service, took on in their districts a face very different from that Paris knows that they succeeded in holding on more or less, with, in his instance, the un-looked-for support of the UNR. Only 9 of 80 deputies who voted for the 'Salan amendment' will return to the Palais Bourbon."[22] Along with sympathizers of the OAS, out went representatives of small shopkeepers, small business, individual farming interests. On the other hand, thanks to disciplined voting by the Communist clientele, deals were arranged for the second round among groups of the Left, which aided the Socialists and kept the Radicals alive. In 103 contests between a Communist and a member of the UNR, the latter won 90, but of 58 direct confrontations of Socialist and UNR candidates, the Gaullists came off better only 23 times. Of all the political leaders to sign the declaration opposing De Gaulle on the referendum, only Maurice Faure, erstwhile Radical, and Guy Mollet, Socialist leader, survived.[23]

22 Pierre Viannson-Ponté, Le Monde, November 27, 1962.
23 Gaullists attributed the relative strength of the Left not only to Communist discipline in voting for Socialist and Radical candidates, but to hidden support by the Secret Army. Before his own defeat Debré, in a debate with Mollet, linked the "cartel of 'noes'" with the OAS, and the UNR's own journal, La Nation, later accused Mollet himself of having made a secret pact with Bidault's CNR. Le Monde, October 26, 1962, January 15, 1963.

Thus, even though it resisted the designation, the UNR had become, by positive and negative developments, the new Right.[24] The UNR, plus its "leftist" affiliate, the Democratic Workers Union (UDT), and a scattering of other deputies supported by Malraux's Association for the Fifth Republic, comprised a majority in the 482-seat Assembly. It was by no means certain, however, that the executive of the Fifth Republic, meaning De Gaulle, would change his opinion of the National Assembly now that there was a "government majority," regarding it now as a constructive collaborator in formulating policy rather than an enemy to be bullied or avoided. Premier Pompidou appeared before the new session with an omnibus and vaguely phrased "program," to which only 268 deputies signified specific approval, a total six less than the supposed Gaullist strength. While the President's message spoke of "cooperation," other passages seemed to circumscribe again the legislative role. "Undoubtedly," De Gaulle declared, "opinions can differ as to the course we should take in order to achieve this [the country's development]. That is why the concept of a single party could not be justified and, furthermore, why deliberation remains essential in order to point the way to decisions. But since progress, in the sense that it is understood in the present era, is henceforth the supreme law of any society, that toward which we must proceed is well and truly determined for us, while the responsibilities, the means and the behavior of the public authority must, by necessity, be adapted to the great effort of renovation."[25]

After the demise of the Fourth Republic, the French executive had ruled substantially by decree under authority recurrently tendered it by the legislature. Thus was the transition to the Fifth Republic arranged; thus was De Gaulle's Algerian policy carried out. Special powers under Article 16 were also invoked in the aftermath of the Generals' Revolt in April 1961. Interspersed among legislative abdications and executive

[24] The UNR refused to sit on the right in the reconvened Assembly, choosing instead to spread itself across the semicircle. On the other hand, by rejecting political identification in the European assembly, UNR delegates isolated themselves in lonely splendor — on the Right.

[25] Translation of Service de Presse et d'Information, Ambassade de France, New York.

arrogations were ratifications by the people through referenda of De Gaulle's right to rule by himself. The referenda of January 8, 1961 and April 8, 1962 both asked the voters, in approving Algerian self-determination, to agree at the same time to government decrees related to that purpose.

On the occasions when the executive did come before the legislature, it increasingly tended to seek approval for *lois-programme* (law-programs)[26] on particular subjects, which, once passed, gave De Gaulle and his advisors power to "legislate" by ordinance. In December 1962 Pompidou indicated he would ask for such authority to cover the diverse intentions of the government in housing and education. More notorious, however, was the *loi-programme* concerning the French nuclear striking force. Submitted in October 1960, it was consistently rejected by the Assembly and Senate. It finally "passed," however, when the deputies could not muster an absolute majority to censure the government. From 80 to 90 percent of the votes in the legislature, it was estimated, were simple ratifications of previous decisions taken under *lois-programme*, whose life continued for several years. Little wonder that veritable debates on the budget disappeared, along with the Fourth Republic. In cases where the Assembly threatened to show signs of selective opposition, the government could and did demand that only a single vote be taken, as with the supplementary credits previously mentioned. Executive-legislative imbalance was so striking that it was likened to the situation in the twilight years of the Weimar Republic. Common inspiration was even found in the drafting of the German and French constitutions.[27]

As with all political systems, especially new ones, however, the Fifth Republic was not totally bereft of counter-weights to executive domination. Re-elected president of the National Assembly after the November 1962 elections, Jacques Chaban-Delmas apparently maintained concern for the stature of the legislature, in spite of his affiliation with the UNR.

[26] A *loi-programme* is a legislative delegation of authority to the executive to issue decrees on certain (frequently vaguely defined) subjects without seeking legislative approval at the time each decree is promulgated. A prominent example of such delegated power was Algeria.

[27] See letter by Henry Ehrmann to *Le Monde*, January 22, 1963.

"It is a fact," he told the Association of Parliamentary Journalists, "that the president of the National Assembly should at all times first take care to protect the opposition so that its rights are respected. He should equally 'restrain' the majority that threatens to bolt . . . Insofar as the majority is moderate in the exercise of its power and the minority is organized, a certain balance is approached which is certainly republican, democratic, parliamentary. As for me, I have decided to work toward that end."[28] Debré's reappearance in the Assembly might also increase the interest, if not the influence, of that body. His skill in debate and preference for the offensive would certainly make him a magnetic target for the opposition.

Conceivably the Senate could also be a moderating force. Among its members were a number of prominent political hold-overs from the Fourth Republic, elected thanks to the indirect system of voting. Relatively longer tenure added to the independence of the Senate; and, unlike the Assembly, it could not be dissolved. At times the senators displayed a certain obstreperous obstinacy. When the government restricted it to only one vote on amendments to proposed military appropriations, the Senate retaliated by reducing the length of compulsory service in the armed forces to one year and knocking out funds for the nuclear striking force. Senators knew that theirs was only a gesture; the government's majority in the Assembly and its constitutional right to resolve an impasse between legislative branches guaranteed its ultimate success.

Where the issue was not either/or, however, and the government consented to make conciliatory gestures, the Assembly and Senate combined could occasionally exert a modicum of influence. For example, each branch individually pressed for changes in De Gaulle's proposed permanent tribunal to try those charged with crimes against the state, and the conference committee representing deputies and senators induced the cabinet to modify its position on details.[29]

"Ladies and gentlemen of the Assembly, I do not doubt that the Na-

[28] *Le Monde*, February 2, 1963.
[29] The substance of the issue involving the permanent tribunal will be discussed in the next chapter.

tional Assembly itself will wish to take inspiration from this result of recent popular consultations," President de Gaulle stated at the conclusion of his message to the new session. It was rumored that he had still other "little" reforms to introduce into the political system, notably the creation of the office of Vice President and the right of the President to appear before both legislative bodies. While the spectacle of De Gaulle enunciating in person homilies such as the one just cited might well inspire even more fervent amens from his fervent followers, it could hardly redress the balance between legislative and executive, both separated and intermingled, Gaullist style. As with so much of contemporary French action, the future depended on one man's wish. It was not very probable that the self-styled "guide" would voluntarily complicate his task so soon after winning an unparalleled, double triumph over an opposition however ephemerally united.

The two quotations heading this chapter are not, then, incompatible. The first, written before the Autumn 1962 referendum and elections, was directed at the absence of autonomous sources of power within the political system and the lack of organized channels of communication between leadership and electorate. De Gaulle's definition of strength, on the other hand, was precisely the situation *L'Express* deplored. To him presidential power was what made the entire structure of the Fifth Republic durable. However much Americans might agree with *L'Express*, however much they might share its preference for such democratic refinements as viable political parties and legislatures that can legislate, they should not ignore the pressures as well as the predilections that lay behind De Gaulle's actions. Although concentration of authority in his person invited gun- and plastic-toting enemies to make him their target, firm and unified direction was demanded for the resolution of the crisis produced by De Gaulle's Algerian policy. Substantial alterations had to be made in the place occupied by the army in French society. Allegiance of the army to civilian leadership had to be attracted, with new and increasingly costly weapons, with new assignments, seeking to reconcile increased material power with diminished operational space. Finally, the army, once endowed with new missions, must be fitted into the pattern of Gaullist statecraft to fulfill the grand destiny France's guide had ordained for his country.

One might break the logic of the argument at any point, as, for instance, on the need for nuclear weapons or the type of bonds desirable for linking the Common Market countries. But it is precisely the connections among the pieces that mattered to De Gaulle, for his was indeed a *pattern of statecraft,* however ambivalent and hesitant some of his individual moves might seem. One could also argue that De Gaulle's heightened power might be at least partially effective over the short run, but increase the odds on eventual disaster. Though perhaps attractive, perhaps perspicacious, such an argument would be doubly irrelevant. De Gaulle has consistently pronounced "democracy" "authoritarianism." And time was not the lightest of his pressures. The army had to be remade quickly. The foundations of Gaullist Europe had to be laid before it was too late.

BACK TO THE

ARMY IN THE

NATION'S SERVICE

Military justice is to justice what military music is to music. —
Clemenceau

*The question is going to arise of whether they will ultimately
give machine guns to young men of the Right and pickaxes to
young men of the Left.* — A French officer

A TERRIBLE logic lay behind the army's challenge to De Gaulle over
Algeria. Were the war to end, much more than a shift of troops and an
assignment of new responsibilities would take place. France could
hardly avoid a re-examination of the relationship between the army and
the society it was dedicated to protect. If the army, perverting notions
about psychological warfare, failed to define its role, the political system would not be able to evade the complex task. What the desperate,
protracted threat by military and civilian elements to the Fifth Republic did was add a new dimension to the problem. Before positive reconstruction could be undertaken, there must be chastisement of those
who defied civil authority. The purpose of punishment went beyond

retribution and defense against repetition of the offending acts. It would enable the President to demonstrate that he could rule the army as well as the other organs of his state. Similar to that waged in Algeria was the struggle between De Gaulle and his enemies to capture the allegiance of the French populace.

Punishment was meted out both collectively and individually. Within the military structure itself units were broken up, re-assigned, dissolved. In 1960 conditions for ending the Barricades Revolt included an opportunity offered followers of Lagaillarde to form a commando outfit attached to the first foreign regiment of paratroopers. Zeal to demonstrate in Algiers for a French Algeria, however, outran enthusiasm for prospective hand-to-hand engagement with the Moslem nationalists in a struggle whose ends were becoming more and more dubious. Only two hundred insurgents even reached the camp at Zeralda. Of these barely more than half signed up for a month. When the group was dissolved at the end of that time, it had participated in no combat or any other kind of mission.[1]

Notwithstanding the Barricades, there was a close connection between insurgency and both paratroopers and Legionnaires. Following the failure of the Generals' Revolt, the two Legion units which had rallied to General Challe were split up and their officers re-assigned. (Marching to oblivion, the first foreign regiment of paratroopers was showered with flowers by Algerian Europeans as it sang, "I regret nothing.") Thus disappeared about one-tenth of the total Legion strength of 20,000. With the end of the Algerian war in sight, the number had been further reduced by temporarily shutting down recruiting stations and refusing all enlistments. Those already in the Legion left its last colonial stronghold by devious routes. Some went south to fight for Katanga and Moise Tshombe. Plans were made to assign others to scraps of French territory around the world, where, it was thought, Legionnaires could be a sort of roving technical aid mission. What a comedown from the brave days of Beau Geste! It was not surprising that large-scale assignments of this nature were cancelled, sometimes in the name of "economy," after colonial leaders had acquainted Paris

[1] Brombergers et al., op. cit., pp. 439–444.

with their displeasure at the prospect. A warmer welcome was out in Corsica, where some 1,500 Legionnaires were assigned in June 1962. About half of that total — the first foreign regiment — were fortunate enough to use Corsica only as a stopping point en route to regroupment in Aubagne, belonging to the Ninth Military District. Some of those remaining behind — over sixty by official count — demonstrated their dissatisfaction at the new circumstances in which the Legion found itself by attempting to desert.

"A period of adjustment is necessary," said the Legion's inspector, "but young men who now enlist in the Legion and take their training in Corsica will do so in a different spirit." Actions by its officers against De Gaulle had had a rational base. Whether the title "Foreign Legion" were maintained or not, its character would be profoundly altered by a deliberate and necessary fragmentation, making of the Legion a subordinate element in other formations with a European base and missions as new as some of their equipment.[2]

At the close of the Algerian war France had almost 40,000 parachutists, of whom about 8,000 were grouped in the Foreign Legion. Because para units regarded themselves as the elite of the elite, whether their enlisted men were volunteers or draftees, they represented in extreme form the maladjustments between the nation and "its" army. Nevertheless, all paratroop units outside the Legion could not simply be dissolved, as was the Fourteenth Chasseur Regiment after the Generals' Revolt. New missions or old missions, they would remain an important element in the country's military strength. They could, however, be disciplined. As part of an effort to make their camouflage uniforms less conspicuous, new dress and new headgear, but not new training methods, awaited paratroopers returning from Algeria. In Biarritz they made a ceremony of burning the now-forbidden red berets in the central square before marching to re-assignment. Temporarily some units were sent to Metz, whose military governor was none other than the notorious paratroop general and one-time Algiers commander Jacques Massu.

---

[2] See *New York Post*, November 6, 1961, June 6, 1962; Paul Hoffmann, "Taps for the Foreign Legion?" *New York Times Magazine,* January 21, 1962; *Le Monde,* June 22, August 21, October 11, 28–29, 1962.

Despite initial assignments, paratroopers would not serve the Metropole as solely a frontier force. They would also be regrouped in formations designed for overseas service in an emergency, or for territorial defense against aggression.[3]

Although they did not present the same problem in discipline after the rebellion, adjustment to life in metropolitan France would certainly be difficult for some 17,000 former *harkis* who, with their families, had abandoned Algeria. They comprised only about one-tenth of the total who had fought with the army against the Moslem nationalists. Few would dare return to their former homes, but their future as French citizens was also bleak. In spite of special schools established for the purpose, there were not enough Moslem officers to make possible regroupment in large, autonomous formations. In any event, the purpose for which they had joined the army had disappeared. New military assignments must now appeal in competition with available jobs in the civilian economy. The attractions of civilian employment were certainly reduced by the several hundred thousand Moslems already concentrated in unskilled industries, most of whom had been supporters of the FLN. The *harkis* might declare, "We are in France. The FLN is thus a foreign party," and De Gaulle's Minister for Algerian Affairs echo the sentiment that in the Metropole the *harkis* were "at home." But "home" during the unprecedentedly severe winter of 1962–1963 in all too many cases meant tents or shacks, while the work of individual screening and classification of skills went on and on. If many *harkis* wound up once more in the French army, it would quite clearly be the result of necessity on one side, compassion on the other.[4]

Punishment of individual civilian and military plotters was a more delicate question, since it involved issues of both judicial integrity and

---

[3] *Le Monde*, October 13, 20, December 1, 2–3, 12, 1962.

[4] *Figaro*, June 26, 1959, February 24, 1962; *L'Express*, August 2, 1962; *Le Monde*, October 4, 7–8, November 17, 25–26, December 6, 9–10, 30–31, 1962. Wherever some semblance of former military unity was preserved, identification and training for new employment could be carried on more quickly and more successfully. The same was true in the rare instances where French officers who had been assigned to the SAS (Specialized Administrative Services) remained in close contact with the Moslems and took responsibility for them, as the SAS had attempted to do in Algeria.

individual rights. It was difficult to find any one tribunal appropriate to try the wide variety of cases involving crimes against the state growing out of the Algerian war. As a result, at one time or another *ad hoc* courts, juries, military courts, and metamorphosing special tribunals were all handed the job. One of the difficulties with reliance on *ad hoc* courts was the optimistic assumption that the threat was limited in time, place, and personnel involved. Moreover, the court established to try cases growing out of the Barricades Revolt was itself a failure, since it neither prevented other revolts nor rallied public opinion behind the President. Its proceedings, "one of the longest in judicial history," did not begin until November 1960, almost a year after the uprising, and then dragged on until March. By that time the plans for the Generals' Revolt were well advanced; and the public had become so tired of the daily battle of defense and prosecution that it had ceased to care about the great issue of the legitimacy of the Fifth Republic. The nature of the verdicts, when finally rendered, reflected the indifference. Thirteen of the defendants were acquitted, while only six were condemned. The latter verdicts were less severe than they appeared superficially, because those convicted, either released from prison or never caught in the first place, had to a man escaped to join the underground Secret Army. "All these acquittals must be loudly applauded," wrote the ultraconservative *L'Aurore*, "but it was painful enough, even nauseating, to see men tried because they loved too much and tried to defend their country, France." To others, however, "the leniency of the judges was a little surprising."[5]

Juries were apt to be equally unsatisfactory judicial instruments. In September 1962 a survey of the French Institute of Public Opinion reported that only 7 percent of its respondents thought verdicts against OAS members were too harsh, while 53 percent thought them too lenient, and a substantial 40 percent vouchsafed no opinion.[6] The poll takes on added interest since it followed on the heels of extremely light sentences handed down by a jury at Troyes to those found guilty of attacking the head of state himself. The large degree of tolerance con-

5 *L'Année Politique, 1961*, pp. 35–36.
6 Reported by *L'Express*, September 27, 1962.

spicuous among the jurors was motivated in part by Salan's success in escaping the death penalty. "Why should one condemn him [one of the plotters] when Salan was able to save his own neck?" asked one juror. "There are reasons why the big shots save their necks and the workers pay," opined another. Sympathy for or fear of the OAS was another reason for moderation. "The OAS is those who wanted to keep Algeria French. O.K., it's like the Resistance, isn't it?" said the wife of the second juror quoted. "It was fatal that they [Salan's judges] were lenient," said the widow of a participant in the Resistance. "I decided on the sentence before the lawyers' pleas. I didn't come there to condemn anyone to death, no sir," she added. Some feared what a secret, ubiquitous organization might do to those who favored heavy penalties for plotters. "They [the OAS] are bastards . . . the OAS is anyone," declared a juror. Finally there was a tendency for the jurors to take a slap at the President. "The real leader was De Gaulle. Wasn't he Salan's chief? Wasn't he the one who told him 'Algeria will be French?' . . . While this [trial] was going on, De Gaulle was throwing himself into the arms of the Germans."[7] Whatever the composite of motives, many on the jury apparently shared the emotional reaction of one member. "These condemnations were scandalous. I wept . . . To my way of thinking two years would have been enough."[8]

As well it might, the leniency of the juries reportedly convinced De Gaulle that regular, civilian, legal processes should be avoided wherever possible.[9] Courts within the military hierarchy, on the other hand, were deemed unsuitable as well as inadequate to try all the civilian and military conspirators rounded up by the police. By a process of elimination, therefore, and seeking to profit by the experience of the tribunal set up for the Barricades revolters, the Fifth Republic, like its predecessors, came to rely on a special court with specially selected judges, trying special cases involving, in the opinion of the government, crimes against the state.

---

[7] The reference is to the President's "triumph" in West Germany, of which more further on.

[8] The inquiry was made by reporters for *L'Express*, September 13, 1962.

[9] *L'Express*, September 20, 1962.

By their very jurisdiction successive courts became a political weapon of the "power." As such, their activities, precedents, and effects on the French judicial system represent one standard by which to assess the Fifth Republic. Any examination of De Gaulle's response to military-civilian plots would be incomplete without consideration of the entanglement therein of the judiciary. As excerpts quoted in earlier chapters have shown, the various proceedings concerned themselves hardly at all with the question of guilt or innocence in regard to omnibus charges. Since, under French procedures, the evidence had been taken and assessed in private session, public hearings not infrequently took on the aspect of a debate. Against judges and prosecutors, somewhat restrained by their responsibilities, stormed articulate military and civilian revolutionaries and their defendants, as eloquent as they were leather-lunged. To the revelation of crimes ranging from insurrection to murder they countered with pleas seeking to advance that same cause on behalf of which insurrection and murder had occurred.

Jacques Isorni's words concerning behavior before the Court of Assizes applies equally well to tactics in all legal contests where French Algeria was the matter really at stake: "The bar of the defense had become the foremost rostrum in France, that from which one's voice carried furthest . . . It was incomparably superior to that of a debased Parliament, where, if some made themselves understood, no one listened."[10] The decline of legal standards resulting from the army's dealings in Algeria with the FLN was evident in the courtroom. Said a lawyer who had once defended Moslem nationalists: "We used all procedural resources, all judicial tricks to slow up as much as possible action of justice against our clients. We cannot decently reproach lawyers retained by activists for using the same methods and seeking the same results."[11]

Since it existed outside the framework of both the judiciary and the military, the jurisdiction of the special tribunals was questioned at each proceeding. The time consumed by imputations of incompetence varied

[10] *Op. cit.*, p. 95.
[11] Quoted by Paul-Marie de la Gorce, "Y a-t-il une justice française?" *France Observateur*, October 25, 1962.

with the extent of public attention focussed on the trial in question, the ingenuity of the defense attorneys, and the patience and experience of the judges. Tixier-Vignancour waged a protracted, if ultimately futile, battle against the tribunal seeking to try Salan. Attacks on individual judges supplemented general claims of lack of jurisdiction. The comparatively superior skill of the same attorney in defending Bastien-Thiry and his cohorts for the attack on De Gaulle's life at Petit-Clamart led to suggestions that the judges and prosecution either learn their jobs or give up.[12]

Supporters of military and civilian conspirators opened a virulent campaign against General de Larminat as soon as he was named by De Gaulle to head the court replacing the one which had aroused the President's wrath for failing to order Salan's execution. De Larminat, not in the best of health for some time, committed suicide, leaving a letter telling De Gaulle he was unable, physically or mentally, to discharge the duty assigned him.[13] Without prior notice, let alone any attempt to verify its contents, Jacques Isorni read to the court trying Bastien-Thiry a letter impugning the fitness of one of the judges to sit on the case. The attorney was immediately silenced and disbarred for three years, the penalty, as will be pointed out below, being fully as questionable as Isorni's already notorious concept of legal ethics.[14]

Understandably, judges revealed a uniform distaste for service on courts charged with dispensing "political justice." "What I want above all is what all my colleagues also want: Not to be involved in it," one judge was quoted as saying. "In such circumstances our freedom seems to us greatly reduced, even if it is not so objectively . . . The tactic of the defense is to limit as much as possible the attention paid to the facts and to enlarge interminably on reasons, motives, passionate or subjective considerations, political maneuvers, ideological controversies . . . The risks inherent in publicity surrounding affairs of this nature limit our alternatives for action."[15]

---

[12] *Le Monde,* February 12, 1963.
[13] *Le Monde,* July 3, 1962.
[14] *Le Monde,* February 8, 1963.
[15] Quoted by De la Gorce, *op. cit.*

The effort of the Fifth Republic to attract the loyalty of metropolitan Frenchmen while punishing its enemies had two deleterious effects. If there was any logical pattern in the sentences meted out, it escaped detection, unless the cynical remark of the Troyes juror that the big shots escaped the guillotine and the small fry paid provides a clue. Regular officers had star character witnesses, skilled defense lawyers, exhaustive searches for extenuating circumstances; and they tended to receive comparatively lighter sentences than humble civilians participating in OAS activities. While some inconsistency was inevitable in view of the variety of courts established, even the judges presiding over the two successive special tribunals established after the Generals' Revolt appeared unable to find any acceptable criteria to determine appropriate punishment for differing degrees of culpability. General Jouhaud was condemned to death; his superior, General Salan, was not. Degueldre was shot; the same sentence on Jouhaud was not carried out. Godot and Robin, assistants to Degueldre, got twenty years; Lieutenant Bernard ten for stealing arms. André Canal, better known throughout France as the "Monocle," was condemned to death as an OAS leader; but Jean-Marie Vincent, who actually carried out many attacks, including one that grievously maimed a little girl, got away with life imprisonment. With Salan and Jouhaud imprisoned, Bastien-Thiry, mastermind of the Petit-Clamart attack on De Gaulle, which killed no one, was shot; the life of his colleague in conspiracy, Bougrenet de la Tocnaye, was spared.

Incoherence of another type attended the two special high tribunals themselves. Established April 27, 1961 to try those involved in the Generals' Revolt, the first court lasted barely a year after its first meeting. It incurred the President's wrath by daring to find the extenuating circumstances to justify sparing the life of Salan and was summarily suppressed on May 26, 1962. Its successor lasted less than half a year. Canal's lawyers took their case against the second court to France's highest administrative body, the Conseil d'Etat. Over government protests the Conseil decided that it did indeed have jurisdiction, and, after upholding De Gaulle's right to establish a special court, it proceeded to throw out this particular one on the grounds that the exceptional procedures followed ran counter to accepted legal practice.

This most unusual display of independence by the normally docile Conseil d'Etat both startled and annoyed the government. A communiqué accused the judges of "at least abnormal" behavior in substituting their own opinion of what constituted threats to the nation for that of the constitutional authorities. "Such decisions," the communiqué concluded, "will of necessity constitute an encouragement to subversion and crime." Promptly De Gaulle took his revenge. When the new National Assembly convened after elections, the government submitted a bill to establish a permanent court to try crimes against the state. In the bill was a provision validating *ex post facto* all ordinances taken under the special powers granted the government by the referendum of April 13, 1962 (which also approved the Evian agreements with the Algerian nationalists). By virtue of this stipulation the old special court, temporarily interred by the Conseil d'Etat, was resurrected. As a final slap at the Conseil, the old court, not the new permanent one, was charged with trying the would-be assassins of President de Gaulle.[16]

"Is there justice in France?" asked writer-journalist Paul-Marie de la Gorce.[17] Like all good questions, it could not be answered simply. Rather did it focus attention on the practical definitions being given "justice" by the Fifth Republic. Under the statute of the new court a suspect could be held by the police for two weeks instead of the old-fashioned one day. While the legislature shortened the "normal" detention time to ten days and provided for the suspect's periodic appearance, an executive decision that a state of emergency existed would still validate the longer period. Increased length of detention naturally entailed a comparable increase in the investigatory power of the police. Although Jean Foyer, Garde des Sceaux in Pompidou's government, claimed — perhaps whimsically — that the police would not be using the extra time of confinement to intimidate suspects into confession, but rather to preserve the secrecy of police operations, charges of brutality were not unknown in France. Concern for the welfare and full legal rights of Moslem nationalists had not always been evident during the

[16] *Le Monde*, May 29, June 1, October 21–22, 23, 28–29, 1962, January 6–7, 1963.
[17] *Op. cit.*

Algerian war, and defending attorneys charged that their Secret Army clients were subjected to similar excesses of zeal. Finally, the jurisdiction of the new courts was widened by the government to include minors from 16 to 18. The legislature objected to this innovation, but succeeded in remanding to another court only those rare cases where minors alone were involved.

The provisions concerning appointment of judges were as questionable as those concerning protection of defendants. Included on the court were to be two officers, in addition to civilian magistrates. All were to be named by the government, and their assignment was to last two years. (The government had wished the term to be one year.) Thus, the army was to have a permanent role in trying cases believed by political authority to involve a threat to the state. In the past, one complaint against both military and mixed civil-military tribunals assigned to such cases had been that their activity had encouraged further politicalization of the army. Now the military was to be regularly involved in the "legal" judgment of political acts.[18]

The conviction of suspects had brought other problems, and these also were now to be permanent. Were political crimes worse, the same, or less important than other crimes? On the one hand, they were regarded as worse, because they threatened the stability, even the existence, of national political institutions. On the other hand, there was cogency in the repeated assertions of defense lawyers that politics had always been politics and today's subversive was tomorrow's hero. The uneasy, unsatisfactory solution to which the government was impelled involved the establishment of two types of imprisonment. Political malefactors, if they were sufficiently notable and if their actions had not been construed to involve infractions of the criminal code, received special treatment in such matters as food, visitors, and radios. They were, as reporter J.-M. Théolleyre put it, the "aristocracy of delinquency," but they still complained. Those who did not benefit from the more lenient classification were, of course, even more aggrieved. Since most acts against the state could easily be tied to common crimes — con-

---

[18] *Le Monde*, January 13–14, 1963 contains the provisions adopted for the new court.

cealed or stolen weapons, stolen automobiles, deliberate assault, etc. — they felt their type of detention to be arbitrary and agitated for a rise in status.

Over both groups hung the explosive issue of the concentration camp. More "civilized" perhaps than a regular prison, the camps nevertheless called unpleasantly to mind detentions by the Nazis during World War II. It was estimated that by 1962, 36,000 Moslems had been placed under "protective custody." As they were released, hundreds of French plotters began to take their place. Since the trials of many had been summary and the courts exceptional, the concept of political justice appeared to be linked to methods of authoritarian control over society itself. Concentration camps, it seemed, were easier to establish than to abolish, grounds for assignment easier to broaden than restrict. The ever-present possibility of selective amnesty introduced the real prospect of yet more discrimination. Would the Nazi experience be duplicated here also: some of the major (military) figures being released, while aides and assistants served out their terms? Would the pliable definition of threats to the state add a new type of clientele to the camps, as, for example, Communists, "Leftists," "political extremists" in a repetition of the terror-filled days of 1939 and 1940? A state considering itself continually in danger, armed with exceptional powers made permanent, would certainly have little difficulty in finding enemies.[19]

Details concerning rights of suspects, appointment of judges, and treatment of those found guilty lead to even more fundamental questions concerning the relationship of political to judicial authority. What were "political crimes," anyway? Critics protested the fact that De Gaulle's special tribunals judged acts which were not recognized as crimes when they were committed. In itself the establishment of particular courts for particular purposes made them less impersonal dispensers of justice than fashioned instruments to punish identifiable individuals. Against the verdicts there was, in the nature of things, no appeal, as the Cour de Cassation (the highest judicial court of appeal) had recognized in disclaiming jurisdiction. Although Roger Dusseaulx,

19 *Le Monde*, August 22, 23, September 28, October 3, 1962.

head of the UNR-UDT (Union Démocratique du Travail) group in the National Assembly, was proud that "for the first time in our judicial history, crimes against the security of the State will no longer be judged by an *ad hoc* jurisdiction, but by a jurisdiction whose bases will have been fixed in advance by law," his welcome to the result of rare executive-legislative collaboration was uncalled for. The list of infractions was long. What determined that those infractions were political was a judgment that they were part of an attempt to overthrow the state. Even if one grants that blocking roads (included in the government's list) in the final version of the act had to entail the presence of firearms, the significant fact remained that it was the political authority itself which was to decide whether it had been threatened. It could then invoke the jurisdiction of a court whose judges it had appointed, albeit for the handsome, independence-encouraging tenure of two years.

Prosecution for attempts to undermine the stability of the state narrowed to the vanishing point the delicate distinction between justice and vengeance. Quite clearly the tribunals that heard cases involving plots against the Fifth Republic were not supposed to find the defendants innocent. Guilty, guilty, all were guilty. Nor were tribunals to excuse, to pardon, to be lenient, to be merciful. De Gaulle reacted strongly to the Troyes jury's decision that those seeking to kill him deserved only twenty years in prison. His dissolution of the court which failed to order the death sentence for Salan was even more indicative of his capacity for swift retribution. From the very beginning, with the arrest of the suspect, provisions for the permanent court showed that evaluation of degree of guilt would be less important than protection of the state by severe chastisement of its imputed enemies. Merely making the court permanent would not in all probability increase its concern to safeguard all the rights of the defendants, including those surrounding the myriad circumstances of attenuation. "Justice of the king is a matter for his judges, but his vengeance belongs to his officers."[20]

Senator François Mitterand, as persistent a critic of De Gaulle as he

[20] So said an earlier Argoud, no relation to the leader of the OAS bearing the same name. Quoted by Paul-Marie de la Gorce in *France Observateur*, November 1, 1962.

was of the military-civilian insurrectionists, advanced this idea further in his exhaustive critique of the proposal for a new and permanent court. There were, he said, two French concepts of justice, one linked to the monarch, the other to the people. Because the former had been embodied in special tribunals established by kings and emperors, and subsequently by Vichy, criticism of the basic concept remained valid even if the court were made permanent by regular statute. The essence of justice derived from the people, Mitterand found in historic efforts to enlarge the role and the independence of the judiciary. That the authors of the constitution of the Fifth Republic had explicitly refused to include provision for dealing with subversion, Mitterand attributed to the preference of the "power" for monarchical procedures: in other words, for political control over the judiciary.

"Hasn't the power in France, under the Fifth Republic, got all it wished for?" the Senator asked. "He has his Constitution, or rather his personal method of interpreting the Constitution. He has his Government. He has his majority. He has his referendum. He has his television.[21] He has his *force de frappe*. He would wish to have his Senate. He has his Europe. Perhaps now, and very simply, he wants to have his own justice? After the executive power, the legislative power; after the legislative power, the judicial power ... 'A society,' says the Declaration of the Rights of Man, 'in which the separation of powers is not determined, does not have constitutional government.' You will permit me to add: such a country, such a society no longer has a Republic either."[22]

One must concede the possibility that some salutary effects might eventually emerge from the entanglement of the judicial and administrative systems resulting from De Gaulle's efforts to solidify the dispensation of political justice. The French judiciary was in its own way as closed a corporation as the army. "Things go on as if there were a

[21] The reference is to recurrent efforts to restrict news and documentary reports carried on the state-owned network.

[22] Text of speech in *L'Express*, January 10, 1963. See also articles by Maurice Garçon, *Le Monde*, June 3–4, 1962; Paul Thibaud, "Les atteintes à la sûreté des Français," *Esprit*, March 1961, pp. 353–381; Casamayor, "La justice vivante," *Esprit*, October 1962, pp. 399–430.

sort of domain reserved for initiates who pass the keys around among themselves and from which others stay aloof, resigned to see in justice only a world apart, a little mysterious and very disturbing, with which it is better to have no contact and, if the case should arise, be reconciled to its unpredictable decisions."[23]

Postwar attempts to ventilate judicial ranks achieved even less success than comparable ones directed toward the military hierarchy. The magistrature remained the preserve of the bourgeoisie, with heaviest representations from the same French districts that produced more than their share of civil servants. Armed with the full powers granted De Gaulle, Michel Debré, then Garde des Sceaux, instituted in 1959 a special school for judicial training, as he had done after the Liberation for civil service. Unlike the Ecole Nationale d'Administration, however, the National Center for Judicial Studies did not prove popular. Qualified candidates were fewer than those accepted for other magistrate courses. Moreover, the number fell by almost fifty percent between 1959 and 1961. Those enrolled were actually fewer in number than the positions to be filled. Higher posts in the judicial system were, in fact, not being filled from any source. "Is this the end of bourgeois magistrature?" asked De la Gorce.[24]

The same question might have been asked of the Conseil d'Etat. Its surprising action in destroying one of De Gaulle's courts had a pervading political aroma that led some to examine that august body as a collection of individuals as well as an institution. Its ancester was said to have been established by Philip the Good, and its contemporary structure, like that of the administration it was designed to oversee, dated from the Napoleonic era. The Conseil was comprised of less than two hundred members ranked by seniority and, along with the Finance Inspectorate, was able year after year to call on the most able graduates of the National School of Administration. By all odds the most important of its five sections was the Contentieux, which heard three or four thousand cases a year. Regular cases were decided by subcommittees, important ones by the full section, and exceptional cases by

[23] De la Gorce, *France Observateur*, November 1, 1962.
[24] *Ibid.*

the plenary Assembly of the Conseil d'Etat. Almost all twenty-five members of the Contentieux had attained the rank of Counsellors of State, that is, they were at least sixty years of age.

In the review of Canal's appeal, one of the sub-sections of the Contentieux had decided on rejection, but this particular matter was then submitted to the plenary Assembly. While the decisions of the Assembly normally were patterned on the advice of the lower group, in Canal's case it went against the report presented to it, and in all probability against the opinion of its president, M. Parodi, as well. The members instead seized an opportunity most fortuitously presented. Ultra-conservative by individual predilection, by experience, by function, by age, the members of the Conseil chose to line up with liberal as well as Right-wing critics of De Gaulle. They had survived the *Front Populaire*, Vichy, and the Liberation, and now they struck a strong blow against the man they could regard as the greatest political troublemaker of their (long) lifetimes. Thereby the Conseil d'Etat, which had beaten back over the years many threats to its autonomy, strengthened in the process its own position of administrative pre-eminence and, in addition, the individual prestige of its members. Like the army, it would continue to stress the permanent State against the ephemeral Government, the permanent Nation against mere mortal components.[25]

In creating a permanent court composed of military and civilian representatives the leaders of the Fifth Republic demonstrated their desire to use the army as an instrument of internal social control as well as for defense against external enemies. The justification, looking beyond the clandestine outrages of the OAS-CNR, was that subversion was a permanent aspect of international politics. In recognition of that fact the army had been given the general mission of cooperating with other groups in domestic defense.[26] The long-range price of intermingling police, political, juridical, and military functions in a unified state such as France can only be surmised. Whether De Gaulle perceived that

[25] *Le Conseil d'Etat, Livre jubilaire: 4 nivose, an VIII — 24 décembre, 1949*, Sirey, 1952; *Le Monde*, October 21–22, 1962; De la Gorce, "Y a-t-il une justice française?"
[26] For details of this mission, see the next chapter.

there was, in fact, any "price" to be paid, whether he had before him any practical alternatives, given the threat of military and civilian elements to his regime — the definitive answers to such questions must await future historians.

Military leaders had sought to use the army as an instrument to purify French society and to change the political system accepted by French voters. Punishment of plotters helped maintain the authority of President de Gaulle, but it only prepared the approaches to the complicated problem of the role which a chastened army should fulfill. Could the army with equal effectiveness discharge foreign assignments and occupy a central position in the socialization of French youth? Unlike its policy on "political crimes," the Fifth Republic seemed to grope toward a definition of the new military establishment without much awareness of the choices to be made and the implication of those choices.

An ordinance of January 7, 1959 had defined national service in far broader terms than military duty. "Obligation for national service exists for male citizens from 18 to 60, if they have the necessary physical capacity," read Article 25. Article 26 continued: "National service includes, on the one hand, military service to meet the needs of the armed forces; on the other hand, defense service to satisfy non-military personnel needs." Most affected by the ordinance would naturally be the ground forces. The navy and air force, at least in times of peace, were able to rely primarily on volunteers. Moreover, they did not have as large a part to play in domestic defense as did the army, although cooperation between individual air and ground units would certainly be necessary.

The Algerian war postponed implementation of the ordinance; at the same time, in this area as in others, it magnified the problems of eventual adjustment. Until 1962 French youth was needed to fight Moslem nationalists. The French army grew to over a million men, making the ground forces, as the largest "consumer" by far, a socializing instrument of a particular sort. With the approaching end of the conflict, however, De Gaulle and his advisors could no longer avoid decisions defining the configuration of an army finally, if reluctantly, at peace, an army to be based primarily in the Metropole. There was a deceptively large area of agreement on steps needed to re-unite France and its army. First, the size of the armed forces would be reduced, with the cuts coming in the units serving the French Community and in the ground forces. In January 1963 the ground forces comprised 721,000, the air force 140,000, the navy 78,500, and combined groups 69,300, a total of about 1,009,000. The eventual goal was stated to be 700,000, a figure to be reached some time during the second five-year military plan for 1965–1970. Since the projected total for the ground forces was estimated at about 400,000, the percentage of total military manpower assigned to that service was to fall from 70 to 57.[27]

A second point generally accepted was that the length of compulsory service should be reduced. When the army was occupied in Algeria, French military service was for twenty-seven months, the longest of all the NATO countries. At that time Great Britain was announcing plans to end conscription altogether. In the latter stages of the Algerian war the government released some military classes early, but it was not until January 1963 that Minister of the Armed Forces Messmer confirmed intentions to lower the term of military service to eighteen months beginning in March. Long-range plans were rumored to call for a further reduction to seventeen or sixteen months,[28] but there was no indication that France would follow Britain's lead and end conscription.

Decisions to continue to require military service were founded on two related, deeply entrenched myths of a partially militarized society: Universal military service, of equal duration and equally applicable for all, was good for Frenchmen and good for national security; and military service was a central feature in the education of Frenchmen for a useful life. Myths born of the origin and ambition of successive generations of French leaders, they had a rich patina of age, which covered dislocations consequent upon attempts to reconcile objective military facts with national values related to successive styles of political and social organization. The demand of the postwar French army that it be

27 *Le Monde*, January 5, 1963, September 22, 1962.
28 *Le Monde*, October 30, 1962, January 25, 1963.

assigned an intimate relationship with French youth, for both military and ideological reasons, caused the intertwined notions to be accepted as effective bases for the modernized, nuclearized, Europeanized army as they had earlier been for forces assembled and thrown into colonial combat.

Thus did the individual sections comprising the area of agreement on the nature of the army provoke dispute. Although the conflicts were apparently over details, in reality they arose from inability and unwillingness to support indicated priorities with consistent policy decisions. On one level universal military service clashed with the objective of military efficiency. For an antiquated or colonial force infusion of manpower was a relatively inexpensive way to fight. France with its 23 military effectives per 1,000 population, as compared to Belgium's 13, Britain's 12, the Netherland's 11, Italy's 8, and West Germany's 5,[29] could "afford" the Algerian war, because it chose not to afford alternatives. When De Gaulle opted for a modern force, France's swollen army was thereby revealed to have, relatively, very low fire-power. When steps were taken to increase fire-power, non-nuclear as well as nuclear, the question then arose whether France could "afford" even the reduced force of 700,000, that is, whether the Fifth Republic really wished to attain its announced goal of a strong, national, multi-purpose army. The easy route between conflicting pressures would be to mollify partisans of substantial military manpower and up-to-date matériel by moderate contributions to both. But the military establishment produced by such a compromise would then, of course, be only theoretically organized for missions assigned to it by political leadership.

Demographic statistics, of which France was so justly proud, interfered with any simple solution. From the mid-1960's on, increases in the birth rate after World War II would every year make eligible for military service more and more young men, just as attempts were being made to reduce the size of the armed forces. By 1976 there would be about one million Frenchmen aged 20, of whom some 900,000 would meet existing physical requirements. Such a yearly call to the colors would create an army of 1,350,000, or close to twice the projected

[29] Gromier, "Une conception archaïque," p. 23.

stabilized size.[30] More exacting standards of selection could be applied
to reduce the number somewhat, but other possible solutions ran head
on into the myths previously mentioned.

Why not make the three services entirely professional by relying
solely on volunteers? Such a change would affect primarily the ground
forces, which would then resemble an elite corps whose potential fighting effectiveness would compensate for any decrease in numbers.
"Equality of service," said General Boussarie, in a round-table discussion, "is a fundamental idea in our country, and it doesn't seem that we
can discard it." However, the General continued, under modern conditions adequate training alone should properly take almost the entire
period contemplated for compulsory military service. Therefore, "if we
could have a career army, we would applaud with both hands."[31] General Valluy expressed the same sentiment. Could not the active, combat
portion of the army be composed of about a quarter of a million volunteers? "Do we want to take in everyone?" Combat readiness, he claimed,
required two enlistments of twenty-four months apiece.[32] What
counted, after all, was manpower that was not only available but
trained and equipped. Those who were planning other activities, said
General Boussarie, were thinking of the "army of papa."[33] "As for me,
I just can't see a modern, motorized regiment, perfectly outfitted, going
to gather in the harvest, after throwing away all its matériel."[34]

The General's imagery was not farfetched; proponents of equality and
universality of service envisaged just such an army. There were long-
standing, vested interests to protect. Without large groups of draftees to
order about, what would become of the horde of junior officers? How
many fewer non-coms would a purely professional army need? Even if
there were a hypothetical place for both types in a new structure, they
would need somehow to acquire different, and quite probably technical,

[30] Colonel E. J. Baude in *Revue de Défense Nationale*, August–September 1962,
pp. 1422–1424; Dullin, *op. cit.*, p. 8.
[31] *Figaro*, June 22, 1962.
[32] "Le nouveau duo, Armée-Nation," pp. 493–494.
[33] A direct allusion to De Gaulle's derision of colonialists as desiring to perpetuate an "Algeria of papa."
[34] *Figaro*, June 22, 1962.

skills. Even if adequate retraining programs were instituted, junior officers and non-coms might still find themselves outstripped by later recruits who had received instructions in the intricacies of modern matériel at the very beginning of their careers. On the other hand, if ordinary foot soldiers coming, presumably, by conscription could be kept as a substantial percentage of the ground forces, presto! superfluity changed to deficiency. Armed Forces Minister Messmer gave out the welcome — and astounding — news: the projected army of 1970 would lack some 30,000 non-coms alone.[35]

Military mythology, however, was probably more important in producing decisions by default than were existing personal interests. Both army and youth, it declared, benefited from enforced exposure to one another. "Military service," said France's High Commissioner for Youth and Sports, Maurice Herzog, "is an enrichment for young men to the extent it intermingles all social classes." Why not, he asked, use part of the time to educate, to open horizons, to develop culture? There is, after all, "no comparison between expense of a cultural center and an airplane carrying atomic bombs."[36]

At about the same time that the Commissioner spoke, reports were appearing about the findings of two committees. The first, established in April 1959 within the national defense structure, was headed by Inspector-General Genevey and included four representatives from the Ministry of the Armed Forces and three from civilian ministries (Interior, Work, Economic Affairs). The committee was asked by the Premier to study ways of implementing the concept of national defense, initiated by the ordinance of January 7, 1959. Two years later, in January 1961, another committee was organized, this one to make recommendations concerning military service. Presided over originally by General Demetz, the military governor of Paris, this committee also had representatives from the Ministry of the Armed Forces, as well as other civilian and military officials. Whatever their titles, the objectives of both groups were, in the nature of things, the same. So, it appeared, were certain of their conclusions, as reported by Le Monde's military

[35] Figaro, June 11, 1962; see also Le Monde, February 18–19, 1962.
[36] Figaro, June 11, 1962.

commentator, Jean Planchais. "First principle established: the system of conscription is to be preserved . . . The tradition of military service is deeply rooted. *The presence of the draftees is, in addition, considered a counter-weight to the present politicalization of a part of the career army.* The government has chosen, and it is very improbable that this choice will be reconsidered in the near future."[37]

If the army were to continue to take in by conscription more men than it needed to perform purely professional functions, more men than could be trained in complicated techniques of modern war, there was only one answer: give the military non-military duties. This was just what the exponents of revolutionary war had demanded, of course, but presumably the same procedure could produce laudable results if there were ideological cleansing along the way. Again, the idea of "national service" helped. Masses of men could be taken into the army for any stated period with no thought that they could contribute to a defense of the country against external enemies. So that they would not get in the way of the real soldiers, they could be trained for home defense duty — whatever that might mean — and then returned to civilian life. Thereafter they would presumably comprise a huge "freedom force," springing to arms when the nation was threatened (if the threat were sufficiently pre-announced, slow-moving and weakly armed).

Although a proponent of professionalism, General Valluy saw the possibility of reconciling a Nation "avid for equality" with an Army "demanding differentiation" by adding to voluntary enlistments draftees obliged to serve about five months so they might receive civic instruction, physical training, and enough military tutoring to turn them into good Swiss militiamen.[38] The operative words in the General's argument were "civic instruction." He, and others,[39] saw dangers in too great a technological revolution in the army. Who would care for people in this machine and direct it toward human, not bureaucratic ends? "The

---

[37] *Le Monde*, June 23, September 22, 1962; italics added. "The 'fundamental reform' announced by official commentaries very strongly resembles a simple compromise," Planchais concluded in September 1962. See also Baude, *op. cit.*, p. 1421.

[38] "Le nouveau duo, Armée-Nation," p. 494.

[39] See, for example, Robert Chapuis, "La jeunesse et l'Armée," *Esprit*, October 1962, pp. 476–477.

individual is one of the values we have to protect, and this cannot be
done by having the protector begin to do away with him!"[40]

Back, then, to the vision of the army as the great humanizer of
Frenchmen. What profit would ensue from training specifically for
territorial defense, particularly if the period were reduced to the extent
General Valluy suggested? Would not the consequent formations be altogether too rational — designed to meet military requirements for fulfilling assigned missions with maximum effectiveness, instead of being
designed "to a myth of equality that only operates during the duration
of service?"[41] Adherents to historic fantasies continued to claim that the
length of service should be the same for all, that it should be long enough
for the army to fulfill its socializing role, that deferments and rejections
should be held to a minimum, that the age of eligibility for service
should neither be advanced nor set back. To promote this ideal they
supported proposals to make the army the antithesis of the paratroops,
to make it a home away from home. "The young Frenchman called to
the colors should be treated like a soldier in all that pertains to technical
training and physical hardening for combat," wrote Jean Planchais.
"Beyond these strict limits, he should be considered as a citizen."[42] Let
him get further away from the base on short leaves. Give him a larger
clothing allowance, as the French navy was beginning to do. Give him
responsibility for multiplying the non-military, cultural, recreational,
educational, esthetic accoutrements of the base. Fix up his barracks.
Work out procedures for collective judgment on appropriate penalties
and punishment. Raise his ridiculously low pay. Put an end to useless
military details, as for example "sentinels" at most metropolitan posts.
In sum, if the army was to be a socializing agent, let it become itself
more socially acceptable.

And "to all the detailed improvements a more profound transformation should be added. Those responsible for the army and the minister
himself appear determined to launch a serious campaign against 'lost

[40] Jean Valluy, "Réflexions sur l'armée de demain," Revue des Deux Mondes,
July 15, 1962, p. 170.
[41] General Béthouart in Figaro, August 18–19, 1962, arguing for just such functional diversification of types and times of compulsory military service.
[42] Le Monde, November 10, 1962.

time.' "[43] "Lost time" certainly did not refer to time away from military activity, but rather to "dead" time: time spent doing nothing at all. Having created the dead time in the first place, those responsible for conscription, far-reaching in scope and relatively long in duration, were naturally assumed to be the ones responsible for filling it.

An army made attractive for every mother's son called to spend a year and a half in it could then hide its austere, professional purpose behind various disguises. It could become a French version of a 4-H club. By September 1960, 31 agricultural clubs had been established in the three services, designed to bring enlisted men and farming organizations together. By 1963 the number had grown to 146 with almost 10,000 members located in France, Germany, and Algeria. The Army-Youth Committee had issued to military bases a do-it-yourself booklet, providing "all information necessary for the creation of a club: the addresses of all public and private organizations which could be helpful . . ." Young farmers drafted into the army could learn to become better farmers. If they were so lucky as to be serving in an agricultural area, they could form work details to help local cultivators sow and reap.[44]

And the army could become a vast *Sportspalast*. In June 1962 the Minister of the Armed Forces announced that a second battalion would be formed of skilled athletes. The specialty of the new unit would be team, not individual, sports.[45] Physical hardening could be fun if accomplished by playing soccer. Although presumably *boules* would not be acceptable, aloof soldiers could go in for tennis, swimming, and the like. Those who knew a game could teach those previously deprived of the opportunity. All could then teach still more after their release from service.

The interest of the High Commissioner for Youth and Sports in continued large-scale conscription becomes readily understandable. One drawback to training future Olympic-games winners might be a shortage of suitable arenas, playing fields, and equipment. While metropolitan France, asked to absorb an army returning from Algeria, had

[43] Planchais, *ibid.*
[44] *Le Monde,* September 23, 1960, June 21, 1962, January 25, 1963.
[45] *Le Monde,* June 23, 1962.

discovered its most fundamental encampment facilities woefully inadequate, a Youth and Sports Commissioner might get more funds by insinuating his way into the military budget than by trying to go it alone.

And the army could become a French version of the Peace Corps. Mention was made earlier of proposals to send Foreign Legionnaires hither and yon to help people in France's few remaining colonies. Objections to the Legion would presumably not apply to *bona fide* metropolitan Frenchmen. In November 1962 Pierre Messmer announced that he was acceding to the request of the Minister of Cooperation to place at his disposal each year a certain number of conscripts who volunteered for special assignment. They would be chosen in the light of the degrees or certificates they had received before entering the service. Engineers and teachers were particularly wanted. To head off a flood of applications, the Ministry's announcement told draftees, "Don't call us; we'll call you." It was estimated that the total number would be small: a few hundred, of whom about 150 would be engineers.[46]

More than anything else, however, the army could be a finishing school, a trade school, and, naturally, an employment service. Calls for courses in health and hygiene were as old as the practice of conscription itself. So was pressure to use the army to overcome illiteracy. Although estimates were that only eight percent of the conscripts were actually illiterate, recurrent suggestions arose that the better educated teach those with less schooling. At least it would keep both groups out of mischief during their spare time. Accompanying these proposals for cultural refinement were others for instructing young men in a useful trade. Training opportunities expanded as the demand increased for soldiers possessing varied technical skills. In presenting his budget, Minister of the Armed Forces Messmer cited figures to demonstrate that "following national education, whose business it is, the army is, of all public organizations, that which is making the most powerful effort in behalf of the education of young Frenchmen."

In paternalistic military thinking it followed that draftees should not simply be dumped on the economy at the end of their period of service. Military and civilian committees established sets of examinations to

[46] *Le Monde,* November 8, 25–26, 1962.

test draftees taking courses in the army and to reward those who did well with certificates of credit transferable to civilian institutions. Pains were taken to acquaint conscripts with employment conditions throughout France in their particular skills. Officers were encouraged to write directly to officials in the various departments, and available information was centralized in the ubiquitous Army-Youth Committee.[47]

Decisions (or lack of them) concerning the type of military service to which French youth would be subjected directly affected the types of officers which would be required. Unfortunately, the demands were difficult to reconcile. The professional corps would need far more technical expertise, a broadened understanding of the place of military force in national statecraft, while still retaining the valorous attributes of leaders in combat. Analogous pressures exist on other Western military establishments, where experience shows that no satisfactory criteria for solution come ready-made.

In the case of France special circumstances delayed rather than stepped up concerted national attempts to modernize training of officers. Protracted colonial combat had monopolized the attention of military planners. Developing ideas concerning "revolutionary war" then perverted curricula and, perhaps more significant in the long run, carried into military schools highly specialized definitions of ideal officers. The ensuing clash between military activists, who were partisans of a French Algeria and frequently also "theoreticians," and civilian leaders hardly helped to establish a rational relationship between various military careers and various types of military training. In the clamor for continued colonial control, competing assignments, as for example European defense in the North Atlantic Treaty Organization, could barely be heard. A general-president continually subduing revolts and frustrating attempts on his life was able to shift officers supervising or teaching in military schools to positions where they could do less damage. But neither he nor his government could, apparently, formulate and enforce graduated programs at the different levels of seniority to reinforce the missions they had since 1959 begun to define and since 1960 begun to implement under the four-year modernization program.

[47] *Le Monde*, February 1, 1962, January 25, 1963.

In addition to the uncertainty of its grip on political and social institutions, civilian leadership was seriously handicapped by the fact that the missions being assigned to the army were specifically *national* missions, taking only minimal account of France's membership in a multilateral Western alliance. Potential supporters of fundamental changes in officers' schools were alienated by Gaullist nationalism. Officers themselves became more suspicious of De Gaulle as a military strategist. Interpenetration of French and other Western military schools, instead of becoming habitual after the end of the Algerian war, became progressively more limited.

Courses in psychological warfare were dropped, altered, sanitized, but the opportunity to make over the officers' schools from top to bottom was not grasped. Changes took place, but adaptations were uneven, delayed, and vigorously challenged in the name of conflicting military mythologies. To those who stressed the need for more and better technical training at the very beginning of an officer's career, opponents gave several answers. On the practical level, they pointed out, stiffening scientific standards were already driving potential candidates away from military service, particularly the latest generation of military families.[48] Furthermore, the best of those who did enter the army were using the skills military education provided to obtain well-paid jobs in private industry just as soon as retirement with pension became possible. As a result there was a danger that the armed forces would be left with mediocre technicians who had been indifferently trained to start with, since no military school could concentrate on scientific subjects to the extent that was possible inside civilian academies.

The argument was also advanced that undue emphasis on non-martial capacities would produce a weak officer corps. In times of national crisis, when the survival of the country was at stake, its members would lack those qualities most needed for successful combat — bravery, leadership, dedication, self-sacrifice. Those who participated in the fifteen years of colonial fighting were quick to remind others that

[48] Strictly military families might be disappearing, but more sons of officers apparently were entering the service. See below, p. 175.

the test of any army remained, as always, its effectiveness in war — and men, not machines, made war.

Far more serious, though naturally not more popular with traditionally minded military leaders, was the suggestion that a modern officer needed to know more than how to fight or how to apply scientific techniques to complex matériel. Social science *requirements*, it was argued, should be substituted for standard literary options offered in military schools. Critics, if not the formulators of military programs, were increasingly convinced that academic disciplines still considered rather esoteric by French civilian instructors should be introduced into courses for officers. Among studies suggested were political science, psychology, and social psychology. The novel idea was broached that the army in a modern state should regard itself as only one facet among many elements of power in a nation which confronted a variety of external menaces to its existence, of which the military threat was but one. Therefore, military schools should instruct future officers in the range of and relationships among the ingredients comprising France's statecraft. From there it was but a short step to the notion that respect for the uniform was won, not just by leading troops on peacetime maneuvers or by decorative commemorations of past battles, but by ability to contribute constructive ideas to civilian-military policy-forming councils at the upper echelons. "Military thought cannot henceforth close itself in a private, narrow circle, for it is at the same time a branch of political thought and a child of general thought."[49]

"In their present education do our military training schools — and, especially, Saint-Cyr — meet these requirements?" asked Tony Albord. "We are forced to answer no."[50] Saint-Cyr, for all its course labels and options, was, in fact, criticized for moving away from, not toward, more education in the social sciences.[51] Narrowly trained officers were apt to become dangerous ones later in their careers, dangerous in precisely the way that their forerunners had threatened the Fifth Republic.

---

[49] Tony Albord, in an article headed "Reconstruction or Tinkering?" *Le Monde*, August 29, 1962. See also François Gromier, "Le 'trouble de l'Armée,'" *La Nef*, July–September 1961, pp. 17–18.

[50] *Le Monde*, August 29, 1962.

[51] *Le Monde*, October 4, 1962.

Ignorant and prejudiced opinion could be stated as forcefully and supported as vigorously as conclusions formed after serious study. "For almost a half-century we have suffered in high military positions from a certain intellectual mediocrity and deficiency of will, which did not, however, exclude a frantic ambition from leading naturally to the political arena."[52] The answer to General Valluy's complaint that Polytechnicians were getting all the top military jobs was not, as the General warned, that there would come a day of political reckoning. Rather was it to make overdue changes in the curricula of other schools, especially Saint-Cyr, so that their graduates would provide candidates worth appointing to the highest positions. Considering the time lag of more than a quarter of a century between training and eligibility for senior rank, one might conclude that it was not too early to start.

Military schools did vary, of course. They attracted different types of students, and their individual programs produced different motivations toward careers as officers. Existing studies of the candidates permit tentative conclusions as to future congruence between leadership of the three services on the one hand and the military direction marked out by political authority on the other. In all military schools the proportion of sons of officers to total students appeared to be increasing since World War II. Saint-Cyr, still regarded as a channel for social advancement, had the greatest proportion of sons of non-coms. The Ecole Polytechnique and the Ecole Navale had a larger share of what might be called the middle bourgeoisie. More than half the candidates at the former and more than a third of those at the latter represented industry and the liberal professions (teaching, government, arts, etc.). In all three institutions the number of sons of workers, farmers, and white collar employees was low, reflecting continued distrust of the military system and the symbolic nature of officially expressed concern for a broadened base of officer recruitment. The few from the bottom of the socioeconomic pyramid who did seek a military career tended to concentrate in the Air School, quite probably because it lacked both military and bourgeois traditions and also because the nature of its technical program offered opportunities for good pay later in the aviation industry.

[52] Tony Albord in *Le Monde*, May 13, 1961.

When the Algerian war was drawing to a close, the ratio of applicants to acceptances was increasing in all the schools.[53]

Under auspices of the Scientific Action Committee of National Defense, the Center of Studies and Psychological Instruction of the Air Force conducted a study of the attitudes of some 1,250 students at various military schools.[54] Asked to list in three categories objectives which had strongly, somewhat, or not at all motivated them toward a military career, respondents placed in the highest rank "patriotic ideal, taste for command, taste for risk and combat, fraternity of arms," all of which could be classed as representing traditional military virtues. One exception, placed in the midst of those listed, was "desire to travel." "Glory of the career of arms, information, and family tradition" were recognized as having had some influence, but "desire for technical specialization" and "search for professional security" were among those discarded. "Desire to travel" had been elevated in the over-all assessment thanks to citation by Air and Naval School students, who, conversely, dropped the notion of the "patriotic ideal" to sixth and fourth places respectively. Air School students ranked "desire for technical specialization" third, while the others, including Naval School students, ranked it toward the bottom.

The study also attempted to rate the students in regard to their "militarism," submitting questions on the relative place of the military in society, attitudes past and present toward the army and military behavior, and student ideas of their personal role in the army. The study concluded that distinctions among the various schools were widespread and pronounced:

> The candidates in the Saint-Cyr History and above all Languages [curricula] appear as future warriors, militarists, and immersed in the patriotic ideal, very opposed to all aspects of technical activity. Candidates

[53] Lothar W. Hilbert, "L'Officier français à notre époque," *Revue Libérale*, 1 Trimestre 1962, pp. 69–76; J. Perret-Gentil, "Armée française: faits d'actualité," *Revue Militaire Suisse*, October 1961; Jean Planchais, "Quelle est cette armée?" *La Nef*, July–September 1961, pp. 57–64. It would be difficult to say whether applications for military schools were increasing because young men eligible for service preferred duty in Algeria as an officer to that of a draftee or because the anticipated end of the war was making a military career generally more attractive.

[54] Combined Forces Special Military School, Naval School, Air School, Engineers-Mechanics Naval School, and Air Base Officers School.

at the Naval and Air Schools, also immersed in the same ideal, are much less militaristic and a little less closed to technical training. Very close to them are the candidates in the Saint-Cyr Science [curriculum], yet less imbued with the idea of "service." Militarism decreases still more clearly with the candidates at the Naval School along with, to a lesser extent, the importance of the political ideal, without this decline increasing the taste for technical training. Finally, with the candidates at the Air School one sees the forward surge of the desire for technical specialization and a new falling off of the patriotic ideal.

There thus appears in the candidates in general a variable but frequent association of the patriotic ideal, combativeness, and ambition, the three aspects of the military career clearly placed in opposition to the desire for technical specialization and the aspiration for professional security . . . Repeated statistical cross-checking confirms that militarism increases as the curriculum becomes less scientific . . . a balance being nonetheless observed in the special case of candidates at the Naval and especially at the Naval Air School.[55]

Punctuating De Gaulle's moves to cement his own political power were efforts at restoring to the army a valued place in French society. Within the government a new national defense structure was created. New military leadership was brought forward. Rebellious military units were shifted or dissolved. Army and civilian conspirators were tried before a series of tribunals, whose failures and successes served as guides to the permanent court established in 1963. Yet, at the same time, a minimum of attention was devoted to examining the army itself, its proper functions, and its patterns of recruitment. Commissions were appointed and studied the subject for years; what emerged was labelled "compromise" or "tinkering." How to account for the determined battle in one arena, inaction or conciliation in the other?

One explanation is that the battle was forced on De Gaulle; it was not of his own choosing. In spite of the claims of men like Tixier-Vignancour and Soustelle, there is little evidence that De Gaulle deliberately set out to fight the Algerian army which had placed him in power. De Gaulle's ambiguities, shifts, and retreats are more logically explained as reactions to unanticipated obduracy encountered in his dealings with both the Moslem nationalists and the military-European

[55] "Attitudes et motivations des candidates aux grandes écoles militaires," *Revue Française de Sociologie*, April–June 1961, pp. 133–152, quotation, pp. 149–151.

alliance in Algeria. When the officers began to appear in the dock, the courts sought to limit condemnation to individuals, not to a movement, let alone a set of interlocking organizations. It was the defense attorneys who forced government-appointed judges and prosecutors to compete with them for popular approval.

Once launched, however, the use of improper legal procedures as instruments of social control was subjected to few restraints by political leadership, largely because De Gaulle and his followers did not acknowledge that there were unacceptable costs involved. A president who could define democracy as the appointment of one, mass-supported, national "guide" could see nothing incongruous in dismissing the Committee to Safeguard Individual Rights and Liberties because this notoriously do-nothing group had "attained its objectives."[56] Restrictions on individual freedom, penalties for defending lawyers, expansion of police powers, use of magistrates for political purposes — all these were not labelled as exceptional, temporary measures forced upon the government by the need to fight OAS-CNR terrorism. It was assumed that beyond the immediate danger of military-civilian plots lay a permanent threat of subversion. A system so rootless that its premier felt compelled to call upon the people of Paris to oppose military landings with their massed bodies could be counted upon to seek security in constraint rather than in freedom. Political parties, labor unions, teachers, farmers, intellectuals, where might not the shadow of illicit activity fall? The leader, and perhaps even the leader's cohorts, might commune with an idealized, undifferentiated "public," but individuals meeting together, exchanging ideas, organizing to obtain goals were potential dangers because their estate, their ordering in society, was not clearly defined.

De Gaulle, it becomes clear, was neither in the business of social revolution nor even in the business of alleviating the social discontent which added to the threat posed by conspirators. His view of the proper nature and composition of his "new" army was fundamentally no less retrograde. Military advice and leadership available for transformation of the army was severely limited, first, by the army's long experience with colonial combat; second, by the diffusion throughout the officer

[56] See *Le Monde*, February 6, 1963.

corps of revolutionary-war ideas derived from that experience; and, finally, by the low standing in military circles of Gaullism in general and De Gaulle in particular. With these handicaps, it would take time for the General-President to create a military mystique powerful enough to attract the loyalty of younger officers who had not passed through the intoxicating years in Indochina and Algeria. It would take all the longer because that mystique would deliberately be built with pieces of equipment on which would be painted the slogan "to be used for national grandeur," not with consistently applied principles to guide the selection, training, and outfitting of a mid-twentieth-century army. "National Service" was only the hoary "Nation in Arms" brushed off and polished up. Most Frenchmen failed to perceive that, in expecting an army to be father, teacher, employer of the nation's youth, they were presenting a terrible indictment of their civilian society. Their unconscious assumption that civilian society was bankrupt could become a self-fulfilling prophecy.

C H A P T E R 7

NEW WEAPONS

FOR A NEW ARMY

*The atomic bomb has no more or less importance today than
Greek fire some centuries ago. It assures its user of a certain
advantage so long as the enemy doesn't know the secret. Once
an equilibrium is re-established, the war of armies resumes.* —
Anonymous French writer

*Obviously we must, during the years to come, provide ourselves
with a force able to operate for our own benefit — what has
come to be called a* force de frappe *. . . The foundation of this
force will be an atomic armament which we shall produce or
which we shall buy — but which should belong to us . . .* —
Charles de Gaulle, November 1959

MILITARY budgets of the Fourth Republic reflected the enfeebled
nature of the Republic itself. They were haphazard, unplanned, belated
responses to compelling external events; above all, they were inadequate responses. Rearmament had hardly begun when France, in 1951,[1]

---

[1] "Sirius." Beuve-Méry (editor of *Le Monde*) derisively compared his nation's
military "effort" to that of Switzerland. *Au fil des semaines*, Paris, Malfère, 1951, p.
80.

was simultaneously confronted with an increasingly severe conflict in Indochina and American demands that the continental allies take seriously the requirements of defense and greatly increase their military contributions to NATO.

The French arms budget did rise in 1952, but it fell in 1953 and remained stationary in 1954. In 1953 and 1954 the military budget represented about one-third of the total national expenditures,[2] a high proportion, but it bought neither victory in Indochina nor a French army on the continent judged adequate by its allies. After the fall of Dien Bien Phu France became even weaker militarily in Western Europe. Although rearmament efforts had noticeably improved the quality of French contingents in Germany, the bulk of these troops were soon transferred to Algeria. Some increases were made in military expenditures, but their percentage of the total budget dropped to about one-fourth. The army's demands for men, men, and still more men to invest in Algeria resulted in a de-emphasis on production of matériel. Personnel costs during the five years 1954 through 1958 increased from 40 to 47 percent, while expenditures on major items of equipment declined from just under 30 percent to 20 percent.[3]

Thus, for the decade 1948–1958 France had a colonial-war budget. Since the Fourth Republic insisted on playing the role of great power with neither the means nor the inclination to pay for it, the budget was also that of an irresponsible mendicant. American largesse allowed France to fight its colonial wars, claim its participating membership in NATO, carry out its successive Four Year Plans for economic development, and finance, in a manner of speaking, its current civilian expenses.[4] In the four years before the Algerian war killed the Fourth Republic, the United States helped France in at least four different ways. There was direct military aid and financial assistance, with a large international loan coming too late to help the beleaguered Pflim-

[2] Jean Godard, "Les budgets militaires françaises," *Revue de Défense Nationale*, March 1956, pp. 327–331.

[3] *Revue de Défense Nationale*, March 1959, p. 534.

[4] American aid in 1954 has been calculated at almost 19 percent of the total French budget. Jean Godard, "La contribution alliée aux charges militaires de la France," *Revue de Défense Nationale*, April 1956, p. 443.

lin government. Equipment supposedly destined for Western defense wound up in Algeria, without the United States being able, whether or not it had wished, to prevent the diversion.[5] The United States, by keeping large numbers of American troops in West Germany, rescued France from the dilemma created by concentrating its forces in North Africa while at the same time masquerading as a leader of NATO. Equally significant in the long run, the United States, backed up by Great Britain, forced France to agree that Germany should be permitted to re-arm. A Bonn-Washington axis thus filled the void left by the Fourth Republic's departure for Algeria.

General de Gaulle and his advisors set out to change all that. Along the way, they also sought to change several other unpleasant characteristics of the military budget, Fourth Republic style. An annual battle royal formerly had raged around the formulation and approval of the budget. The first round pitted cabinet minister against cabinet minister, the two foremost antagonists being the Minister of the Armed Forces and the Minister of Finance. An indefinite number of succeeding rounds saw a shaky, divided cabinet try to salvage some of its financial proposals from a series of assaults by the parliament. Even if it survived temporarily, the so-called executive was often fatally wounded. So prolonged was the process that the budget was never voted on time, at the beginning of the calendar year; the government was forced to live on an improvised hand-to-mouth basis for as long as half a year. By contrast, the Fifth Republic proposed to plan in advance a substantial proportion of military expenditures. These would then be authorized at one time by the National Assembly in the form of a *loi-cadre*. Annual budgets were to be voted before the beginning of the fiscal year. In sum, De Gaulle, not the legislators, would control the size and allocation of military expenditures.

Secondly, the arms budget was to be *for* not *in spite of* the economy. When he was Finance Minister, Robert Schuman had called for a delay of "several years" in all military programs "that use too many men, too

---

[5] While France professed to resent any American "intrusion" into its "domestic" affairs, its North African departments were, like France itself, covered by the North Atlantic Treaty.

much matériel, or too much money in relation to the limited and reduced resources of the country." In 1950 it was argued that, despite the
needs of the Indochinese war and European defense, no increase at all
in military expenditures was possible. Reasons given were that the
French economy was too weak to support an armaments industry, and
foreign indebtedness did not permit France to buy equipment abroad.

Belated economic prosperity and rigorous financial measures instituted by the Fifth Republic changed somewhat the substantive relationship between the economy and national arms production. What
changed more drastically, however, was the psychological approach of
the government. Leaders of the Fifth Republic saw in certain types of
arms expenditures, not a dead weight, but a source of stimulation supplementing and as valuable in its way as the continuing Four Year
Plans. Moreover, Gaullists saw the possibility of *selective* stimulation;
military modernization could advance general modernization by spur-
ring the shift from small, archaic, economically marginal plants to those
designed for a greatly expanded market.

In 1959 Minister of the Armed Forces Guillaumat stated, "We intend
that the armament industry be able to participate in the general expansion of our economy, by adapting under-developed sectors toward new
activities and by doing away with useless and non-profitable branches."[6]
A year later the head of the Senate's Finance Committee was more
specific. Studies and production in such varied fields as aeronautics,
chemistry of metals, and plastics, said Henri Dorey, "can play the role
of accelerator as much in the development of techniques as in increasing production." Policies of buying items produced in France, even if
they cost more, and of seeking export markets for military equipment
"cannot fail to produce chain reactions, increasing production considerably in certain sectors."[7] It was certainly no coincidence that the coterie
surrounding De Gaulle came increasingly to represent the modern
financial and industrial sectors of the economy.[8]

[6] Quoted by Maurice Megret, "Questions et réflexions sur le programme français
de force nucléaire," *Politique Etrangère*, No. 1, 1960, p. 17.

[7] Quoted by J. R. Tournoux, "Force de frappe," *Revue de Paris*, December 1960,
pp. 114–115.

[8] Witness the departure of Pinay and the arrival of Georges Pompidou as Premier,
with Giscard d'Estaing as Finance Minister.

Another feature of Gaullist budgets was their national rather than colonial character, a feature which, perhaps fortunately for the President, was initially obscure to legislative and military leaders. Military expenditures came to reflect changing priorities among the branches of the armed forces and military missions basically European in character. The budgets were to carry forward De Gaulle's policy and his policy alone. While their underlying philosophy reflected in considerable degree De Gaulle's battle with the army, it was *his* battle brought on by *his* maneuvers in Algeria. American experts, who predicted that the end of the war in North Africa would see France re-enter NATO with all the strength its relatively large, combat-trained army could command, were never more wrong. The policy of national military power was for national autonomy, not for continued second-class status in any coalition run by the Anglo-Saxons. French military strategy would be defined in Paris. If definitions of strategic goals appeared curiously unrealistic, it was because the observer was reading them as objective military statements, not as detached sections of an essay in political philosophy.

After 1960 the French parliament saw military expenditures in three forms: annual requests as part of the regular budget, requests for supplementary appropriations during the year, and requests for implementation of the four-year arms program.[9] In the beginning, over all three areas of military costs hung the shadow of the Algerian war. Defense Minister Guillaumat, in presenting the 1960 regular budget, warned that "the effort at modernization will unhappily remain symbolic insofar as the ground forces are concerned, since their equipment must principally be directed toward material means for the conduct of operations in Algeria."[10] The influential *Revue de Défense Nationale* used words often to be repeated: "The 1960 budget appears to be a holding budget that will allow living from day to day . . ."[11] Requests for the next two years were also "holding budgets," since they focussed on manpower needed in Algeria at the expense of camp construction, specialized training, and modernization of French forces in West Ger-

[9] Passed as one enabling act. See discussion below.
[10] *Revue de Défense Nationale,* January 1960, p. 171.
[11] July 1959, p. 1294.

many, to which some units were being transferred from Algeria. Increases — 200 million francs for 1961 and 360 million for 1962 ($40
million and $72 million respectively) — reflected rising costs of equip-
ment, increases in pay, closing of bases in North Africa, and repatriation
of troops.[12] Far from objecting to the price of national defense, Gaullist
style, deputies assailed during these years the meagerness of expenditures slated for military pay and purchase of matériel (with the exception, to be examined later, of funds for the *force de frappe*).

The Algerian shadow did not disappear after the official end to hos-
tilities. Defense Minister Messmer calculated that the 1963 budget
would reveal savings of about 205 million francs ($41 million) by re-
ductions in the length of military service and preservation of equipment
now not involved in combat. On the debit side of the ledger, however,
would appear 180 million francs to build and modernize camps and
arsenals in France and another 80 million to make the Mers-El-Kébir
airfield in Algeria operational.[13] "In spite of the war in Algeria," declared André Maroselli of the opposition Democratic Left, "the military
budget increased only 10 percent during the period 1959–1962, while
the total budget charges went up 23 percent."[14]

Not only were defense expenditures relatively constant, but also,
Messmer claimed, they would continue to remain so through the life of
a projected, second *loi-programme* slated to run to 1970. The army had
absorbed and would continue to absorb about 6 percent of the gross
national product, assuming a 4 percent annual increase in future years,
or between 20 and 25 percent of total expenditures. Both ratios were
roughly the same as those of Great Britain and West Germany.[15] The
following table presents the picture for the years 1958–1962. It should
be taken as illustrative only, since the gross national product represents
an estimate which may well be on the low side, especially for 1962,

12 *L'Année Politique, 1960*, pp. 103, 138, 175; *1961*, pp. 173, 184; Perret-Gentil,
op. cit. New francs are referred to here and subsequently, unless otherwise specified.
13 *Revue de Défense Nationale*, August–September 1962, p. 1422.
14 *Le Monde*, February 3–4, 1963.
15 Pierre Messmer, "French Military Establishment of Tomorrow," *Orbis*, Vol.
VI, No. 2, Summer 1962, pp. 207–209; Messmer's statements in presenting the
1963 budget, *Le Monde*, January 12, 25, 1963.

while figures for defense and total expenditures are approximations only.

(*Billions of Francs*)

Year	Gross National Product	Total Expenditures	National Defense Expenditures		
			Total	As Percent of GNP	As Percent of Total Expenditures
1958	240	58.0	14.5	6.0	25
1959	285	66.2	16.1	5.6	24
1960	308	66.8	16.2	5.3	24
1961	331	70.5	17.1	5.2	24
1962	332	75.0	17.3	5.2	23

What was changing behind the generally stable budgetary façade were relative priorities accorded the branches of the armed forces and the types of military equipment. The first *loi-programme*, presented in 1960, gave a sketchy indication of the new directions to be followed. The government asked for advance authorization to spend 11,790,500,000 francs between 1961 and 1965, or somewhat less than 40 percent of the estimated 31,160,000,000 total for the years concerned. The largest single category was 4,928,000,000 francs for "special studies and special missiles" (related to nuclear weapons and delivery systems). Next in line was the air force, with 2,730,000,000 francs. Another 1,407,000,000 francs was to be spent on aircraft research and equipment not formally assigned to the air force. The army was to receive 1,778,500,000 francs, and the navy 947,000,000. During parliamentary debate the government was induced to transfer 120 million francs from the "special studies" category to the navy for planning and producing marine ballistic missiles. Another 280,000,000 was taken from the air force and given to the army for its modernization program. Both transfers represented small concessions by Gaullist leadership to the parliament's manifest antipathy toward the *force de frappe*. (Of this, more below.)

No sooner had the first program been launched than study on the second began. Estimates of expenditures under it were 43 billion francs. The 12-billion-franc increase, so the government said, was to go toward completing modernization of the army, for naval construction, and for ballistic missiles. Especially noteworthy was the claim that expenditures for the nuclear program and the air force would become stabilized between 1965 and 1970. It was planned that both the air force and navy would remain at approximately the same strength until 1970, but not so the army. In 1962 there were 78,000 in the navy, and it was hoped that 1970 would find 83,000 to 84,000 in this service. Indications were, however, that the total had actually slipped to less than 77,000 by 1963. Some unwelcome contraction was also taking place in the air force, whose personnel was supposed to remain at approximately 140,000. In 1963 the number had fallen to 127,755. As indicated in the preceding chapter, the ground forces were to be cut back from 721,162 at the beginning of 1962 to about 450,000 in 1970. In the two years 1962 and 1963, directly following the end of the Algerian war, reductions of over one-third were scheduled. The infantry total was to fall 42.9 percent, artillery 36.8, armored and cavalry units 33.8, engineer corps 26.4, service corps 22.6, communications 21.0, health, postal, and other miscellaneous services 22.0. These reductions were seen as prerequisites to, not accompaniments of, the modernization process. By 1965 Defense Minister Messmer expected that units in West Germany would be re-equipped, but the large-scale transformation of the ground forces would have to await the progressive implementation of the second *loi-programme.*[16]

It was this delay in modernizing the ground forces which opponents of De Gaulle's government continually criticized. They suspected that priorities, once established, meant greater delays than anticipated in reaching military categories placed toward the bottom of the list. Once begun, favorite programs would be found to cost more and more, and the government would then re-assign funds originally allocated to less favored sections of the armed forces rather than request commensurate

[16] Messmer, "French Military Establishment of Tomorrow"; *Le Monde,* January 25, 1963.

increases in total military expenditures. Constantly rising costs, it was feared, would ultimately cause the government to call ground-force modernization complete when it actually fell far short of original intentions. An unsigned article in the periodical *Armée*, published under the general supervision of the ground forces command, gave a mournful warning of what was to come. The portion of the military budget going to the ground forces was estimated at 8 billion francs, of which 4.5 billion would be spent in paying, housing, and outfitting officers and men. The remaining 3.5 billion would not come near buying what the government claimed it was going to provide. "The number of modern, mechanized divisions that we can equip will most certainly come closer to five than to ten, and the other forces we are assembling will have to content themselves with equipment, now in our supply dumps, which is still operational."[17]

Modernization, in other words, smarted even while it soothed. The nature of the sensation was determined by the extent to which a given branch of the armed services or a given section within one of the three branches could be tied to what had become after the Algerian war the dominating concern of successive military budgets, development of nuclear weapons. French armed forces faced the same prospect as had the American, British, and presumably the Russian before them. Least involved were the ground forces. Nuclear equipment for them was in all probability a decade away, dependent upon still-unproven French scientific and technological ability to mass-produce missiles and reduce the size of nuclear warheads. Should progress in these directions be rapid, the ground forces might still lose out to the air force or the navy as the result of governmental decisions concerning which few weapons systems should be carried from drawing board to operational status. In the foreseeable future the ground forces would have to be content with conventional equipment. Items on order or already being produced included trucks, tanks, anti-tank weapons, light Alouette helicopters, and automatic machine guns. Programs for heavier trucks and tanks had been abandoned, and the schedule for anti-tank weapons ap-

[17] Reported in *Le Monde*, August 11, 1962.

peared uncertain early in 1963.[18] Also lagging were programs for base construction.

Beginning in 1959, plans had been made for streamlining divisions in a compromise between the overly expensive American and, in the eyes of the French, the under-manned West German organization. Each of the French brigades was to be capable of autonomous combat for from three to five days. Hence the plans called for large-scale improvement in motorization, armor, fire-power, repair facilities, health provisions, and, ultimately, for nuclear weapons allocated to the brigade level. In fact, however, ground force formations would during the 1960's largely play a supporting role for advanced defense in West Germany, and an "interventionary" role outside Europe. Their largest single responsibility would remain the relatively primitive, relatively low-priority defense of France itself against subversion and guerrilla activity. Military mythology, previously discussed, together with the long years of colonial combat would assign to "modernization" a primarily conventional meaning.[19]

The navy was definitely scheduled to enter the nuclear age, but the delayed date of its arrival would necessitate temporary sacrifices. As Defense Minister Messmer delicately put it, "For the first time in many years, the French Navy will be assigned a permanent and critical mission in the national defense, namely that of supplying a considerable portion of the deterrent force. The Navy will thereby acquire enhanced prestige and increased material resources; but the entry into service of nuclear-powered missile submarines will place so heavy a financial burden upon the French budget that the Navy will be forced to curtail expenses on other items of its program."[20]

There was pie in the sky, but meanwhile there would be stew. The carrier *Clemenceau* was put into service during 1962; the *Foch* underwent tests. Two modern cruisers, the *Colbert* and *De Grasse*, four frigates, assorted escort vessels, and sub-chasers were also scheduled for

[18] *Le Monde*, October 21–22, November 10, 1962, January 25, 1963; *Revue de Défense Nationale*, November 1962, pp. 1777–1778.

[19] *Revue de Défense Nationale*, February 1960, pp. 360–361; Etienne Anthérieu in *Figaro*, October 18, 20, 1960; *Le Monde*, January 25, 1963.

[20] *Orbis* (translation), *op. cit.*, p. 211.

production. But total tonnage fell in five years from close to 400,000 in 1958 to 169,000 in 1963. This was in marked contrast to the 540,000 tons proposed by France a decade earlier at NATO's Council Meeting in Lisbon. Although estimates had fixed the number needed at 30, submarines of the *Daphné* type scheduled for production were cut from 11 to 9, and quite possibly the latter figure was still too optimistic by about 3. Modern aircraft support was represented by the *Etendard IV,* which was born from a union of *Mystère* and *Mirage,* both air force planes. The *Etendard,* which existed in both assault and reconnaissance versions, was not produced in quantities large enough to meet requirements. One hundred had been ordered; price increases reduced the number to 90; only about half that number would be available by 1963. To fill out the minimum complement France was forced to buy from the United States 46 *Crusaders* (fighters) for delivery during 1963 and 1964. Less spectacular in performance than the American *F-4,* the *Crusader* had the advantage of being lighter, and above all cheaper.

The explanation of the navy's problems is simple. Missile and nuclear weapons were slower to enter its arsenal than French optimists had anticipated. Whether 1970 would see the long-awaited missiles and nuclear-powered submarine (one) was problematical. "With financial means it wished were larger but whose limits it objectively understands, the Navy is now forging the instrument best suited to its tasks," Admiral Cabanier told the Institute of High Studies of National Defense. Obviously a great deal depended on the precise definition given the phrase "now forging" and the word "tasks."[21]

In contrast to the ground forces and the navy, the air force was obviously benefiting from the changing spectrum of military expenditures. Throughout the pre-missile age, the air force had epitomized French modernization efforts. If it could use its vested interests to full advantage, this branch of the military establishment might well dominate, at least until 1972, national decisions regarding the types of missile systems to be produced. The favorable position of the air force had been

[21] *Figaro,* November 17, 1960; *Le Monde,* November 11, 1962, January 13–14, 19, 25, 1963; *Figaro,* March 17–18, 1962; *Le Monde,* January 19, 1961; Perret-Gentil, "Vers la force de frappe," *Revue Militaire Suisse,* June 1962, p. 282.

attained, not only through De Gaulle's general determination to provide the armed forces with new equipment, but, most importantly, from his decision to institute the changes with a bare minimum of international cooperation.

Glamor weapon of the glamor service was the *Mirage*. It had succeeded the *Mystère*, which in turn had followed the *Ouragan*, the first French plane to break the sound barrier. The *Mirage* made its maiden flight in June 1959; production began in 1960; two years later the output had reached ten a month. Versions of the *Mirage* included trainer, reconnaissance, and attack planes, but the *crème de la crème* was the *Mirage IV*, the so-called "strategic bomber." Although Defense Minister Messmer claimed that production of the *Mirage IVA* was proceeding on schedule, and planes would be operational in desired quantities after the end of 1963, the Senate rapporteur for the air force budget stated that the plane was "still far from being produced in regular series." The "desired quantities" appeared to mean as many as three by 1964, but already the successor, *Mirage IVB*, was being programmed. Initially, the range of the aircraft was stated to be only 1,500 kilometers (900 miles),[22] but new engines would raise that limit, as could a system of aerial refueling. It was hoped that by 1966 fifty *Mirage* bombers would be in service. Once they were a part of the air force or, in the case of the *Mirage IVB*, in production, the life of the aircraft would presumably be prolonged by equipping them with air-to-ground missiles, assuming that problems of nuclear miniaturization had by then been overcome.

Familiar difficulties were delaying and reducing production of other modern planes. The number of *Mirage III's* on order fell from 130 to 116 early in 1963, with further cuts possible. France and Germany cooperated in building the twin-engine transport *Noratlas*, of which over 300 were in service or on order in the two countries. However, the successor *Transall*, suffering from postponed decisions and lack of coordination, did not even get off the ground until the Spring of 1963. It would not be in service in quantity until late in the 1960's and at costs greater than those of the comparable American *C-130*, which could

[22] 2,500 kilometers was another estimate.

have been produced in France under license. High on the list of military requirements were planes needing only limited space for take-off. A light transport, the *Spirale III*, was approved by the Debré government in 1962 after one year of debate and an investment of 180 million francs, in preference to the *Super-Broussard* and the *Breguet 945*, both judged too expensive. Also approved was the *Super-Frelon*, a heavy helicopter, which began to undergo tests at the end of 1962. Although NATO circulated specifications for NMBR's (NATO Military Basic Requirement) Three and Four, both vertical take-off planes, or short take-off planes with unusually heavy load capacity, France was ignoring the Organization in favor of its own, projected lighter versions.[23]

"As regards missiles, our situation is not brilliant," Premier Debré told the Finance Committee of the National Assembly in 1960. "We still have a rather long row to hoe before arriving at the production stage." In July 1959 a private company, but one acting under government auspices, had been formed. As its name implies, the Société d'Etudes et de Recherches sur les Engins Balistiques (SEREB) was designed as coordinator and supervisor of research. It was concerned with development of space vehicles, as well as with military missiles. Firms represented included Dassault, Breguet, Matra, and the Société d'Etudes de la Propulsion à Réaction (SEPR) and also public representatives from nationalized aviation concerns, the Office Nationale d'Etudes et de Recherches Aéronautiques (ONERA) and the Service des Poudres. Funds to be made available from the government between 1960 and 1964 were estimated at one billion francs, which might well err on the low side, considering the difficulty of tracing funds parcelled out to government agencies, nationalized industries, private companies, the armed forces, and groups concerned with space exploration.

In the field of conventional, mass-produced missiles was the Ameri-

[23] Mark Lambert, "The French Industry in 1962, I," *Flight and the Aircraft Engineer*, July 5, 1962, pp. 11–14; P.-M. Gallois, "Long-Term Program for the French Industry," *Interavia*, June 1959, p. 646; *Interavia*, May 1961; *Flight*, November 15, 1962; *Interavia*, October 1961, p. 1343, May 1962, p. 593; *Le Monde*, February 8, 16, July 17, November 16, 1962; Perret-Gentil, "Vers la force de frappe," pp. 280–381; *Le Monde*, January 19, 24, February 3–4, January 25, 1963; Contre-Amiral Lepotier, "La force de 'dissuasion' sous-marine," *Revue de Défense Nationale*, November 1962, p. 1672.

can-developed *Hawk,* an anti-aircraft weapon, manufactured in Europe by an international consortium representing France, Belgium, Italy, Holland, and West Germany. France's own Nord company had been in the missile business since 1955, acquiring an American subsidiary and planning for one in Germany. Its product was purchased by American and Belgian as well as French forces. By 1963 it had added to its anti-tank project programs for air-to-surface and surface-to-air missiles, the last a direct competitor to the *Hawk.*

Initially it had appeared that the main problem in long-range missile research was to develop one weapons system: a ground-to-ground weapon (SSBS). Such a judgment was naive, however, since it reckoned on neither the appetite of competing services nor the vested interests of producers and purchasers in existing systems. The navy insisted on getting into the act with a nuclear-powered, missile-armed submarine, while the air force and plane manufacturers demanded that the *Mirage* series not be rendered prematurely obsolete. Missiles would therefore be air-to-ground and sea-to-ground as well as ground-to-ground; they would also complement some operating systems, while serving to enhance the rationale for the production of others.

The first experimental missile was the *Agate,* successfully tested in 1961. Weighing 3,200 kilograms, the *Agate* attained an altitude of 67 kilometers with a pay load of 400 kilograms. By the end of 1963 it was hoped that a second missile, with a tele-guided engine, the *Topaze,* would be ready. Close on its heels was expected to come the liquid-fueled *Emeraude.* The *Emeraude* plus the *Topaze* would in turn comprise the *Saphir,* which, with the addition of a third-stage engine, would be succeeded by the *Diamant,* the "precious stone" of missile-satellite research. The *Diamant,* whose arrival was confidently predicted first for 1964, then 1965, and then 1966, would hopefully boost a 110-pound satellite into a 250–750 mile-high orbit. In the meantime, France successfully tested three solid-fuel rockets during 1962 — the *Bélier,* the *Centaure,* and the *Dragon.* With other European nations France was also cooperating in a program that would ultimately launch Europe's own satellite. This intermingling of research and production, earth-bound and space, military and peaceful preoccupations in France was analogous to procedures followed by other Western countries. It also realistically reflected the concentration of the Fifth Republic on military power as an accessory to diplomatic aspirations for European leadership and great-power status.[24]

Nowhere was the blending of military and political motivations better illustrated than in the nuclear effort undertaken by the Fifth Republic. Ignoring the alarm of many countries at the advent of a fourth nuclear power, De Gaulle exulted in the explosion of the first primitive device on February 13, 1960. As presented in the *loi-programme* later in the year, funds for atomic armament were but the small nose of a very large camel pushed under the flap of a medium-size tent. The *force de frappe*, said the government, would take less than 1.5 percent of total state expenditures.[25] Funds involved comprised 7 to 8 percent of the total defense budget, or an amount equivalent to what the United Kingdom proposed to spend on its *Blue Streak* missile between 1955 and 1965.[26] By June 1962, however, the government was seeking supplementary sums for its nuclear plant at Pierrelatte.[27] Three months later a bulletin of the Ministry of the Armed Forces was calling for careful budgeting to accomplish the desired military modernization, *after the priority accorded to the nuclear force*.[28] Debate on the budget for 1963 focussed on the possibility that nuclear programs might increasingly dominate future military expenditures.[29]

Previous pages have suggested the manner in which other aspects of military modernization either became pointed toward the nuclear arsenal or took a back seat. Atomic tests were carried out in the Sahara in 1962 and 1963. The underground test in the Spring of 1963 provoked

[24] Mark Lambert, "The French Industry in 1962, II," *Flight and the Aircraft Engineer*, July 12, 1962, pp. 56–58; Nicolas Vichney in *Le Monde*, July 10, 1962; Perret-Gentil, "Vers la force de frappe," pp. 281–287; *Revue de Défense Nationale*, August–September 1962, pp. 1424–1425; *New York Times*, January 29, February 24, 1961, April 1, December 7, 1962; *Le Monde*, November 11, 1962, January 3, 9, 1963; *Figaro*, March 27, 1962; *Combat*, October 23, 1962.

[25] *L'Année Politique, 1960*, p. 103.

[26] Leonard Beaton, John Maddox, *The Spread of Nuclear Weapons*, London, Chatto and Windus, 1962, p. 92.

[27] *Le Monde*, June 12, 1962.

[28] *Le Monde*, September 22, 1962.

[29] *Le Monde*, January 15, 25, February 2–3, 1963.

protests from Algeria as well as from neutralist countries, although France had obtained in the Evian agreements rights to the sandy site until 1967. Simultaneously a search was on for alternative places to test both hydrogen and atomic bombs and to launch long-range missiles; one possibility was the Gambier archipelago south of Tahiti in French Polynesia.[30] French research and technology had produced an operational atomic bomb in May 1962; in 1963 and thereafter production would keep to the stately pace of *Mirage IV* fabrication.[31] Armed Forces Minister Messmer claimed that studies concerning the "second-generation" nuclear arsenal, featuring the hydrogen bomb, were one year ahead of schedule.[32]

By the 1970's, therefore, Gaullists expected France to possess several nuclear weapons systems. Ground-force units would be armed with battlefield nuclear weapons. Under the ocean would be one or more of the projected series of atomic submarines, each equipped with sixteen nuclear ballistic missiles and having a ninety-day cruising capacity.[33] On the ground other ballistic missiles would be in place. Airborne would be nuclear-armed versions of the *Mirage* bomber, by this time presumably capable of greater range and speed, and new vertical take-off planes.[34] "Since when," asked De Gaulle on January 14, 1963 in commenting on the December 1962 Anglo-American agreement at Nassau concerning the Polaris missile-submarine weapons complex, "has it been proved that a people should remain deprived of the most effective weapon for the reason that its chief possible adversary and its chief friend have means far superior to its own . . . The French atomic force, from the very beginning of its establishment, will have the sombre and terrible capability of destroying in a few seconds millions and millions of men. This fact cannot fail to have at least some bearing on the interests of any possible aggressor."[35]

---

[30] *Le Monde,* January 10, 12, 1963.
[31] *Le Monde,* January 25, 1963.
[32] *Le Monde,* January 24, 1963.
[33] *Interavia,* August 1962, p. 965.
[34] Messmer, "French Military Establishment of Tomorrow."
[35] Service de Presse et d'Information, Ambassade de France, New York, Speeches and Press Conferences, No. 185.

But why a nuclear striking force for France and for France alone? The idea aroused strong opposition on several scores. It represented a wasteful allocation of scarce resources. Economic, technical, and scientific advances could be fostered more effectively by other programs. Although the country should certainly proceed with research and production related to peaceful uses of atomic energy, decisions to develop an atomic arsenal, far from contributing to this endeavor, actually delayed and distorted advances. The government's determination to acquire weapons as fast as possible must only compromise the ultimate national strength to be derived from diversified uses of atomic energy. A case in point was the uranium plant at Pierrelatte; its commitment to the nuclear arsenal was said to be impairing its value as long-run fuel producer and stimulator of more advanced research and production.[36]

At ruinous cost, critics maintained, France would obtain a feeble military instrument. Again Pierrelatte was Exhibit A. Called the "most complex and costly industrial installation ever built in France," its annual expenditures were expected to reach four and a half billion francs a year, "three times what has been foreseen and six times what has been announced."[37] Similar extrapolations applied to all parts of the nuclear weapons program. Continued sacrifices of conventional weapons would weaken French power without producing any compensating atomic strength. "A certain number of specialists and representatives of the high command," reported Jean Planchais, "believe a nuclear force of the type France could produce would represent more of a danger to the country than a protection."[38] Such had been the opinion of General Valluy. "It does not appear," he wrote in 1960, "that the French *force de frappe,* as envisaged, can be attained for several years and then only at a price beyond our normal resources."[39]

The experience of other countries, opponents continued, supported their contentions. The United States, they pointed out, was spending on missiles alone a sum equal to the entire French budget. The Ameri-

[36] L. Leprince-Ringuet in *Le Monde,* July 25, 1962.
[37] Nicolas Vichney in *Le Monde,* June 27, 1962.
[38] *Le Monde,* June 12–13, 1960.
[39] *Figaro,* October 15–16, 1960.

can outlay for nuclear weapons between 1950 and 1960 would match
the total French expenditures for fifteen years, even allowing a 20 percent margin for error. As for Great Britain, with a national defense budget 40 percent higher than France's, it was still forced to abandon element after element in its own nuclear arsenal.[40] Jules Moch pointed out
that one American laboratory, specializing in guidance and reporting
systems, itself employed 400 engineers and 4,000 technicians. In five
years this one laboratory would spend six times as much as France intended to spend on all its missiles. "No matter how competent our engineers are, isn't it a mockery to pretend to create the delivery system
of a deterrent weapon with means beyond our possibilities, with one-
tenth or less what the Americans have spent with success and the British without success?"[41]

The French vision of crossing a threshold and entering the select company in the atomic clubroom was illusory. France had a late start; to catch
up with the two nuclear giants was impossible. After weakening its conventional arms and drawing funds away from much needed social,
economic, and scientific projects, France would produce a nuclear force
falling further and further behind the United States', the Soviet Union's
and even Great Britain's. The small quantity of French bombs which
might be produced in 1970 would already have been obsolescent for at
least a decade. Delivery systems — planes or missiles — likewise would
be outmoded before they became operational. Land and air forces
would be vulnerable because of their relative concentration; the damage they could inflict would be large by conventional standards, but
minimal in the nuclear age. Submarines would be so few in number that
they also would present small threat to an opponent.

What potential enemy would be deterred by the belief that France
would actually use a force of this type? Instead of serving as a deterrent,
feeble French armament more likely would be a positive incentive to
a powerful aggressor to launch a surprise, pre-emptive attack. "Is it
reasonable," asked Daniel Dollfus, "to suppress almost all programs for
naval equipment, for armored divisions and artillery in order to permit

[40] Daniel Dollfus, *La force de frappe*, Paris, Julliard, 1960, pp. 25–43, 53–55.
[41] *Le Monde*, December 6, 1960.

the nation to have a striking force whose ineffectiveness and uselessness has been demonstrated?"[42] Dollfus' conclusions were unanimously approved by the Study Committee for the Republic, presided over by the Socialist Christian Pineau and with representatives from other parties and from workers, farmers, producers, cooperative organizations, and civil servants. So weak was the force that it was labelled by Jules Moch a "first strike," not a retaliatory force at all. "When a missile that flies 25,000 kilometers an hour is launched toward a target located at least 1,000 kilometers away," he told the Assembly, "the warning time is two minutes. You would not have time to get your reprisal force started. The *force de frappe* can only be offensive."[43]

In the view of the opposition the international price of a nuclear force was as ruinous as the domestic price. "In the matter of European defense," Premier Debré declared during the 1960 debate on the government's military program, "France has no lesson to learn from anyone, not even from a French deputy."[44] The obstinate refusal to learn or even to listen was exactly the point at issue. Gaullists seemed determined to flout world opinion by continuing tests in the Sahara, to wall the country off from its best allies, Great Britain and the United States, to weaken European unity on the continent itself, and to pull apart the North Atlantic Treaty Organization.

The time to put a stop to anachronistic nationalism was, some argued, before it got started. "If we today allow the *force de frappe* to be prepared in the same silence [as greeted the first French atomic explosion in the Sahara]," André Fabre-Luce wrote prophetically in 1959, "next year we shall feel obliged to defend it. How many errors have been made and aggravated in the name of this worthy sentiment! Let's break this vicious circle."[45] Three years later Daniel Dollfus was arguing the same thing. The deputies, he wrote, should refuse to appropriate more money for the Pierrelatte nuclear plant, even though the President had

---

[42] *Op. cit.,* p. 84.
[43] *Le Monde,* January 25, 1963. Minister of Armed Forces Pierre Messmer was inclined to debate the point, citing possibilities of constant air alerts and also atomic submarines.
[44] *L'Année Politique, 1960,* p. 106.
[45] *Le Monde,* December 5, 1959.

cleverly included financing for social and economic programs with his Pierrelatte request. Legislators were deceived if they thought it possible to separate the external from the internal manifestations of *grandeur*. While courageous deputies daring openly to oppose De Gaulle would be the object of special presidential wrath, the entire legislature was losing ground anyway, he argued, as De Gaulle trampled on all who stood between him and authoritarian rule.[46]

As Fabre-Luce and Dollfus had predicted, original opponents of the nuclear striking force found it progressively less realistic to argue that money requested should be directed to other purposes. The mere fact that so much had already been invested in the *force de frappe* made continuation, even at greatly increased cost, easier to accept than abandonment of the effort. Said Maurice Schumann, president of the National Assembly's Foreign Affairs Committee, in January 1963: "The French atomic effort is now more justified than in the era when a government of the Fourth Republic made the decision to undertake it."[47]

Opposition to De Gaulle's nuclear program came from three directions. Some Frenchmen were, quite simply, against any atomic arms program. Others had no objection to the program in itself, but quite logically concluded that it would reduce French concentration on Algerian affairs. Still others, like the MRP, were prepared to endorse a French-built force only if it were part of an integrated European defense system. Between 1960 and 1963, as the proposed nuclear arsenal came closer and closer to reality, the Algeria-firsters lost out. The alternative then was between a national and a European force; to say that the "Europeans" lost the battle with De Gaulle would be an understatement. Contradictions in their case, softness exploited by seemingly conciliatory nuances occasionally introduced into the discussion by government spokesmen, and the fragility of the platform from which they argued utterly routed the "Europeans."

The first engagement with Gaullist policy came in July 1960, when

[46] *Le Monde*, July 24, 1962. Dollfus' prognostication was accurate. De Gaulle, as discussed in a previous chapter, did indeed seek, and successfully so, to obtain a more docile parliament.
[47] *Le Monde*, January 17, 1963.

Premier Debré consented to inform the National Assembly of his government's domestic and foreign policy. By rules adopted under the Fifth Republic the Assembly was prevented from using the occasion to open a general debate; it was forced to select only one deputy to speak for all. Said Socialist Arthur Conte: "Europe will be integrated, or there will be no Europe. Our conception corresponds to our idea of national security. To reinforce it, and to lighten the burdens which weigh on working people, we much prefer a European striking force to a national striking force."[48] One might presume there was in the Assembly a "European" majority to force on De Gaulle a choice of integrated nuclear force or no force at all. But there were more battles to be fought.

In the Fall of 1960 the parliament debated for two months the Gaullist *loi-programme* to modernize the army, centering its fire on projects to produce nuclear armament. Speaking for the Assembly's Finance Committee, Henri Dorey of the MRP said France would be unable for years to fulfill its commitments to Western defense if the government had its way. "Deterrence is a poker [sic] game," he declared. Far less Gaullist than the Assembly, the Senate voted overwhelmingly to shelve the entire program until the legislature had approved an executive definition of the European and world policy it was planning to follow.[49]

Eighteen months after the *loi-programme* became law without specific legislative approval, "Europeans" launched their third, this time a double-barrelled, attack. In June 1962, it will be remembered, the MRP's secretary-general, René-Maurice Simonnet, mustered a majority of the Assembly for a "manifesto" demanding that France adopt a foreign policy based on "the methods and principles which have succeeded in the Common Market." When the government next requested more money for a number of items, including the nuclear power plant at Pierrelatte, the opposition, led by Henri Dorey, who was still special *rapporteur* on military credits for the Finance Committee, castigated a policy that would, by slighting conventional armaments, deliberately default on France's obligations to the Western European Union and to

---

[48] *L'Année Politique, 1960*, p. 526.
[49] *Ibid.*, pp. 106, 117.

NATO. The only solution to Pierrelatte was to make it a European, not purely a French, enterprise. "You call yourself a 'sincere European,' Monsieur Nader," said Mollet to the UNR deputy. "Believe me, the only answer . . . is Atlantic and European integration." The motion of censure declared: "This exclusively national *force de frappe* is condemned to remain a military illusion . . . Between the nuclear monopoly of the United States and the proliferation of national deterrent forces toward which the government's policy leads, there is room for a [European] community solution."

Outside the Assembly prominent Independent and one-time Premier Antoine Pinay expressed similar sentiments. Pinay had been Debré's Minister of Finance and Economic Affairs, but was ousted because of his objections to the government's economic policies and also to the derogatory remarks De Gaulle insisted on making about European unification. French representatives to the Western European Assembly meeting in December 1962 voted for a resolution which, in condemning the proliferation of nuclear arms, was clearly aimed at France. "The majority of Frenchmen are opposed" to the nuclear policy of the French government, Marius Moutet, Socialist Senator, reassured the European Assembly.[50]

"I do not know of a single [Gaullist] UNR deputy who campaigned [in the Assembly elections of November 1962] on the *force de frappe*," wrote Jean-Jacques Servan-Schreiber, himself an unsuccessful candidate. "On the contrary, I knew many who, confronted with insistent questions by voters on this enormous expense that mortgages the future, replied evasively . . ."[51] However, since De Gaulle did not choose to submit *this* issue to a referendum, there was little the people or their representatives could do. In 1960 the government program "passed" the legislature after three times confronting a hostile Assembly, after having been rejected by the Senate, and after having failed to obtain approval from Assembly-Senate conferences. It survived only because an absolute majority could not be found for any of three motions censuring the government. During 1962 a re-run of the same drama (bathos?)

[50] *Le Monde*, June 15, July 12, 13, 14, 18, December 6, 1962.
[51] *L'Express*, December 6, 1962.

presented a "European majority of the corridors," which fell apart when it returned to the floor of the National Assembly. The people could not be expected to comprehend complex military problems, concluded General Pierre M. Gallois, articulate advocate of the French nuclear force.[52]

Although arguments against the *force de frappe* may have had compelling appeal to Frenchmen from most parties and social levels, those favoring the national "deterrent" had the advantage of supporting the conviction and power of France's self-styled "guide." In considering the propositions advanced by various proponents one must bear in mind that some were designed for public consumption, others to weaken legislative opposition, and still others were shaped for the benefit of foreigners, especially the "Anglo-Saxons." Therefore, it is desirable to concentrate on the effects which official utterances had on the French domestic and international environment, rather than to attempt to disentangle "real" justifications from "propaganda" and both from the thinking of the one man whose opinion on the subject was determining.

One type of justification for the nuclear force deserves to be called "negative." Within this type the most disingenuous contention was that the Fifth Republic simply carried on where the Fourth Republic had left off.[53] The projected picture of President de Gaulle, quite ready to manipulate the Constitution or to alter its provisions, standing firm against the army and the OAS, yet withal so meek that in a matter of this magnitude he followed an imputed decision of the detested Fourth Republic, simply because that decision had already been made — such a picture is so distorted as to be unrecognizable.

Then there was the argument that France should get into the nuclear arms race because the spread of atomic weapons was inevitable. "Is it

---

[52] "Les sophismes de M. Macnamara (sic) et le départ du Général Norstad," *Revue de Défense Nationale,* October 1962, p. 1460.

[53] See "investiture" address by Premier Debré in January 1959; also, Raymond Aron in *Figaro,* November 14–15, 1959; Tournoux, *op. cit.,* p. 11. For the history of the French decision not to rule out the possibility of atomic armament (something quite different), see Bertrand Goldschmidt, "The French Atomic Energy Program," *Bulletin of the Atomic Scientists,* September 1962, pp. 39–43; Beaton, Maddox, *op. cit.,* pp. 81–98; George A. Kelly, "Political Background of the French A-Bomb," *Orbis,* Fall 1960, pp. 284–307.

right," asked Raymond Aron in a curiously ambivalent article specially tailored for an American audience, "that the Europeans should forever renounce possessing their own means of defense, when there is a possibility that ten years from now one or two states outside Europe may have acquired an atomic capability?"[54] A variation of the theme of inevitability was sounded by Jacques Vernant, head of the Center for Studies on Foreign Affairs. "In a sense, from the historical point of view," he wrote, "the realization of the French nuclear program is for France the liquidation of the aftermath of the war; it is the end of the postwar period."[55]

Related also was the proposition that no viable alternative existed. Adding to the fervor of the 1960 debate over the government's program was a report by a "Study Group for Strategic Problems," formed by members of the Center for Studies on Foreign Affairs. The report accomplished the not-inconsiderable feat of reconciling, in nine points, the views of veteran diplomat René Massigli, Generals Gallois, Gelée, Nicot, and Valluy, Controller General Genevey, and Vernant himself. Point six stated that a nuclear force integrated with NATO had never been proposed, that the United States and Great Britain would not abandon control of nuclear weapons to any third power, hence that "direction" of such weapons by a NATO commander would be purely symbolic. Point seven held that a "European" force would require "the existence of a federal state," and concluded that "it is not reasonable to subordinate production of French nuclear armament to the realization of a situation which will not occur in the near future."[56]

Finally, in the negative category was the rather plaintive plea that French science deserved to be rewarded with a panoply of nuclear weapons. The explosion of the first bomb had produced the fall-out of a "White Paper" lauding prewar accomplishments of French science

[54] "De Gaulle and Kennedy: the Nuclear Debate," *Atlantic*, August 1962, p. 36.
[55] "De l'entente française-allemande à l'armée nucléaire française," *Revue de Défense Nationale*, August–September 1962, p. 1388.
[56] Text in *Le Monde*, November 12, 1960. The last point stressed the need to reconcile in "this defense policy ... requirements of the indispensable allied solidarity ... and national imperatives." Asked "A.F." (André Fontaine) in a blandly worded footnote, "Hasn't this agreement been accomplished at the expense of realism?" (p. 14.)

and linking them to the successes of Anglo-American-Canadian nuclear efforts during World War II. In spite of its contributions, continued the White Paper, "France was completely isolated, kept ignorant of the important achievements made by the Anglo-Saxon countries under the stimulus of a gigantic war effort."[57] Anglo-Saxon desires for exclusiveness were nevertheless thwarted; the bomb had been built "by our experts and our technicians with no foreign aid, in less time than had been thought possible."[58] France could take its place proudly at the celebration in Chicago of the twentieth anniversary of the first nuclear chain reaction, offering the "unexpected spectacle of a French atomic exposition enclosed within the American exposition."[59]

President de Gaulle himself ignored most but not all the negative reasons for possessing an independent nuclear "deterrent." His views on European integration and NATO were no secret.[60] At his important press conference of January 14, 1963 the President declared that the "so-called" multilateral nuclear force advocated by the Anglo-Americans in their agreement on the Polaris submarine would place the weapons under an American commander, would leave most of American military power outside NATO, and would allow both the United States and Britain to recapture control when supreme national interests so required. More than three years earlier he had told officers at the Ecole Militaire: "The system that has been called 'integration' and that was inaugurated and even to a certain extent practiced after the great ordeals we have experienced, in a period when one might believe that the free world was confronted with an imminent and immeasurable menace and when we had not yet recovered our national personality — that system of integration has had its day."

His 1959 speech illustrates President de Gaulle's penchant for accentuating the positive. A nuclear force in France's hands would bring with it vast diplomatic advantages. The issue, in fact, was great-country or no-country. Without France's own nuclear armament, De Gaulle

---

[57] "France's First Atomic Explosion," English translation, pp. 3–5.
[58] Vernant, *op. cit.,* p. 1389.
[59] *Le Monde,* November 29, 1962.
[60] Their significance will be explored in a later chapter.

told the people of Chambéry, "we would no longer be a European power, a sovereign nation, but simply an integrated satellite." In a confidential letter to the central committee of the UNR, Debré is reported to have accused the United States of wishing to colonize Europe militarily.[61] Again, writing in *L'Echo de Touraine*, the former premier labelled the alternative to a national force "acceptance of status as a foreign protectorate" and "neutralism."[62] The appeal of such expressions to non-Gaullists and even anti-Gaullist nationalists was exemplified by the statement of Jacques Gagliardi. "My comrades and myself," he wrote, "passionately resisted the abandonment of Algeria. We nourish no excessive tenderness for the Chief of State . . . But De Gaulle for some years will constitute the only obstacle to the dilution of France in a vast Atlantic market where we will only be a subsidiary of the United States."[63]

With the bomb, however, France was leader of Western Europe, Gaullists argued. The only viable European system of defense was based on national cooperation, since integration was as undesirable as it was impossible. French atomic weapons, far from weakening the defense of the continent, would add greatly to it and therefore, rather than destroy the North Atlantic alliance, would make it more effective. This was the soothing syrup fed the Assembly when the opposition became too harsh. The suavest purveyor of this line was by all odds Foreign Minister Couve de Murville; indeed, opponents of De Gaulle found it hard to believe that this professional diplomat could harbor the same nationalistic sentiments as his chief. Europe, he told the deputies in June 1962, before the "European" majority walked out, "should have a defense policy. She should little by little become, in the heart of the Atlantic alliance, an equal partner of the United States of America. She should finally represent within the continent and toward the Soviet Union a stable element of equilibrium, and the creation of this equilibrium will thereby foreshadow the peaceful arrangement

[61] *L'Express*, July 26, 1962. We shall encounter the charge of attempted economic colonization later.
[62] *Le Monde*, July 14, 1962.
[63] *Le Monde's* "Libres opinions," November 29, 1962.

from the Atlantic to the Urals that must one day be defined."[64] "Never,"
said Premier Pompidou in defending the nuclear policy, which was now
"his," "has France felt herself so closely linked to this continent that is
Europe. This is the first fact on which you will have to reflect."[65]

The crux of the matter, of course, was the United States. France was,
could be, or would be an equal of Great Britain, but equality with the
United States was impossible to imagine. The United States had taken
"draconian measures . . . to preserve its monopoly of this power of apoc-
alyptic destruction and thereby impose a 'pax americana' on the
world."[66] Furthermore, the United States upset both the potential balance and entente between Great Britain and France by continually
discriminating against France in favor of Britain. With its own nuclear
force, however, France could both influence and escape the United
States. Americans, suggested Raymond Aron,[67] feared national nuclear
forces less than the development of several atomic strategies, each independent of the others. Since Europeans agreed on the need to define
and execute together one common strategy, the way was open for negotiation.

The Study Group for Strategic Problems in its eighth point supplemented Aron's view: An atomic armament would "make relations between France and the United States closer by removing the obstacle to
the tightening of those relations that the nuclear secret constitutes."
Then, reflecting some doubt that the American policy would in fact be
modified, the Study Group added, "France *is right* in thinking that the
sacrifices she has undergone to attain her nuclear armament will permit
her, like Great Britain, to benefit in her production of arms from the
scientific and technical aid of the United States."[68] The apprehension
of the Study Group was, of course, justified. "Everyone knows, I may
say in passing," De Gaulle told his press conference in January 1963,
"that this collaboration has never been proposed to us, and everyone

[64] *Le Monde,* June 15, 1962.
[65] *Le Monde,* November 6, 1962.
[66] Contre-Amiral Lepotier, "Pourquoi la 'force de frappe'?" *Revue de Défense
Nationale,* March 1960, p. 429.
[67] *Figaro,* June 20, 1962.
[68] *Le Monde,* November 12, 1960.

should know, in spite of what certain people relate, that we have never asked for it."

There was, perhaps, more cogency in the argument that a deterrent would move France away from, not closer to, the United States. To Walter Lippmann's claim that "little nuclear *forces de frappe*" could never be independent, the journal of the UNR replied: "The great European peoples, who are powerful peoples with enormous material resources and techniques, will never accept indefinite dependence on an ally whose interests are already not exactly the same as theirs and could become very different in the course of a future whose unfolding no one can predict."[69]

Specifically, continued the Gaullists, independent nuclear power would prevent another shameful capitulation such as France was forced to make over Suez.[70] "Only the possession of nuclear weapons can enable a modern army to avoid constituting a costly front obliged to give way before the least atomic blackmail," wrote General Charles Ailleret, the "father" of the French A-bomb.[71] North African troubles, said Admiral Lepotier, "would certainly have ceased as if by magic if our response to Nasser's forceful coup had been immediate and terrible."[72] Defense Minister Guillaumat told the Senate on December 3, 1959: "Nuclear intervention and national forces should be powerful enough to be feared at the international level, well enough equipped to be a sought-after contribution to a coalition, coherent enough, finally, to protect the *autonomy which will eventually permit [the nation] to act outside all organizations.*"[73]

Another area where American and French interests potentially diverged was, in the view of proponents of atomic armament, European defense itself. American disengagement was always a possibility, even a probability, they contended. Even if disengagement did not formally take place, there would certainly be occasions when the United States

[69] *Le Monde,* December 29, 1962.
[70] Britain, of course, drew the opposite conclusion.
[71] "De l'Euratom au programme atomique national," *Revue de Défense Nationale,* November 1956, p. 1321.
[72] "Pourquoi la 'force de frappe'?" p. 417.
[73] Quoted by *Revue de Défense Nationale,* February 1960, p. 363. Italics added.

and France would interpret threats to Western Europe in different ways, when the geographic position of the United States would cause it to place a relatively low priority on matters France considered related to its very survival. "The new strategic situation created by Soviet-American nuclear parity poses in new terms the problem of deterrence," declared the Study Group for Strategic Problems, most politely. "American cities are henceforth under the direct menace of Soviet missiles, as Soviet cities are under the direct menace of American missiles, with the result that recourse to nuclear force will end in the mutual annihilation of the two belligerents. Hence the guarantee that all members of the alliance draw from the existence of these arms in the arsenal of some of them is no longer absolute."[74]

Defense Minister Messmer, in an interview granted to *U. S. News and World Report*,[75] was somewhat more direct. The "balance of terror," he said, made it no longer possible to depend on the old NATO strategy of the shield and the sword. Therefore, the United States began to search for a more flexible strategy, and "it isn't surprising that certain Europeans started asking themselves questions. And some of them reached a conclusion that this change made it necessary for those countries with the capacity to create their own nuclear force. In that way they would be able to answer threats to their existence which the United States might interpret differently from them." Characteristically, De Gaulle was bluntest of all. "In these conditions [of possible, direct destruction] no one in the world, especially no one in America, can say if, where, when, how, to what extent American nuclear armament would be employed to defend Europe."[76]

If in a crisis the United States did "opt out," France must be able to undertake its own defense. One finally arrives at the claim that military protection is gained even by armament called by an English critic an "obsolete, semi-demi-credible 'deterrent.' "[77] Most brilliant expositor of "adjusted" or "small power" deterrence has been retired Air Force

[74] *Le Monde*, November 12, 1960.
[75] September 24, 1962, p. 72.
[76] Press Conference of January 14, 1963.
[77] Maunsell, *op. cit.*, p. 10.

General Pierre Gallois. It was not necessary, he argued, for a nation's nuclear striking force to be as large as that of a potential adversary. The Soviet Union would be deterred from attacking France if France could, in retaliation, inflict heavier damage on the Soviet Union than the USSR's estimated gain from its attack. Granted that the USSR could, if it wished, totally devastate France, any advantage in so doing would be more than offset by the partial destruction the French *force de frappe* would inflict in return. "Even with limited resources," General Gallois told the Royal Canadian Air Force Staff College, "France believes she can establish a balance between the value she represents to a potential aggressor and the 'quantity of destruction' she could inflict if she were totally threatened . . . It is their realization of this strange law of equality with inequality that impels the smaller nations to acquire or develop an atomic arsenal — although it may be limited and proportional to the stakes they represent or believe they represent."[78]

As with the Soviet or American force, what counted was the credibility of the deterrent. The Russians must believe that France would retaliate, that its nuclear striking force could do so, and with the power France claimed to possess. Soviet leaders must, in other words, make the same calculations of advantage versus cost which French leaders were making in building their atomic arsenal. The Russians then must be convinced of the capacity of the relatively small deterrent to survive a sudden, all-out attack, to leave the devastated country behind, penetrate Soviet defenses, and strike large population centers with accuracy. As Defense Minister Messmer frankly explained, concentrations of people were the only sensible targets for a nation seeking with a small force to deter a large potential enemy.[79]

Military logicians like General Gallois felt that the French force could in fact meet all the aforementioned standards. If such were indeed the case, De Gaulle's nuclear program would greatly assist in

[78] "French Views on a National Policy of Deterrence," *RCAF Staff College Journal*, 1960, pp. 26–27.
[79] *New York Times*, April 30, 1963, reporting an article by Messmer in the May 1963 issue of *Revue de Défense Nationale*.

holding the Western alliance together. Provided others, particularly the
United States, permitted, France could cooperate in research, development, and production of weapons, in strategies to fill the dangerous gap
between defense with conventional weapons and multi-megaton hydrogen bombs, secure in the knowledge that in the last resort France and
France alone could make the ultimate decision of its own life or death.[80]
General Gallois held the same opinion as UNR deputy Sanguinetti: the
defect in the military modernization program was that it did not go far
enough down the nuclear road.[81]

Other Gaullists reasoned similarly. Claude Delmas' article "La 'force
de frappe' nationale," which appeared in the Revue de Défense Nationale during the great debate of 1960,[82] is replete with "Gallois says"
and "Gallois likens." Like the General, Delmas bewailed the dangerous
ignorance of public opinion, which, by attacking the proposed nuclear
program, threatened to weaken the credibility of the desired deterrent. De Gaulle himself occasionally adopted the language of
small-power deterrence. At the end of his rejection of the Anglo-American proposal from the Bahamas, he said, "Besides, the atomic force
appropriate to it [France] has a certain efficacy and a measurable terror
even if it does not approach the maximum imaginable."[83]

For the most part, however, De Gaulle's position avoided reliance on
Gallois' most arguable thesis, that the Russians would believe a French
force could somehow survive their pre-emptive attack and, although
there was no longer a France to avenge, penetrate Soviet defenses to
exact disproportionate retaliation. Rather did the President's actions
appear to accord with ideas expressed by another air force general: "I

[80] For other Gallois presentations, see "Limitations des armes à grand pouvoir de
destruction," Revue de Défense Nationale, December 1956, pp. 1485–1497; "Lois
nouvelles, autres forces," La Nef, July–September 1961, pp. 79–97; "The New
Weapons and the French Military Policy," The Fifteen Nations, No. 19, n.d. (May
1961 ?), pp. 104–107.
[81] See Gallois' answer in Le Monde, August 11, 1962 to Leprince-Ringuets' attack, July 25, 1962 Le Monde, on the Pierrelatte power plant. M. Sanguinetti's
views were expressed during the debate in the National Assembly on the military
budget. Le Monde, January 25, 1963.
[82] October 1960, pp. 1549–1566.
[83] Le Monde, January 16, 1963.

could take five hours in enumerating the technical reasons that militate against a national *force de frappe*. After which I would conclude: nonetheless it is necessary from a political point of view to create this force."[84]

There were two important domestic considerations motivating the Fifth Republic's nuclear program. Not only was international recognition of France as a great power a part of his grand design, it was also indispensable if De Gaulle were to solve the great problem which has provided a theme for these chapters: the revolt of the army against himself and his regime. On November 23, 1961 at Strasbourg De Gaulle addressed some 2,000 officers.[85] Evoking the liberation of the city by French forces under General Leclerc, De Gaulle drew the lesson — just as he had done earlier in his memoirs — *national* policy needs a *national* army. "Resistant and combatant in the depths of her being, despite a momentary disaster and public surrenders that followed it, France saw her own force reappear to serve her and to serve only her. Thus, having lived through long centuries and great dramas, she knows that the Army should be only hers . . ." After the task they had performed "with courage and with honor" in Algeria, officers should renew their pride in a military establishment he was providing with new and most powerful weapons. "As appalling as are these means of destruction — and precisely because they are — a great State that does not possess them does not control its own destiny."

The various branches of the armed services had, in fact, already begun to absorb the message before the President drove it home at Strasbourg. The air force, concluded an analysis of the Barricades Revolt, had not concentrated all its thoughts on North Africa because it knew it was the arm of the future.[86] Sarcastically wrote "Lieutenant X" in 1961: "Those of us who stay in the army, the former killers of the fellagh, the former revolutionary apprentices, will listen very attentively to the lessons given by the technicians of thermo-nuclear war. They will teach us the use of missiles. That will be a great consolation to us.

[84] Quoted by Tournoux, *op. cit.*, p. 117.
[85] Military expert Jean Planchais commented on his talk: "In the long oratorical career of the former head of Free France, the Strasbourg speech certainly ranks among his most brilliant." *Le Monde*, November 25, 1961.
[86] Brombergers *et al.*, *op. cit.*, p. 71.

We didn't know how to beat several dozen fellagh. But the ministerial generals will teach us how to win the war against the Russians."[87] "I am convinced," said Colonel Gilles Anouil, "that his [De Gaulle's] aim in creating a national deterrent is as much for psychological reasons as for strategic and political ones. His purpose is obviously to appease and win over the military by giving them a really ambitious program which will demand all their energies — energies which might find an outlet elsewhere if allowed to go unused. To those of us who were afraid of a listless, boring life, he is offering brand-new techniques, enormous scientific toys, and a theory of war that is changing from day to day."[88]

For obvious reasons leaders of the Fifth Republic could not stress the military modernization program as a purchase price for the army's forgetting Algeria. Nor did they need to. Apparent to all was the shift in priority among the armed forces which the type of modernization being effected by De Gaulle entailed. The nature of vested interests and of actuarial prognoses was also readily apparent. No matter what their initial motivations and military education, more and more officers would find their careers dependent on positions in modernized units, while age, as well as distaste for the *nouvelle vague,* would remove at the other end of the hierarchy senior officers whose experience had been centered in colonial warfare.[89]

The first domestic concern was, then, the army. A second was the economy. Far from anticipating any danger in progressive militarization, Gaullist leadership planned enthusiastically to use various government programs as instruments for economic manipulation. Added to the *loi-programme* of 1960 was an article requiring the government to document the economic and social incidence of military expenditures and the part thereof which directly or indirectly benefited the civilian sector. Two primary examples of military impact on the economy were the aviation industry and atomic research. At first, it was reported, air-

[87] "Pourquois nous avons 'perdu' la guerre d'Algérie," p. 38.
[88] *Réalités,* February 1963, p. 24.
[89] General Valluy's previously cited critiques of new weapons and organization are an indication that modernization was beginning to have precisely the effects anticipated by Gaullists.

craft producers read the *loi-programme* as bad news, believing that part of the credits they normally might expect to receive would go instead to missile manufacturers.[90] In the short run, at least, they need not have worried. The government carried out an administrative re-organization, centralizing authority in the Chairman of the Ministerial Committee for Armaments, thus eliminating the supervisory responsibility of the Minister (Secretary) of State, or Ministerial Committee for Air. Aircraft was raised to an equal position with general armament construction, improving coordination among the various departments concerned, such as the Technical and Industrial Direction of the Air Force (DTI), the Direction of Studies and Arms Fabrication (DEFA), the Central Direction of Construction and Naval Armament (DCAN), the Direction of Explosives (Poudres), and the Direction of Military Applications of Atomic Energy (DAM).[91]

Official support was not confined to those plants producing components of military aircraft. Agreement was made with the British to produce a *Super-Caravelle* transport able to fly at twice the speed of sound. Each step in the planning of this commercial plane involved military participation. In fact, Sud-Aviation, builder of the original *Caravelle*, was said to be under "triple tutelage" of the government: by the Ministries of Finance, War, and Transport. When the head of the company, Georges Héreil, resigned in protest over Franco-British plans to rotate the chairmanship of the group supervising the construction of the *Super-Caravelle*, he was succeeded by General André Puget, formerly chief of staff of the Air Force.[92]

With government assistance an industry had developed whose prosperity depended in large part on sales of both military and civilian planes outside France. One reason for pushing ahead with France's own vertical take-off plane was the hope that buyers could be found for 1,200 to 1,300, enough to ensure the future of the industry to 1970.[93] M.

[90] Jean Planchais in *Le Monde*, July 16, 1960.
[91] Georges Février, "The French Industry's Program," *Interavia*, May 1961, p. 596.
[92] Jules Roy in *L'Express*, December 7, 1961, July 5, 1962; *Le Monde*, June 30, July 13, 1962.
[93] J. F. Simon in *Le Monde*, July 25, 1962.

Bonte, president of a national committee for the expansion of the aeronautical industry, reported to the Ministers of Finance, Armed Forces, Public Works and Transport that exports in 1961 had been a billion and a half francs. Exports for 1962 and 1963 were expected to be a billion francs. Half of the employees of the aeronautical industry, reported M. Bonte, worked for export. Clouds, however, were appearing on the horizon. Orders for the *Caravelle*, from the United States especially, had not been as large as expected; the United States might all but eliminate the market for the *Super-Caravelle* by producing a transport able to attain speeds of Mach 3; the British had projects for their own vertical take-off plane. And there were the missiles still to come. One reason for rejecting out-of-hand the Anglo-American overtures concerning Polaris missiles was the catastrophic effect they would have on the *Mirage IV* bomber series.[94]

Here, indeed, was a vicious circle. The Fifth Republic had stimulated the aircraft industry for military and economic purposes, but the very nationalism that had inspired increased production threatened to reduce foreign markets. An expanded industry, concentrated in fewer and fewer companies, was most probably heading for economic difficulties. By 1965, said M. Bonte, sales abroad might fall to half the estimated figure for 1963, itself one-third of the 1961 exports.[95] Changes within the aeronautical industry were urgently needed, Defense Minister Messmer told the National Assembly. "The aid of the State will be more than ever justified as this industry intensifies more resolutely its already important efforts at decentralization."[96]

One minister was charged with direction of "scientific research and atomic and space questions." Gaston Palewski used funds at his disposal to promote research in such areas as electronics, molecular chemistry, and engineering, as well as various aspects of atomic research. Assistance to private industrial research included guarantees against financial loss as a result of investments in this activity. In the nuclear and space programs cooperation with private groups represented addi-

[94] *Le Monde,* June 30, October 12, 1962; *L'Express,* December 27, 1962.
[95] *Le Monde,* October 12, 1962.
[96] *Le Monde,* June 25, 1962.

tional responsibilities. An estimated two-thirds of the 3.5-billion-franc atomic budget was directly linked to the government's military program. Nonetheless, it was the Fifth Republic's calculated policy to hand over funds and release technical information to commercial concerns, rather than to make the burgeoning atomic industry a national undertaking. Of the government support for the Pierrelatte nuclear power plant, for example, 90 percent went to private companies.

"Either you are going to die," the French Atomic Energy Commission is reported to have told industrial representatives, "or you are going to profit from the billions in business we propose to give you to place you on the international map." The choice was not difficult for them to make. Why is national defense the prime propellant of scientific and technical progress? a scientist asked. "Because in a society dominated by the power of money, only the military and its research are not submitted to the criteria of profit-making in the short- or medium-range."[97] As was already the case in other Western nations, "modern" industry in France was coming to be defined as military-related industry, and the health and progress of the economy was coming to depend on continued large national defense budgets.

Possession of atomic weapons "very probably permits the attainment of national defense while at the same time realizing tangible economies as compared to the costs of classical weapons systems," declared General Ailleret in 1956.[98] As any English or American student of the problem could have told the General, there were several defects in his forecast. In the atomic age national defense could be weakened or strengthened; it could hardly be "attained," particularly by a Western European country. Far from being cheaper, a nuclear arsenal, as France began to discover in 1963, was much more expensive than conventional armaments. The disparity in cost, furthermore, would become ever greater and at an accelerating rate.

Then there were the succeeding or missile generations to cope with.

[97] Michel Bosquet in L'Express, January 24, 1963. Also Nicolas Vichney in Le Monde, November 7, 1962; Combat, October 27–28, 1962; Le Monde, September 25, 1962, January 9, 12, 1963.
[98] Op. cit., p. 1321.

Although Gaullist leaders moved blithely toward the missile age, the experience of the United States and Great Britain should have been discouraging. Rich as it was, the United States, as it approached the period when missiles were to replace bombers, was forced to some painful re-examination of types, quality, and quantity of defense it could afford. Though France insisted that it did not aspire to nuclear armament comparable to that of the United States, its resources were so much less that it could not avoid severe financial problems. Seeking only a small deterrent to call its own, Great Britain, standing on the very threshold of the missile age, had to look deeply into the recesses of its pocketbook — with results that the Bahamas conference revealed for all who cared to see.[99]

The standard of nuclear living to which the Fifth Republic aspired demanded unsatisfactory choices. Some would be faced deliberately; others would come belatedly through postponement of positive action. As repeated complaints from the National Assembly indicated, parts of the modernization program for conventional armament were delayed or pushed aside altogether. Construction of new camps and arsenals was slow; procurement of various types of motor vehicles lagged; plans for some types of planes had to be scrapped. Authorities were also forced to select particular weapons systems from limited numbers of prototypes. Any competing systems left could then only be subjected to limited testing before options for production were made. Again for financial reasons, great pressures existed to retain weapons systems in the arsenal once they had finally reached the production pipeline. France was, therefore, pushed toward a pattern of continuous weapons systems at best (discontinuous at worst), instead of the overlapping, partially duplicative pattern which the Soviet Union and the United States had decided they could afford. "As regards atomic energy, we are in the race," Premier Debré had told the National Assembly. If he meant the race with the other nuclear powers, he was wrong. France was running in a race all by itself, and against itself.

The experience of other countries indicates that De Gaulle would have difficulty in slowing or re-directing French re-militarization, even

[99] There is nothing like acute financial pain to bring on an attack of conscience.

if he should wish to do so. Under the Fourth Republic the Four Year
Program for Economic Development could be planned without regard
to military requirements. Under the new dispensation the priority was
reversed, and the Program would in time become a supplement to
armament projects. The new army was to be substitute-father. State-
fostered arms production was to be educator, employer, decentralizer,
amalgamator, re-locator, urban renewer, not to mention bearer of
civilization's mushroom cloud to the Polynesians. Would these roles be
played as well as they would be if the actor had civilian welfare in
mind? There is little reason to posit an affirmative answer. For decades
authorities had wrestled with the problem of economic stagnation in
the southern half of France. A study made in 1962 showed that three
out of four French departments were still largely underdeveloped in-
dustrially. The location of military units, the flood of refugees from
Algeria, the requirements of military production — particularly as related to nuclear weapons and the urgency officially imparted to the effort — all would tend to increase the disparity already existing between
different sections of France.

France's position among Common Market countries illustrates the
painful dilemma of a nation caught between defensive requirements it
could never satisfactorily meet and a domestic economy recurrently
threatening to fall behind its continental competitors. Despite significant increases, especially from 1954 to 1960, France ranked fifth of the
Six in growth of gross national product over the decade 1952–1962.
French growth of 47 percent exceeded only that of Belgium and was
far behind the 80 percent increase recorded by its ally and rival West
Germany. *Le Monde's* economic commentator Gilbert Mathieu assigned the blame to France's relatively heavy arms costs. "It is certain
that a link can be established between the considerable weight of military expenses in France (and its weak investments) and the lighter defense charges of Germany (with heavy expenditures for equipment).
While Germany increased her national product about twice as quickly
as we did, she lowered her military expenditures from 5.5 percent to
3.6 percent of that national product. Our country, on the contrary,
whose expansion went less quickly, only reduced its defense costs from

6.9 percent to 5.5 percent of her national product. Funds available for equipment of the nation found themselves that much more limited. Today the statistics show the economic cost of this political choice."[100]

Equally significant was the interaction between De Gaulle's military program and his diplomatic design. A strengthened army, possessing nuclear weapons, was to serve the ideal of *grandeur* by making France once more leader of Western Europe, and, as such, a power on the world stage. To promote France's position on the continent, ties were cut with Great Britain and the United States. But the military foundation for national strength could only be delayed and enfeebled by narrowly nationalistic policies. As a part of modern technology, armament, particularly nuclearization, reached beyond frontiers. Consortiums were needed for research, still others for production. The final product, whatever its national label, was quite apt to require international marketing. Might it not soon be that the diplomatic design became the servant of the military program? De Gaulle's gamble that just so much cooperation and no more, among just so many states and no more, could be organized and controlled by his country and none other takes on new dimensions, which succeeding chapters will explore.

[100] *Le Monde*, February 10–11, 1963.

MILITARY MISSIONS—
THE MEANING OF
NATIONAL DEFENSE

Intellectual discipline lies in total intellectual adherence to the purposes of the Leader, to the goal he sets himself, to the general plan he establishes . . . — General Paul Ely

IN THE assignment of missions to the army the Fifth Republic was influenced by a number of considerations. The missions were in part designed to be transitional, taking account of the exit of the army from Algeria and the exit of French Africa from the Community. Simultaneously, military missions had to anticipate what it was hoped the army might be able to do when re-implanted in France and re-equipped. They thus were to depend heavily on the success of military modernization programs. In addition, the statement and substance of military assignments were both necessarily propagandistic in their appeal to an officer corps sullen or in clandestine revolt over De Gaulle's "abandonment" of the army's "one and only mission" — envelopment of Algeria. Propagandistic too in their attempt to reconcile the army's concern for shaping French society with civilian concern that military objectives not become dominant. Missions were of course framed to support Gaullist diplomacy: the relationships the President sought with his neighbors, his more distant trans-Channel and trans-Atlantic allies, and the Western alliance's adversary to the East. Finally, and given lowest priority by the government, military missions had to assume some relevancy to the nation's economic capacities, else the other purposes would be jeopardized.

A great nation must have great missions, military as well as diplomatic. A nation summoned to a leading role on the world stage must therefore have military missions which are both national in their exclusiveness and global in their inclusiveness. Ordinance 59-145, issued January 7, 1959 by the Fifth Republic, read in part: "The purpose of defense is to assure at all times, under all circumstances, and against all forms of aggression, the security and integrity of the territories as well as the life of the populations. Also it is founded on respect for alliances, treaties, and international agreements." Notwithstanding the ordinance, however, the official policy was at this time still focussed almost exclusively on French Algeria and the French Community. "The first mission falling to the military establishment," Defense Minister Guillaumat told the National Assembly in November 1959, "is the Algerian mission." Secondarily, he continued, there was Europe, to whose defense France in 1960 would assign the same forces as in 1959 – i.e., hardly any. Finally, there was protection of the Community.

Longer-range government intentions concerning missions were revealed toward the end of 1960 in the *loi-programme* submitted to parliament. "In the framework of its defense policy," ran its preamble, "the Government has determined for our armed forces, beyond the task of carrying through the pacification of Algeria, three essential missions: To defend national independence; to meet our responsibilities for defense in Africa and our obligations toward the Community; to meet our commitments for the defense of Europe and the free world." If one assumes that the words of the preamble were not haphazard, they impart the flavor of Gaullist military policy. "National independence" assumed first place, with Algerian pacification reduced to a dependent clause, whose phraseology implied a limited time span. Defense of Europe and the free world were regarded as "commitments," contrasting with "responsibilities" and "obligations" in Africa. The implied distinction was between single direction and leadership (tutelage?) in the Metropole and Africa and the duty to contribute some force to a multilateral alliance.

Nineteen-sixty saw both the Barricades Revolt and the abortive discussions at Melun with the Provisional Algerian Government. Nineteen sixty-one followed the same pattern: the Generals' Revolt and the suspended negotiations at Evian with representatives of the Provisional Algerian Government. Nonetheless, De Gaulle made great progress during 1961 in freeing his statecraft from the incubus. By November the President was outlining military missions to officers at Strasbourg as though the war had already been ended. "It was imperative," he said, "that our army never be defeated and that, on the contrary, it should everywhere and always control the field." With military control guaranteeing the "solution laid down by the Chief of State," namely "the right of the Algerians to manage their own affairs, leading in the end to the establishment of a sovereign state," the army could for the first time become an instrument for metropolitan defense. This was its first duty. "We find France once again threatened in body and soul. We find her in most terrible proximity to a totalitarian bloc that seeks to dominate and brandishes terrible weapons . . . Most certainly the Atlantic Alliance is absolutely necessary . . . But within this concert, this preparation, and this combining of efforts, France must retain for herself her will, her countenance, and her army."

Beyond maintaining France's territorial integrity, the army had responsibilities outside Europe. Contrary to bitter accusations by partisans of French Algeria, these responsibilities were not ending with the end of the war. The establishment of an Algerian peace was actually making their discharge possible for the first time. "As the relative distance between continents is constantly diminishing, there are no longer any dangers or conflicts, wherever they may be, that do not concern every world power and, thereby, France. What is more, in new ways adapted to this century, France is, as always, present and active overseas. The result is that her security, the assistance that she owes her allies, the aid that she is committed to furnish to her associates, may be called into question in any part of the world." General Challe, General Zeller, their followers, apologists, and many military analysts had presented the battle for Algeria as the most important aspect of the Western struggle against international communism. Success in the struggle against the East, De Gaulle was saying, must begin with national strength. From power in Europe came military protection of France's individual and collective Western interests on other continents.

Although a direct connection was denied,[1] the last months of the Algerian war brought governmental decisions which gave concrete meaning to the 1959 Ordinance, the preamble to the *loi-programme*, and official speeches such as that by De Gaulle at Strasbourg. Protection of national integrity emerged, quite logically, as two closely related but separable military missions, with overseas responsibilities constituting a third. First was *external* defense of France against military attack. To this mission were assigned forces then and in the future to be stationed in Germany and in the frontier areas of France. These forces, in turn, were divided into two categories. Under NATO control were two divisions of three brigades each. Behind this covering shield would be four divisions, also of three brigades each, as soon as re-deployment from Algeria was completed. While the four divisions were to remain under French control, the Supreme Allied Commander for Europe (SACEUR) could, said the government, count on them in his planning under the North Atlantic Treaty Organization.[2] All six divisions were to be modernized and supported by tactical and transport air units. In addition, and most important, support was to come from the notable *force de frappe* (when built). "Major instrument of governmental policy, freed from all external dependence but able to be employed in the framework of the alliance, it will be able to act at all times and in all places."[3]

The second mission involved in maintenance of national integrity was defense in depth of France itself, a responsibility named by the Fifth

[1] *Le Monde,* February 2, 1962.
[2] See interview of Defense Minister Messmer, *U. S. News and World Report,* September 24, 1962, p. 73.
[3] *Information Bulletin of the Armed Forces,* September 20, 1962, quoted in *Le Monde,* September 22, 1962.

Republic "Operational Defense of Territory." In principle each military region was to have a protecting brigade of combined forces adapted to its defense requirements, for example an Alpine brigade for the eighth region. In each subdivision was to be stationed an infantry company which could provide the core for expansion to regimental strength if required. Equipment would come for the most part from "existing stock." Special commands could be established for sensitive areas, and provision was made for schools to instruct specialized personnel needed by the various components of the combined forces. Air units, equipped with planes (missiles later) suitable for attacking intruding forces, were also to stress detection, communication, and aid to navigation. In addition to the strictly military forces, the gendarmerie was to be incorporated as an integral part of internal defense. Total peacetime manpower requirements were estimated at more than 700,000. Initially, emphasis was to be placed on developing an effective Operational Defense of Territory for the central region of France.

Both external and internal defense missions might, if necessary, receive support from forces officially earmarked for the third military assignment — intervention outside Europe. Scheduled for location in the third military region in the West and the fourth and fifth military regions in the Southeast of France were ground force units with means of transport by air or sea. The navy's role in overseas operations was to continue to be a large one. Modernization plans included a mobile, logistic base to compensate for the reduction in numbers and technical shortcomings of remaining bases outside France. All in all, the equivalent of one division was to provide the spearhead for the protection of French interests throughout the world, including cooperation with nations of the Community, toward which France had assumed special defense responsibilities.[4]

In terms of De Gaulle's foreign policy the mission of the army to defend the frontiers of France was by far the most significant. (To its implications the next chapter will be devoted.) But the configurations

[4] Missions and forces allocated to them are summarized in *Figaro*, February 26; *Le Monde*, February 27, September 22, 1962; by Col. E. J. Baude, *op. cit.*, pp. 1421–1422.

of the internal and overseas missions, which developed directly from De Gaulle's confrontation with the army over Algeria, provided the foundation and part of the motivation for the President's "grand design." These will now be examined.

For France, as for other Western nations, internal defense was not entirely, perhaps not even primarily, an objective which could be gained by military means. Success involved cooperation of the most intimate kind between military and civilian authorities. Planning for a bewildering variety of contingencies over a large geographic area entailed both centralization and decentralization of authority, assignment of responsibility among local, regional, and national officials representing practically all aspects of governmental activity, and stand-by machinery for mobilization of resources under what could only be foreseen as chaotic conditions. Since the survival of the entire population was potentially at stake, success also demanded the mutual respect and confidence of military forces, gendarmerie, police, and organized civilian groups. Any republican state would have difficulty in meeting the requisites for internal defense, but for the past quarter-century, at least, few had fallen so far short of the mark as France.

Whence came the threat; what forms might it take; what should be the order of priority among forces designed to meet it? In the seventeen postwar years four types of answer were given. After De Gaulle had resigned in protest at the reappearance of "the exclusive regime of parties," Communists, Socialists, and the MRP cooperated until 1947 in running the government. As befitted the era of "tripartism," internal defense took on a French-revolutionary coloration, but the threat could not, of course, be specified. "Everything leads us to the eminently democratic conception of the nation in arms," declared Defense Minister and Communist François Billoux. "There is only one way of assuring both local defense and maintenance of work: that is to prepare and organize in time of peace local security forces around the shop, the plant of the village, of the quarter. In becoming part of those forces, young people will be in that framework carrying out their military preparations . . . The population would thus be ready to intervene immediately against air-transported troops, detachments of parachutists, attempts at sabotage, and all other forms of hostile action. It would also be ready to carry on guerrilla activity behind enemy lines in case of total or partial occupation, for resistance to occupation should henceforth become a sacred duty for all."[5]

Emergence of the Soviet Union as the primary postwar enemy coincided with the imposed departure of the Communists from the French government into opposition. The succeeding executive coalition moved one notch to the Right, bringing the Radicals into partnership with the MRP and Socialists. Internal defense measures, when finally defined formally, reflected three years of violent protest by the extreme Left against, first, the Marshall Plan and then the North Atlantic Pact. On September 29, 1950 the government of René Pleven created a bureau of psychological action in the permanent secretariat of national defense. Defense zones were established, with civil-military staffs, and a general was named as inspector. In addition to regular military forces, the gendarmerie, the Republican Security Guard, a "territorial guard," and "regional battalions" were all to be involved in protecting the country. Regional battalions were to be composed of reservists from former military classes; the territorial guard, in addition, was to admit people who had not been eligible for military service. "Surface defense of the metropolitan territory," said Defense Minister Jules Moch, "includes the range of measures undertaken to assure the security of communications, struggle against foreign elements dropped, disembarked, or infiltrated, to oppose all attempt at sabotage, assure the maintenance of order."[6]

In formulation the design was grandiose, but there it stopped. The territorial guard and regional battalions could hardly be recruited without careful distinction among the French people themselves between loyal friend and potential foe. Prating loudly of class conflict while participating in Rightward-trending bourgeois governments, the Socialist Party was in no position to make such a distinction; and for all his use of troops to break miners' strikes, Jules Moch was still a Socialist. Nor could military participation be obtained, let alone an

[5] Quoted by Jean Planchais in *Le Monde*, October 13, 1962.
[6] *Ibid.*

228 De Gaulle and the French Army

acceptable division of military and civilian responsibility be drawn up. The army had no time for such diversions; it was off fighting in Indochina. What was left in Europe was a second "Luxembourg" army. To defend the Metropole most effectively this remainder, it was suggested, should be organized as guerrilla units of from 500 to 600 men. Dispersed, they could live close to the national soil of France and be able to confront the Russians, not with a ludicrously weak, entirely ineffective barrier to invasion, but with the prospect of perpetual, well-orchestrated, suitably equipped, underground resistance. "Intimately united with the Nation, [such an army] will save it or perish with it."[7]

Needless to say, neither the army as a whole nor its European segment was regrouped into guerrilla formations; instead colonial goals were pursued with increasing obsession. In metropolitan France coalition governments moved another step to the Right with the inclusion of former participants in De Gaulle's Rally of the French People (RPF). Attempting to placate elements determined to destroy the Fourth Republic, Socialist Guy Mollet capitulated to the mob in Algiers and, with fellow Socialist Christian Pineau, directed France's outrageous experiment in military aggression, the assault on Suez.

Another action of Mollet's government was a decree enlarging military responsibility for internal defense. The decree stated that in normal times authority would rest with the Minister of the Interior on the national level and with government representatives on the regional and departmental levels. But "after the declaration of the state of siege, this responsibility and this direction are to be transferred to military authority under conditions anticipated by the law of August 9, 1849." Regional representatives of the Government were to "hand over their powers to a general officer of combined forces and become his civilian aide." The scope of the army's power was also broadened by inserting the word "implanted" where the 1950 version read "foreign." In maneu-

---

[7] Colonel X, "Positions et propositions," *Esprit*, special issue: *Armée française?* May 1950, pp. 820, 829–832. Even greater coolness greeted George Kennan's later application of the same idea to general European defense. By 1957 NATO had become committed to doctrines of defense by nuclear weapons and to West German rearmament. See *Russia, the Atom and the West*, New York, Harper, 1958, pp. 63–65.

vers held in October 1957 the importance of the change in phraseology was demonstrated. The exercise posited guerrilla activity and "subversive strikes," in conjunction with an atomic attack. Official commentary, which was released to the public, defined the maintenance of order as "quieting social, economic, or political troubles, *preventive* or active intervention against the *eventual* accomplices of the foreign enemy."[8]

Cheered on by civilian extremists inside the last governments of the Fourth Republic, the army's psychological service began a hunt for *its* ideological enemies in France, as it had done in Algeria. In the process, social stability was undermined, democratic justice subverted, and human dignity violated. When, in May 1958, there was real need to place in operation a program of internal defense, the army could not be given the job. To have done so would have meant handing over the house of government to the termites. While the army was destroying the Fourth Republic and placing De Gaulle in power, Jules Moch, now Minister of the Interior, could not even count on the loyalty of the Republican Security Guard and the gendarmerie; and to have armed civilian militia units would have initiated civil war. Three years later, when Challe, Zeller, Salan, and Jouhaud attempted to eliminate De Gaulle in his turn, no one considered setting in motion the old system of internal defense.

Governments of the Fourth Republic showed themselves as incapable of dealing with the problem of internal defense as with the entire structure of national defense. Established plans were recurrently scrapped and new ones adopted, only to be ignored. The potential external enemy (the Soviet Union) was easy to identify; unfortunately the actual internal enemies of the state turned out to be extremists of the Right as well as of the Left. The Fourth Republic could not dictate meaningful cooperation between civilian and military officials on the local, departmental, regional, or national levels. It certainly was unable to insure civilian primacy in strategic policy-making. Nonetheless the Gaullist Fifth Republic, undeterred by the failures of its predecessor, set out to establish its own definitive system to protect the country from its internal enemies.

[8] Quoted by Jean Planchais, *Le Monde*, October 13, 1962. Italics added.

Decisions taken by the government in February 1962 reflected its awareness of the new circumstances which the nuclear age had brought to the problems of internal defense. No longer was there to be any distinction between military and interior zones, since the country as a whole was considered threatened. The threat itself was adjudged to be all of one piece, not nuclear and non-nuclear, military and subversive. Hence, the government concluded, Operational Defense of Territory should rely greatly on close cooperation with modernized military units formed for external protection. The Gaullist regime continued to recognize the need to provide in emergency situations for rapid and effective decentralization of responsibility, but it now placed greater emphasis on centralized planning and on the prevention of conditions which might endanger national security.[9]

Although the regions of France had to be provided with the capacity to act autonomously should communications with Paris suddenly be destroyed, the highly centralized administrative system maintained its peacetime directing authority. The national government also set out to re-instate civilian control, which the final internal defense plan of the Fourth Republic would have forfeited. Within the cabinet civilian responsibility was located in several offices. An inspector general was to be attached both to the Premier's office and to that of the Defense Minister. In addition, a senior civil servant was to serve under the Minister of the Interior. The inspector general was to have at his disposal a military staff whose members represented each of the three branches of the armed forces. In times of crisis he was to assist the chief of the general staff of national defense in matters of internal defense. The supervisory position of the Premier in both peace and war was thereby protected.

The official in the Ministry of the Interior was, like the Ministry itself, to direct and coordinate the defense work of geographic subdivisions. France was divided into six zones, comprising ten regions, each zone to have its own civilian and military officers. In the event of a crisis the civilian authority, representative of the Minister of the Interior, was not to hand over power officially to his military counter-

[9] *Le Monde*, February 2, 1962.

part. Rather was he to assume responsibility for meeting internal defense requirements as established by the local army commander.[10]

The end of the Algerian war provided an opportunity to hold three successive military maneuvers in a brief space of time, two by the army and air force, the other primarily by the navy. They were the first in France since 1958, and De Gaulle considered them so important that he attended all three.[11] The lead-off maneuver, entitled "Valmy," was essentially an exercise in carrying out the first military mission — to protect the frontiers of France. Directed by the ubiquitous General Massu, the schedule called for initial successes by the "red" invaders, but the arrival of General-President de Gaulle happily coincided with the triumphant counterattack by the defending "blue" forces.

"Assas," which directly followed "Valmy," posited an invasion of central France by hostile paratroops at the same time as "Valmy's" hypothetical attack against frontier defenses. It was a highly specialized test of concepts designed for Operational Defense of Territory. Fifteen teams of "foreign" commandos were supposed to destroy communications, after which a regiment of paratroops was to attempt to reduce local resistance. Defending groups were to spot and report the invaders, and then mobilized forces were to lead the successful resistance. Several types of forces were involved. Initial defense rested largely on the gendarmerie and the Republican Security Guard. Acting on their information, the nation-wide system for internal defense went into operation, supervising the assignments of air units, the mobilization of local military personnel, and the dispatch to the threatened zone of outside reinforcements, among which were included segments of forces designed for overseas intervention.[12]

Externally focussed or internally focussed, "Valmy" and "Assas" were

[10] Le Monde, February 26, October 13, December 4, 1962; Figaro, February 26, 1962. Both newspapers have maps showing internal defense regions and zones. Revue de Défense Nationale, November 1962, p. 1775, contains a list showing corresponding departments.

[11] In the process he left Pompidou with no one to receive his formal resignation after the National Assembly had censured his government.

[12] Jean Planchais in Le Monde, September 29, October 7–8, 13, 14–15, 16, 1962; Paul-Marie de la Gorce in France-Observateur, October 11, 1962; Georges Chaffard in Combat, October 19, 1962.

related in more than theoretical testing of military missions. One important purpose they shared was to make the army happy. The maneuvers followed a schedule which had been meticulously worked out so as to leave little to chance or accident. At the conclusion of "Valmy," "Assas," and the navy maneuver "Linnois," President de Gaulle congratulated Defense Minister Messmer on the "perfect organization and presentation of the various aspects [of the maneuvers] at which I was present." All troops — active and reserve, enlisted men and officers, ground, air, and naval forces — were saluted by the President for the "initiative" they had shown.[13] Inspector General Noiret agreed. After the "Valmy" exercise he said: "There has been much written about the uneasiness (*malaise*) of the French army, but I am pleased to think that whatever the anguish some have experienced, the quality of the armed services and their desire to serve are intact." He followed these words with a eulogy of General Massu.[14]

The maneuvers introduced the army to its new missions, hopefully demonstrating that they were equally if not more demanding than the single one of colonial combat. "Valmy" emphasized the *national* nature of the army's mission of external defense in positing the destruction of 70 percent of NATO's air forces and the withdrawal of the remainder to bases in France, Great Britain, and Italy. Prescribed limitations on the hypothetical nuclear attack in turn permitted the infiltration of the "reds" into central France, with which the "Assas" maneuver was concerned. Not only did the two exercises develop in a nuclear "environment," but new French equipment was brought into play wherever possible to point up the intention of the Fifth Republic to modernize all units, not just those associated with the prestige-laden *force de frappe*.

All the activity associated with the maneuvers was in itself of psychological significance. After their days of combat in Algeria, officers could see that they were not doomed to become mere paper-shufflers. "Valmy's" leader, paratroop General Jacques Massu, epitomized the vigorous leadership the Fifth Republic wished to associate with the new missions. The former Algiers commander also represented the incorpora-

13 Text in *Figaro*, October 18, 1962.
14 *Le Monde*, October 6, 1962.

tion of colonial units into forces located in Germany and in the Metropole. The maneuvers were thus a test of the success of redeployment.

Specific evaluation of "Assas" must begin with acknowledgment that it was a demonstration of Operational Defense of Territory, not a solution to the problem of internal defense. Certain technical defects were quickly noted. Air defense by both planes and missiles was obviously weak. Air transport of small groups was inadequate. Larger, heavier aircraft summoned from outside the infiltrated zone were tardy and had difficulty in locating assigned points. Likewise, initially alerted ground forces were slow in ferreting out "red" invaders; hostile commandos had a far easier time than was called for in the script. "Here is what we hope to be prepared to do in five years," was the most optimistic conclusion derived from a detailed analysis.[15]

A more fundamental judgment was made by General Valluy before the maneuvers even took place. "A territorial defense is being prepared against internal agitations and foreign parachutists," he wrote, "but against missiles — nothing! One has the slight impression that what is being prepared is the 'Army of yesterday.' "[16] This critic of the President's Algerian policy was asking him an embarrassing question: Do you really propose to defend *European* territory this way? Against the violent opposition of most professional officers, De Gaulle had decreed against colonial combat, which he found unproductive, insupportable, and unrelated to the exigencies of national defense. Colonial troops he had described as obsolescent, their mission the impossible one of preserving the "Algeria of papa." From this archaic battle he had summoned the army back to Europe, to continental defense (except for the one unit designed for overseas intervention) with modern weapons grouped around a purely French panoply of nuclear power. So be it. But if this were indeed the "real" world that the army was supposed to confront, what was it doing with infiltrated commandos, implanted saboteurs, parachuted guerrillas? Was it possible that De Gaulle was dreaming of another World War II, which France would this time win

[15] Georges Chaffard in *Combat*, October 19, 1962; see also Jean Planchais in *Le Monde*, October 16, 1962.
[16] "Réflexions sur l'armée de demain," p. 166.

by itself? At the very least, General Valluy implies, plans for Operational Defense of Territory would make sense only when the army was reconciled with the nation, restored to a status in society that wartime and postwar experiences had taken from it.[17]

On the level of civil-military relations, others raised a different set of questions. Although, as previously mentioned, an elaborate organization had been established to assure civilian direction, centralize authority, assign regional responsibility to teams of civilians and army officers, the "Assas" maneuver had been purely a military demonstration. Could it, therefore, be called a test of plans at all? Did Gaullist leadership envisage defense of the French population without involving the people? So obvious was the answer that some interesting off-stage noises were heard at the time of the exercise. *L'Express* claimed to have laid its hands on official, printed "instructions which explain the maneuvers and create the climate for them." That climate, *L'Express* reported, posited a general strike called by the CGT (Confédération Générale du Travail), subversive tracts, sabotage, *local* guerrilla forces, and clandestine radio broadcasts. "All the 'exercises' envisaged by [National Defense officials] rest on 'incidents' in France," wrote Claude Krief. "What is now admitted under the Operational Defense of Territory is the politicalization of the Army, which is engaged in this combat. A combat where election results, union action, street demonstrations will be 'military signs.' The idea of a *putsch* is outmoded, 'sectioning' (*quadrillage*) appears much more useful.[18] According to the texts of the General Staff itself this is one of the aspects of the reconversion of the Army that has been talked about since the end of the war in Algeria."[19]

Now, interestingly enough, "Assas" actually had none of the characteristics predicted by *L'Express*. Far from ascribing subversive acts to any groups, the maneuver, as Georges Chaffard pointed out in *Combat*,[20] carried the explicit hypothesis that "the population has been and remains completely loyal." Writing for a journal that could not be accused of militaristic or even Gaullist sentiments, Chaffard concluded

[17] *Ibid.* See also "Le nouveau duo," p. 491.
[18] The reference is to the envelopment of Algeria section by section.
[19] *L'Express*, October 4, 1962.
[20] October 22, 1962.

that the military command observed "perfect neutrality" regarding competing political and social groups throughout the entire exercise. It would appear that *L'Express* was wrong, spectacularly and totally wrong.

But not so fast. Whatever the specific misinformation contained in the "documents" it had laid its hands on, can one say *L'Express* was in error concerning the basic nature of the Problem? Though Chaffard had criticized *L'Express* (without naming it), he also found defects in the exercise, beyond the purely technical failures. "The clearest information one can draw from the 'Assas' maneuvers is the unsuitability of the forces for internal defense at the lowest echelon (subdivision or department) to fight guerrilla action." Instead of regular troops rushed in from outside, there should be local gendarmes and mobile companies. As it was, 11 of the 15 foreign commando groups were not even located. Gendarmes were not trained and lacked "imagination." The people themselves felt only faintly concerned. "The peasant who one evening thought he saw a plane flying above a neighboring forest or who came across two suspicious 'strangers' in the village square, wasn't going to ride his bicycle in the middle of the night five or six kilometers to brigade headquarters. He would await the next day and the daily round of the gendarmes . . . The worker in the urban industrial area would feel himself still less involved in the action, his feeling intensified because he was aware that the military authority distrusts him because he was recorded as voting Communist or as affiliated with the C.G.T."[21]

Chaffard has made *L'Express*'s thesis again relevant. "The error is probably to place Operational Defense of Territory in an exclusive hypothesis of a Soviet aggression instead of presenting it as a system to resist *all* aggression, leaving to the population the pleasure of filling in the 'blank' as they choose, inscribing according to the convictions of each the nationality of the eventual adversary. From the Chinese to the Germans, from 'perfidious Albion' to 'American imperialism,' without forgetting the Russians, there are enemies for all tastes, for all idiosyncracies, for all phobias."[22] Just so. How is it possible to plan internal

[21] *Combat*, October 19, 1962.
[22] *Ibid.*

defense without a vast espionage network, spying, not on the imputed Eastern enemy, but on the French people? Since the threat to the state comes from Left and Right, with a onetime leader of a Center party directing attempts to eliminate De Gaulle, should any section of the French political kaleidoscope be exempt from surveillance? Who should direct the operation to collect data on potential traitors? How could Operational Defense of Territory become operational without provoking civil war or militarizing society? The questions of 1947, of 1950, of 1956, of 1958, and of 1961 remained.

The mission of the army overseas was comprised of three parts. Some vestiges of empire lingered on after the loss of Algeria. There were areas which, in the constitutional referendum of 1958, had opted neither for status as French departments nor for membership in the Community. Bits of French territory scattered around the world — in the Western Hemisphere, Africa, Oceania, Antarctica — contained some 500,000 inhabitants. Four old possessions had chosen to remain French departments — Guiana, Guadeloupe, Martinique, and Réunion. Together their population was one million. Toward all these "far away and forgotten lands"[23] France presumably still bore at least theoretical responsibility for defense. Their size, population, and economic value were inconsequential compared to the support they gave to France's claim that it, like Great Britain, remained a colonial power whose direct interests existed in all quarters of the globe.[24]

A second part of France's overseas mission concerned Algeria. The Evian agreements of March 18, 1962 contained certain provisions for continued French military presence in Algeria during a transitional period. For five years air bases at Colomb-Béchar, Reggane, and In-Amguel were to remain in French hands. During the same period France was to retain landing rights at Bône and Boufarik. At the end of five years the first three bases were to revert to Algeria, with France still

23 Philippe Decraene in Le Monde, June 13, 1962.
24 While Algeria was disappearing from French control, the Press and Information Service of the French Embassy in the United States issued in English illustrated pamphlets describing each of France's territories in detail, not neglecting welfare efforts undertaken by the mother country.

possessing landing rights. The large base at Mers-El-Kébir was to be under French control for fifteen years. In addition to allowing these substantial facilities, the Provisional Algerian Government agreed that for five years France could continue "scientific experiments" at Reggane, Colomb-Béchar, and In-Ekkar. Some portions of the French army were also to remain in Algeria. For obvious psychological reasons the Provisional Algerian Government had wanted the number reduced to that present at the outbreak of the rebellion in 1954 — about 50,000 — but France had argued that to man its military facilities would require at least 120,000. Final arrangements called for a reduction to 80,000 by July 1, 1963.[25]

On January 1, 1962 there had been 441,346 French soldiers in Algeria. By the date of Algerian independence (July 1) the number had already been cut to 280,000. Regroupment from some 4,000 centers in French hands at the moment of cease-fire (March 18) took some time and produced the inevitable incidents and mutual recriminations. However, considering the conditions obtaining in Algeria — the struggle for power within the Provisional Government, bloody vengeance against some *harkis* and their families, the widespread efforts of the OAS to involve French forces in clashes with the Moslems — the exodus of the army must be called a model of swift efficiency. On January 1, 1963 only 144,192 troops remained, and the reduction to 80,000 was achieved on March 1, four months ahead of schedule.[26]

Bombs and bases, not troops, caused the trouble. Evianic euphoria inspired the French conclusion that "these arrangements . . . assure France of satisfactions many did not expect from a policy of negotiation and judged incompatible with the demands of Algerian nationalists. The general nature of the agreements gives the impression that the G.P.R.A. [Provisional Government] has perfectly understood — and admitted — the implications of a policy of cooperation in the military field as well as in the economic . . ."[27] But a year earlier there had been an ominous

[25] *Le Monde*, March 3, 1962.
[26] Defense Minister Messmer during debate on the military budget for 1963, *Le Monde*, January 25, 1963; also *Le Monde*, July 3, October 7–8, 1962.
[27] Alain Jacob in *Le Monde*, March 3, 1962.

sign of what even moderate North African nationalism could mean: Tunisian President Bourguiba provoked a bloody battle in his recurrent efforts to drive the French out of the military base complex at Bizerte. On the other side of Algeria the Moroccans, thanks in part to the United States, had dispossessed the French from military facilities and now sought to get rid of the inheriting Americans in their turn.

No sooner had Algeria become independent than the French government re-organized its command in this erstwhile territory prior to settling down to enjoy its five or fifteen years of rights to military bases.[28] Two months before the changes were announced, however, the Fifth Republic had acted in a manner best calculated to make the period of base rights far from enjoyable and quite possibly shorter than anticipated. One must conclude that De Gaulle anticipated what the Algerian reaction to a French atomic test would be, even though it was an underground one and was technically sanctioned by the vague phraseology of the Evian accords. Algerian leaders proceeded to broaden the issue from one of nuclear explosions to one of all French facilities on Algerian soil. In France to request more economic aid, Foreign Minister Mohammed Khemesti told *Le Monde:* "In our concern to promote optimum conditions for augmenting security and peace in the world, our policy of non-alignment regards the existence of foreign military bases as being an element potentially contrary to this objective of security and peace . . . The principle of their [the Evian agreements'] possible revision is virtually conceded; we do not exclude the revision of military clauses."[29]

As announced in May 1963, the Franco-Algerian agreement was silent on the subject of bases and bombs. It was reported, however, that France had undertaken not to hold any above-ground tests. Also, as the Algerians knew, France was embarking on plans to construct new facilities in far-off Oceania.[30] Whatever the short-range outcome, Algerians had reiterated a familiar point: nationalism, neutralism, Islamic unity, however defined, were all incompatible with the presence of any for-

<hr/>

[28] *Revue de Défense Nationale,* August–September 1962, pp. 1423–1424.
[29] *Le Monde,* November 30, 1962.
[30] *New York Times,* May 2, 1963; *L'Express,* March 21, 1963.

eign military bases, especially ones held by France. "Imagine for a moment that I personally am indifferent to these explosions," Premier Ben Bella said. "Do you believe that I can ignore the reactions of the Algerian people, the sentiments of the Arab and African nations, of all the countries of the in-between ["third"] world, and of the Eastern powers? Do you want me to let it be said our sovereignty is not complete and I let things be done in my own country and by foreigners that I condemn everywhere else?"[31]

In sub-Saharan Africa, also, nationalists opposed a protracted or significant French military presence. By creating the institution known as the Community, De Gaulle had attempted what none of the governments of the Fourth Republic had dared — to get a jump on the forces of nationalism by offering a special association with France that would look attractive but still fall short of complete separation and independence. As embodied in the Constitution of the Fifth Republic, "the area of the Community's competence includes foreign policy, defense, currency, common economic and financial policy, as well as policy concerning strategic raw materials."[32] All the countries of French Africa, save one, voted overwhelmingly to join the Community. The lone exception, Guinea, in effect ceased to exist, since it was excluded from De Gaulle's contemplation.

The French President led, as well as inspired, the Community, collectively and individually.[33] But he found, in Africa as in Algeria, that not even he could arrest nationalism short of its goal — formal independence. Scarcely had the institutions of the Community been officially established, when member chased after member to request recognition of full sovereignty. Not one to let constitutional niceties stand in the way of statecraft, the French Community President acceded to their pleas with individually negotiated agreements transferring to the separate states the powers initially assigned to the Community collectively. Under the provision of these agreements each country was to have its own armed forces, which France would assist in creating by

31 Jean David, interview, *L'Express*, April 11, 1963.
32 Article 78.
33 Articles 80, 81, 82.

supplying military matériel, by transferring nationals from the French to the new army, and by training officers and men. While each new nation expressly assumed responsibility for its own internal and external defense, it could ask for help from France, and it also agreed to participate in defense of the Community. France received the right to maintain and occupy certain specified military installations. Finally, arrangements were made for periodic review of military matters and for a permanent bilateral military committee.[34]

The process set in motion within French Africa by the military agreements was not much different from that which was to be initiated about a year later in Algeria. France released native recruits from its forces stationed in the various states and stopped recruitment. Those serving in French forces outside their country were returned. Notwithstanding the agreements, France either shut down facilities and reduced personnel on bases that it had been granted or handed the bases over completely to local jurisdiction. In Sénégal, for example, installations at Rufisque and Saint-Louis were surrendered; even the great naval base at Dakar was all but emptied. In the Ivory Coast Bouaké was turned over to national forces. Partial exceptions to the diminution of French military presence existed on the island of Madagascar, off the East coast of Africa, and sandy Mauritania, hardly more than an imprecisely defined piece of desert, but, for all that, coveted by its neighbors for the valuable mineral deposits supposedly located there. By the beginning of 1963 only 13,600 French troops remained in the former African territories. At the end of the decade France planned for a total of only 4,000 men, based in the Malagasy Republic, Djibouti (Somaliland), Chad, and Mauritania.[35]

In spite of the withdrawal of forces and facilities, one of the army's missions remained the defense of French and Community interests. Planes and ships were to be kept available so that France could bring specially designated troops from the Metropole to any threatened area

[34] The brief history of the Community is reviewed and the nature of the agreements set forth in Ambassade de France, Service de Presse et d'Information, *Community Affairs*, No. 13, New York.

[35] *Le Monde*, November 25–26, 1962; report to the National Assembly by M. Fosse in connection with the 1963 military budget, *Le Monde*, January 25, 1963.

around the globe. The third military maneuver of 1962 was an exercise to test the navy's ability to protect a convoy proceeding from Mers-El-Kébir to Toulon. Included in operation "Linnois" were the aircraft carrier *Clemenceau*, escort vessels, and some land-based planes. The maneuver helped support the navy's optimistic judgment that, unlike the ground forces and the air force, it required no reconversion or re-education to rid it of the Algerian infection. Provided that construction proceeded as scheduled, it would have a "powerful, multi-purpose, wisely articulated interventionary force . . . able to carry out all the missions which would fall to it in a major as well as a small war . . ."[36] That capacity to intervene in Africa would be an increasingly minor responsibility for the navy was indicated in the announcement that by 1965 elements of the fleet would have been transferred from Toulon to Brest and that in 1963 France would allocate only 800,000 francs ($160,000) to the naval base at Mers-El-Kébir, as compared with almost 4 million ($800,000) in 1962.[37] Like its sister services, the navy was being rapidly Europeanized.

In large part the purpose of positing a continuing overseas mission for the armed forces was to reduce their brooding over Algeria. Involving relatively few men, scarcely any of them from outside the Metropole, and requiring little matériel, the mission still offered a degree of psychic satisfaction. De Gaulle wished the army to believe, at least for a time, that the irreversible metamorphosis of empire had brought with it changes in the *means* of defense, but not in the *responsibility* for defense.

In 1961 a "senior officer" in Algeria suggested that emphasis on the military's role in underdeveloped countries would help bring the army back to "legality," meaning that it would end its plots to overthrow or assassinate De Gaulle. But what of long-range plans? Some believed the mission would continue indefinitely. In presenting his government's proposal to modernize the armed forces, Premier Debré certainly did not envisage the bill as part of a program to limit the scope of France's

36 *Revue de Défense Nationale*, November 1962, p. 1788; Jean Couvreur also describes maneuver "Linnois" in *Le Monde*, October 12, 1962.
37 *Le Monde*, February 12, 1963.

power. On the contrary, "if we wish to preserve our influence and keep the African states and Madagascar around us, we have a fundamental duty to make their leaders know that in critical hours they will find France at their side." It was also pointed out that De Gaulle and his military enemies had one view in common: NATO's strategy was only as good as its effectiveness in non-NATO areas of Africa and Asia, where colonial emancipation was creating opportunities for Communist advance. Behind the President's insistence that a Franco-Anglo-American triumvirate design the defense of Western interests throughout the world stood a battle-hardened infantry and first-class parachute corps far more suitable to allied action overseas than were overly mechanized, European, nuclear-trained formations.[38]

To others, however, it appeared that lasting military compensation for the loss of Algeria could come only from the army's reconciliation with the nation, and that this required the mission of internal defense. "For a quarter of a century," Louis Dullin wrote, "the French Army was used up, consumed in a desperate struggle to try to maintain certain bases of a conception of a world more than menaced . . . It was repeatedly told that it was participating in a titanic struggle which was shaking the world, that it was participating in the modern crusade against Marxism. It believed that the true, the only goal of that struggle must be the holding of all lines previously occupied . . . Our Army must be told that since the end of World War II it has fought rear-guard battles of yesterday's world, or better still advance-guard battles of today's world, which should take up the burden and follow up its action . . . And when one asks our young officers to revive moral values in our society, we must understand that they are also given the mission of protecting society and men against the dangerous inroads of technocracy that leads to the depersonalization of man."[39]

If the overseas mission was an unsatisfactory cure for the Algerian disease afflicting the army, Dullin's (and Valluy's) was worse than the

---

[38] F. O. Miksche, "Frankreich trumpft gegen England auf," *Aussenpolitik*, September 1959, pp. 557–570.

[39] *Op. cit.*, p. 83.

disease. Taken together with proposals on recruitment and training of a large standing army, acceptance of the full responsibility contained in the internal defense mission would invoke a militarization of French society, the wholesale abandonment of domestic freedoms. Fortunately, France's guide, although he deliberately weakened competing and antagonistic groups, held no brief for dictatorship. Thus the mission of internal defense remained largely a theoretical one. There remains to be considered the third, and final, military mission, the contribution of the army to De Gaulle's European statecraft.

C H A P T E R 9

IMPLICATIONS OF

GAULLIST STRATEGY

It is a fact, not only for the French, but for the Germans, that they have never done anything great, either from the national or the international point of view, without the military factor having an eminent part in it. — Charles de Gaulle to German officers, September 1962 as reported by Joseph Barry in the *New York Post*

PREVIOUS chapters have considered two of the three military missions Gaullist France envisaged for an army forced and cajoled into accepting the Fifth Republic. Neither "operational defense of territory" nor overseas commitments, it has been pointed out, could compare in importance to the third military mission — external protection of France on the continent of Europe. The first involved the dilemma of using a recently rebellious army as an instrument of social control; the second, even if Algeria were included, was becoming much less significant as erstwhile colonial territories defined sovereignty as the exclusion of foreign troops and bases.

In contrast, there was the continental military mission. The argument is not that the mission of protecting France from invasion was capable of being discharged under any and all circumstances. Still less is it that the nationalistic means chosen — aloofness from the allied coalition — and the priorities in military equipment assigned — nuclear weapons and delivery systems — increased French security. Rather have the configurations of the Fifth Republic's military policy in Western Europe been predicated on the need to provide substitute satisfactions for the professional army corps and the desirability of weaving that policy into the general pattern of national statecraft.

Just as he has had a clear view of his personal destiny, so has De Gaulle unequivocally envisaged the destiny of France. The increased strength and stubborn determination he brought to French statecraft have tended to obscure the degree to which his objectives in foreign affairs coincide with those of his political predecessors. They, too, had believed that France could become again a powerful nation, leading Western Europe. They, too, had come into conflict with France's two major Western allies, since Great Britain and the United States saw for France a small speaking part in the chorus. If the Anglo-Americans were to rewrite the play to accord with what they regarded as unwarranted presumptions by the French, their own prominent roles would suffer. Moreover, if major recasting did prove necessary, many Americans saw France's trans-Rhine neighbor and historic enemy as more appropriate for the third lead.

The Fifth Republic, however, pursued the goal of *grandeur* with greater flair and greater success than its forerunner. France, De Gaulle and his followers contended, was not just a country — a piece of real estate. It was a *nation*. One function of statecraft was to keep it so. The theme was repeated tirelessly: "France does not intend to lose her character," De Gaulle said at Grenoble. "In that alliance it is necessary that the nations, and especially our own, have their character, their armament, and their responsibilities." (Chambéry) "France should have once more her character and her soul. That is indispensable." (Thonon-les-Bains). To this end De Gaulle sought to build France's military and economic strength. Herein was found the intimate, reciprocal relationship between France and its army. The army made French nationhood possible. Conversely, because France was a nation, it must have its own army. Finally, the purpose of intra-European economic arrangements was to strengthen the national economy; economic capacity was not being created for the greater glory and independence of Western European institutions.

De Gaulle's emphasis on nation carried with it a special view of the world. International relations were just that: relations among nations, with individual states as the basic ingredients. For all the pretense by some members — particularly former colonies and the United States — the United Nations was only a device contrived by separate nations. France was perfectly within its right when it paid no attention to the "sensational speeches, blackmail, and worse menaces" that emanated from "tumultuous and scandalous sessions" of that "ridiculous forum."[1] Regional groupings, of course, had the same character: their value could only lie in the effectiveness with which allied cooperation assisted the participants.

In this world of old and new, dying and emerging nations, conflicts arising from competing statecrafts were a fact of life. No nation had a right to expect others to advance any but their own interests. If interests coincided, fine, but divergence was more normal, even among friends. While there might come a day when peace and harmony would prevail, pending the arrival of the millennium, we live, as De Gaulle has repeatedly declared, "in our time." "She [France] must become wedded to her times and adapt herself to the circumstances — hopeful but ruthless — that are re-shaping the world."[2] "Man 'limited by his nature' is 'infinite in his desires.' The world is thus full of opposing forces. Of course, wisdom has often succeeded in preventing these rivalries from degenerating into murderous conflicts. But the competition of efforts is the condition of life. Our country finds itself confronted today with this law of the species, as it has been for two thousand years."[3]

"Fairly great" describes De Gaulle's view of the relative strength of France. Only two countries, the Soviet Union and the United States, were of continental proportions, while France, which had at one time

---

[1] De Gaulle's speech at Chambéry and his April 11, 1961 press conference.
[2] December 20, 1960.
[3] May 31, 1960, following failure of the East-West "summit" conference.

been as strong as any nation on earth, now quite obviously, in and of itself, belonged to a second rank. The President stressed this realistic view in connection with his national nuclear program. "It is true that the weapons she [France] is building and which she can build will be only a very small fraction of what the others have built," he said in 1961, when announcing that, despite protests, atomic tests would continue in the Sahara. "It is a relatively modest force, it is true," he told his press conference a year later.

Nonetheless, military modernization, increasing economic power, and political transformation had made France the equal of any other state in the "fairly great" category. Specifically this meant equality with Great Britain and equality or superiority vis-à-vis West Germany. It was not British national capacities that led English leaders to act at times as though their country were stronger than France. Rather was it the memory of past greatness, surviving ever-green because of Great Britain's close association with the United States. In respect to West Germany, France, given unified direction, had nothing to fear. Policies begun by the Fourth Republic with the negative purpose of preventing another war between the two could now be directed toward positive partnership.

France, then, was European, continental in location if not in national scope. Its most intimate connections were with its European neighbors. To rise above its second-rank status and to confront on a basis of equality the two nations which were in themselves of continental dimensions, France needed the association of other European states. Since the nation was the only reality, an association that went so far as to submerge sovereign identity would be doomed to frustration and impotence. On the other hand, only through close partnership could Western European countries escape a dependency relationship with one or the other colossus; and dependency was not conducive to survival in a dangerous age, let alone to attainment of national interests. Of the potential European participants France alone was equipped to serve as leader, for West Germany suffered from legal, geographic, and political disabilities. France and only France had world-wide responsibilities. With the cooperation of other Western European countries, its power could be expanded to match its responsibilities. Because the purpose for which power was pursued was the peace and progress, not only of France, but of all its associates, no irremedial conflict need arise between the leader-guide and the followers.

Central to Gaullist thought was the position of France within the framework of Western defense. Here a distinction should be made between the North Atlantic Treaty *Organization* and the *alliance* its members had formed in 1949. The former was obsolescent, the latter as necessary as ever. In 1949 the world had been a bipolar one, dominated by the United States and the Soviet Union. The United States had posed a unilateral threat to the Russians through its monopoly, then, subsequently, its overwhelming superiority in nuclear weapons. In that era Western Europe was weak, recovering but slowly from the worst of its civil wars. Therefore, the presence of the Soviet Union in the heart of the continent had placed in great jeopardy separated, relatively small states still outside its orbit.

The Organization had developed from the exigencies of the time. Because only the United States could counter-balance the Soviet Union, the United States led, indeed controlled, the alliance. Since it was Western European survival which was at stake, the Organization was limited to Europe and to the military defense of its members. The nations of the continent, in view of the small military resources they then possessed, had perforce to place them in a pool at the disposal of the Organization. In contrast, most American and considerable British forces remained outside its purview. The result was an unequal, disparate commitment. The European states found themselves entirely involved in the structure of defense, while the United States, and to a lesser extent Great Britain, dominated the command system, without nearly the same degree of commitment.

Soon after he returned to power, De Gaulle began to argue that the Organization needed to be revised to bring it into line with the current, much more complex, international environment, one no longer adequately to be described as either bipolar or Europe-focussed. The nature of the Soviet threat had broadened in technique and in geography. Russian nuclear power could now threaten the United States directly and immediately. European security could be undermined by developments taking place great distances from the continent. Moreover, the nations of Western Europe, thanks in large part to American assistance, had recovered much of their former strength. To De Gaulle this meant that they were once again aware of their own character, of their own individuality, of the contribution it was possible for them to make to protect and advance their own interests. If the United States were realistic, he concluded, it would recognize these changes and welcome the gains made by Western European states. But whether it accepted the fact or not, the United States was now more limited in what it could do. In fewer areas was its voice controlling; in more areas was its diplomacy dependent on persuasion, not direction.

Behind the Organization lay the Treaty. It, too, was obsolescent and should be revised, as its terms provided. The Treaty, in turn, was but the capstone of the alliance, which De Gaulle continued to regard as crucial to France's and the West's survival. The alliance was nurtured by a network of bilateral and multilateral agreements which bound together the variegated positions, powers, and purposes of fifteen nations, stretching from Alaska to Ankara. The Treaty must be made flexible, like the overlapping, discontinuous, evanescent agreements themselves, else it and the Organization it created would become repositories of archives interesting the historian or, depressingly, the archeologist. To hold its members in their widely varying relationships with one another, the alliance, through whatever instruments it was expressed, must be multi-purpose, not exclusively military, must be world-wide, not just European in purview, and must be capable of equating status with differing responsibilities and national capacities.

Emphasis on the alliance, as against the Organization, accorded perfectly with Gaullist ideas concerning the nation as the basic international unit. His desires to strengthen the alliance were therefore consistent with measures which seemed to weaken NATO. In defending in October 1960 the government's military modernization bill, Premier Debré was pressed to outline his President's policy, yet again. His remarks resembled a lawyer's brief:

"First point: the Western Alliance must be maintained and developed. The Atlantic Pact is its legal and political form. Today as yesterday, this pact meets the fundamental requirements of world strategy. It is essential to the security of Europe and, consequently, of France. Does this mean it is perfect?

"First imperfection of the pact. It is considered only as a regional pact, whereas the Western Alliance . . . will be firm and lasting only if it expresses the solidarity of the free world all over the earth.

"Second imperfection: the political and strategic organization of the Alliance gives its partners roles which are too unequal. There is no question . . . that the political and material capabilities of the great American Republic give it privileged rights in the Alliance. But there are limits to inequality. The partners of the Atlantic Pact, especially those whose interests are complex, should have a greater share in directing its strategy; this is in the interests of the Alliance itself . . .

"We unhesitatingly proclaim our fidelity to the Alliance and our attachment to the principles of the pact, but we ask that — after the twelve years it has been in effect — certain problems should be re-examined. Should not the pact be extended to other regions? We answer 'yes, in the interest of the Alliance.' Should there not be a political 'head' at the top, while avoiding excessive inequalities and while permitting further agreements between the powers — our answer is again 'yes.'[4] Is it not necessary, while coordinating and while unifying, to leave certain responsibilities to the Governments of each country? Here, too, we say 'yes,' for the West is not like the Communist world, and the first evidence of a nation's freedom is for it to take part in its own defense; its responsible command must, therefore, have its share in the fundamental decisions. To express desires for reform, hopes of improvement, political directions — this is not to weaken Western solidarity."[5]

Along the way, Debré defended specific policies regarding the French fleet and the stationing on French soil of foreign-built atomic weapons, both of which had adversely affected the Organization. "What is the fleet?" De Gaulle had asked at his press conference the month before the Prime Minister spoke. "It is a means for remote action. And why imagine that France should leave this means for remote action at the discretion of an organization exclusively European, one which has nothing to do with Africa, while she herself, by her interests and responsibilities, is continually involved in Africa?"

[4] The reference is to the Franco-Anglo-American "triumvirate," proposed by De Gaulle in his memorandum of September 1958.

[5] English translation, Service de Presse et d'Information, Ambassade de France, New York, Speeches and Press Conferences, No. 156.

The placing of nuclear arms and their delivery systems was an even more important issue. If located on French soil, "these arms," said De Gaulle, "should be in her [France's] hands. Given the nature of these armaments and the consequences that their use could have, France obviously could not leave her own destiny and even her very life to the discretion of others." Debré followed De Gaulle's thought to the same conclusion reached by the President. "American atomic power," said the Premier, "is one of the fundamental guarantees of Western security. There is no doubt of this; but is it necessary, on that account, for the use of the atomic weapon, at all times, in all cases and for all purposes, to depend on a decision in which the other nations have not taken part?" A compelling reason for placing a political triumvirate at the head of a NATO broadened in scope was to give France a say in the use of any nuclear weapons by any Western power anywhere in the world.

Removal of French naval units in the Mediterranean from peacetime assignment to NATO, restriction to two divisions of ground forces under NATO command, temporary refusal to participate in coordinated air defense — these acts were all designed to underline Gaullist objections to what was called "integration." "It appears to us," said De Gaulle, "that the defense of a country, while naturally being combined with that of other countries, should have a national character." Debré told the National Assembly, "There is no concept which it is more necessary to analyze [than integration]. If it means close collaboration for defense and even a single command, if it leads to certain arrangements for armaments, studies, plans, and logistic organization, of course we are in favor of it. We give proof of this by the arrangements that we sign with other Governments. But must the French command, the French Government, the French Parliament abdicate all responsibility in the organization of defense? We do not think so, quite the contrary."

De Gaulle charged his opponents, foreign and domestic, with fashioning "integration" into a device for permanently down-grading the French army and France itself. Supporters of NATO replied that the French President pretended not to comprehend the actual meaning of the word when applied to Western defense and that he used it as a smokescreen behind which he concocted schemes for national aggrandizement. De Gaulle's insistence on an independent nuclear striking force was attributed to an archaic, futile wish to control the behavior of other states. These suspicions of Gaullist objectives lay behind the bitter two-year battle in the National Assembly against the government's atomic project. Before Debré was able to declare the enabling act passed in November 1960, he had felt constrained to accept a new article (which the legislators inserted as the first Article). "The defense policy of the Republic," Article A read in part, "is based on the decision to assure national independence and to reinforce the effectiveness of the alliances which guarantee the security of the free world." In the concluding paragraph the same goal was posited: "The object of the program laid down by the present law is notably to permit the Government to undertake, in concert with the allies of France, the common organizational effort necessary, as much from the point of view of political objects as of strategic means, for the defense of the free world."

Ironically, there was nothing in the phraseology which De Gaulle could not accept. His aim was an alliance re-shaped to his blueprint, one in which primary responsibility for decision and action would rest on close consultation among the United States, Britain, and France. Furthermore, use of the plural "alliances" in Article A fitted the President's conception of a Western system which encompassed several multi-national groupings.

Occupying a central place in the North Atlantic structure was the European bloc. De Gaulle's idea of the proper relationship among the Six (the Common Market countries) conflicted also with the desires of French "Europeans," to say nothing of partisans of "unification" in other countries. The issue was not whether there should be cooperation that went beyond the specific economic forms institutionalized in the Coal-Steel Community, the Common Market, and Euratom, but rather the organizational form further cooperation should assume. "If the Atlantic alliance is at the present time necessary for the security of France and other free people of our old continent," said De Gaulle, "they should, in the shelter of this shield, organize for common power and development . . . They will rediscover that *grandeur*, the genius and habit for which past centuries have given them."

"Europe," Foreign Minister Couve de Murville told the National Assembly, "should also organize itself and unite [in addition to the economic field] in the monetary field, the cultural field, perhaps in the field of defense, finally and certainly in the political field . . . The basic point remains . . . the political problem. It opened last year when we met with our partners to organize regular meetings of Foreign Ministers to discuss together international problems. If one wishes to be realistic and thus effective, the basis of our action should be an active cooperation among States, therefore among governments."

Since Gaullists and "Europeans" alike wanted closer relations among the continental countries, how did it happen that by January 1963 — four years after Debré's installation as Premier and almost three years after the statements just quoted — all that had emerged was a Franco-German treaty, whose clauses in themselves meant little? As Couve de Murville said, the heart of the matter was the form of political cooperation to be institutionalized. At such international gatherings as the Council of Europe and sessions of NATO Parliamentarians, time-hallowed proposals for a popularly elected Assembly were dusted off. Gaullists' reaction was "what's the use?" "I don't see what would be added by the election of an Assembly by universal suffrage," said Debré, as he emphasized the need for executive organization.

In contrast, proponents of European unification made much of the three international, technical, economic directorates. From their origin they were designed to operate in the interest of the three respective "Communities," not for individual governments, just as the Communities themselves were economic means toward a political end. "The integration of economic and social aspects of the policy of the member States was desired by the Treaty of Rome [creating the Common Market] as a means of accomplishing the political unity of Europe," declared the Executive Commission of the Common Market in 1962. In a direct reference to De Gaulle's ideas the Commission added, "No extension of integration to new fields (defense, culture, non-economic aspects of foreign affairs) should have the effect of placing in danger or weakening the foundation, functioning, dynamism, and development of the existing communities..."[6]

Well might these agencies protest, for cutting the Communities and their directorates down to size was exactly what De Gaulle had in mind. He argued that their ostensibly technical decisions were in reality political. "It is a political action when tariffs are dealt with in common, when coal-mining areas are converted, when wages and social welfare funds are made the same in the six states, when each state allows workers from the five other states to settle in its territory, when decrees are consequently taken, and when Parliament is asked to vote necessary laws, funds, and sanctions."[7] Decisions of "High Authorities" or "Executive Commissions," therefore, had no legitimacy unless and until they had been accepted by the states. "It is true that one has been able to set up certain organisms more or less supra-national, but they do not have, they cannot have any authority and consequently any political effectiveness."[8]

De Gaulle's conviction that irresponsible international "technocrats" must be made subordinate to responsible national governments was illustrated by the fate of Etienne Hirsch, the French head of Euratom's Commission. Addressing the European Parliamentary Assembly, Hirsch had made bold to say: "The German president of the European Economic Commission is not in the service of Germany; the Italian president of the Coal-Steel Community is not in the service of Italy; the French president of Euratom is not in the service of France ... In all cases I was conscious of defending at one and the same time the interests of the Community and the *true* interest of France." In a sarcastic allusion to Premier Debré's formula of a "Europe of countries," Hirsch concluded by asking where the sixty sovereign nations that Julius Caesar had found in Gaul were now. Hirsch was not nominated for a second term; in his place France proposed (and the other governments ac-

[6] *Combat,* October 30, 1962.
[7] Sixth Press Conference, May 15, 1962.
[8] Third Press Conference, September 5, 1960.

cepted) Pierre Chatenet, not an expert on atomic matters, but a lawyer and former Minister of the Interior.[9]

To "European" ideas of a unified political executive De Gaulle answered, in effect, "utopian illusion." "You see, when one's mind dwells on matters of great import," he said, "it is pleasant to dream of the marvelous lamp that Aladdin had only to rub in order to soar above the real. But there is no magic formula that will make it possible to build something as difficult as a united Europe. Thus, let us place reality at the basis of the edifice, and, when we shall have completed the work, that will be time for us to lull ourselves to sleep with tales from *The Thousand and One Nights.*"[10]

In place of utopian illusion, De Gaulle proposed agreement by the Six to regular consultations by appropriate representatives, including the heads of state, in the fields of foreign, cultural, economic, and defense policies, with permanent secretariats to organize the consultations and supervise the implementation of decisions reached. In November 1961 a committee of experts, under the chairmanship of Christian Fouchet, produced a draft treaty, after working almost a year in the stormy political climate of the Six. The treaty provided for an indissoluble Union, whose institutions were to be a Council, the European Parliamentary Assembly, and the European Political Commission. The Council was to be composed of the heads of state or the foreign ministers and could make binding decisions by a unanimous vote. Like the Assembly of the Council of Europe, the Union's parliamentary body could ask questions of or send recommendations to the Council, which would be obligated to tell what it had decided to do with these *billets-doux* and would also report annually to the Assembly. The Political Commission was designed as a secretariat, whose members were to be senior officials of the six foreign services. Open to adherence by other participants in the Council of Europe (meaning Great Britain), the treaty was to be revised after three years with a view to moving still further toward political unification.[11]

---

[9] *L'Année Politique, 1961,* pp. 626–627.

[10] Replying to a question concerning Paul-Henri Spaak's opposition to French proposals for European cooperation. Sixth Press Conference, May 15, 1962.

[11] Text in the London *Times,* December 1, 1961.

The fate of the Fouchet draft was exactly the same as that met by the proposed European Political Community Treaty eight years earlier — an unquiet grave. "Europeans" in other countries were caught in the same dilemma as De Gaulle's domestic opponents. During the negotiations the French had proposed to reduce in importance all three Communities and their Executive Commissions. Moreover, there was no provision for universal election of a common assembly or for a unified political authority. The text emanating from the Fouchet group did not go very far toward satisfying proponents of unification on these points. On the other hand, French representatives had wished to enlarge the competence of European institutions to include military matters. The draft treaty had specifically mentioned among the aims of the Union, "To reinforce, in cooperation with other free nations, the security of member states against any aggression by means of a common defense policy." The value of the subsidiary phrase was eliminated by the last three words. France's partners feared that De Gaulle sought an autonomous, continental, military grouping that would support, at NATO's expense, his views concerning the proper form of the alliance and the proper position of France therein.

Hence the dilemma of the "Europeans." They favored a political union which Great Britain had frequently stated it could not join, but they equally favored British admission to the Common Market, an institution which they wanted to keep strong as a firm foundation for their political union. They wished more matters to be settled by supranational organs, yet they equally wished to except issues of defense, where the looser, more broadly based Atlantic alliance should, they believed, remain paramount.

De Gaulle saw no reason to concede a thing to inconsistencies of this sort. For all its timidity, he found the Fouchet draft objectionable and unnecessary. Early in 1962 French representatives therefore proposed a "substitute," which in essence reverted to the President's original ideas of separately organized cooperation in each functional field, including the political and military. Seeking to move forward, Europeans now found themselves thrust backward. Crying betrayal, they rejected the newest version of the "Europe of countries," whereupon De Gaulle turned to the one nation he regarded as fundamental to his own design

— West Germany. Following the annihilation of the "European major-ity" in the French elections of November 1962, he felt the time was propitious to sign a formal Franco-German agreement.

The modern rapprochement between the two countries, like many other aspects of De Gaulle's European policy, dated from the Fourth Republic. Its line of origin may be traced through Foreign Minister Robert Schuman's proposal for a Coal-Steel Community to reluctant French acceptance of Germany's participation in the Council of Europe. Not until 1954, however, when France ran out of devices for preventing German rearmament, did bilateral cooperation between the two coun-tries move into high gear. Joint military exercises were held in West Germany and France. While most NATO members were raising a furor over German efforts to obtain bases in other countries, including Spain, France quietly made some of its own territory available. Agreements were signed for the exchange of officers, for the trial integration of military units, for common manufacture of numerous weapons, includ-ing heavy helicopters and vertical take-off planes. Against opposition within his own government, Adenauer accepted French interpretations of the timing and types of moves toward full implementation of the Treaty of Rome.

On two major issues potential conflict existed between France and Germany. Adenauer was a partisan of British entry into the Economic Community. Also, the elderly German leader explicitly espoused a North Atlantic Treaty Organization, which was anathema to De Gaulle. "It is impossible," Adenauer told the Foreign Press Association of Bonn in November 1960, "to let the Atlantic alliance dissolve into a coalition of national armies. Military integration can never go too far. It was normal that the United States took the lead of the Atlantic Organization when they were the only ones to possess atomic arms; it remains no less normal that they keep this position of leadership today."[12]

However, serious as were the general points on which Adenauer and De Gaulle did not see eye to eye, the two dominating leaders had formed the habit of frequent personal meetings to reassure each other of their respective intentions, reinforce their mutual interests, and re-

[12] *L'Année Politique, 1960*, p. 577.

new *quid pro quos*. It was natural that one such exchange of visits
should follow the rejection by France's partners of De Gaulle's alternative to the Fouchet draft treaty. Adenauer helped prepare the ground
for a special Franco-German arrangement as preliminary to any general
Western European political association. "I lay great value on the need
for close friendship between Germany and France, and I have done so
since 1925," he said in June 1962. "That was my wish, stemming from
history, and from my desire that we achieve a united Europe. But a
united Europe cannot exist unless France and Germany are real friends,
and that is our aim."[13] On his tour of Germany in the Fall, De Gaulle
deliberately cast himself in the role of popular spellbinder. Ignoring
reactions he might arouse elsewhere, including those among his own
French supporters, he wooed the Germans as workers, as nationalists,
even as militarists. He won an immense personal triumph.[14] In the out-
pouring of affection German doubts concerning French statecraft and
the wisdom of a purely bilateral tie were swept away. President Luebke
stated De Gaulle's policy as clearly as the French leader ever had: "The
alliance of the free world, the reciprocal commitment of Europe and
America can only preserve its confidence and solidarity in the long run
if there exists on the old continent a center of power and prosperity
akin to that represented by the United States in the New World."[15]

Events then moved rapidly. France made specific proposals to Germany in October. A tentative, affirmative reply in November was followed by more specific German acceptance in December, after the
Chancellor had digested the results of the French National Assembly
elections. On January 22, 1963 the agreement was signed, at Adenauer's
request, in the form of a treaty. Its terms were a virtual replica of De
Gaulle's repeated suggestions for arrangements among the Six. Heads
of state and government were to meet "each time that it will be neces-

[13] *New York Times,* June 2, 1962.
[14] De Gaulle entered Munich as a king, reported *L'Express* (September 18, 1962),
which went on to remark how courteously De Gaulle had received the German
government on German soil. "Daily German life will never be quite the same
again," concluded a German newspaper (as quoted by P.T. in *Esprit,* October
1962, p. 503).
[15] *Esprit,* October 1962, p. 504.

sary, and in principle at least twice a year." Regular reunions were also to take place between the ministers of foreign affairs, education, youth, and defense. Supplementing meetings of defense ministers were to be conferences by the military chiefs of staff every two months. Diplomats were responsible for preparing the various meetings, while ministerial committees in both France and Germany were to follow the progress of bi-national cooperation.

So much for what was grandiosely called "Organization." A second section listed objectives in the fields of foreign affairs, defense, education, and youth, the first two being the most important. In foreign affairs the goal was no less than a common position on such matters as the European Communities, East-West relations, aid to underdeveloped nations, and topics coming before multilateral organizations, including NATO, WEU, OECD, the UN, its specialized agencies, and the Council of Europe. Defense cooperation was to aim at a common military doctrine. Franco-German institutes for "operational research" were to be created, military personnel and military units exchanged, common production of equipment planned; even civil defense was to be studied.[16]

While the treaty was being signed, agreements on military cooperation were being reached in what was described as a "very friendly atmosphere." German troops were to train at French bases, as they had been doing since the agreement of October 25, 1960. More officers were to be exchanged back and forth, and naval cooperation was to get under way. Beginning in 1963 French and German staff officers were to be graduated together after completing a common "theoretical and at the same time practical" curriculum at higher defense institutes. Once again mention was made of joint manufacture of the *Frelon* helicopter and the *Transall* transport, of German production under license of the *Alouette* helicopter, the Nord-Atlas transport, the *Fouga Magister* trainer, and anti-tank weapons, and of German participation in the construction of the NATO aerial refueling plane *Breguet-Atlantic*.[17]

Officials wished it understood that the Franco-German Cooperation

[16] Text of the Treaty in *Le Monde*, January 24, 1963.
[17] *Ibid.*

Treaty did not imply any lessening of an *ad hoc* cooperation already taking place or in prospect with other countries. "It goes without saying," President de Gaulle told his press conference a week before the treaty was signed, "that there is nothing there that either resembles or tends toward the building between Germany and France of any kind of exclusive community . . . But it is true that in tightening their cooperation, Germany and France are providing an example which may be useful in the cooperation of all." The lesson was, of course, that no wedge could now be driven between France and Germany, at least while De Gaulle and Adenauer held power. That went for the United States on issues of Western defense. It went for the Benelux countries and Italy on questions related to the unification of Europe. And it went for Great Britain — closely aligned to both the United States and Benelux — on its application to "join" the European Economic Community.

In the Gaullist view, therefore, the logical shape of the North Atlantic alliance was the United States on the one hand and a continental grouping on the other, with France providing the bridge between. This symmetry was marred, however, by the enigmatic position of Great Britain. Did Britain belong inside or outside the continent? Since World War II the unsatisfactory answer British governments had given was "yes." Fourth Republic or Fifth, Socialist or Gaullist, France could hardly be satisfied with so ambiguous a statement. For the attraction and the repulsion of Britain were both strong. As a participant in continental affairs, the cross-Channel ally could balance a potentially powerful and irredentist West Germany. Because it had no desire to be shut up in a small black box ("little" Europe) with the Germans, the French Socialist Party had made British association with the European Defense Community a condition of its support. Yet later, during the four-year discussion of Great Britain's relationship to the Common Market, the English preference seemed to be for an Anglo-German, not an Anglo-French, duo. Nor would a shift from Conservative to Labor control affect British attitudes. Considering its past position on the Coal-Steel Community, Labor, for all its Socialist cant, would feel more affinity for the relatively capitalist form of German economic organization than for the relatively state-directed French system. So France feared, at least.

Relations among the Atlantic trio were just as difficult to predict. A Britain closely tied to France could provide the latter entrée to the United States, could present to the powerful but somewhat naive newcomer on the world scene viewpoints derived from continental wisdom. At the same time, an Anglo-French entente could protect the two against unreasonable demands and irrational policies of the trans-Atlantic ally. Thus, whenever France had difficulties with the United States and saw that Great Britain was in similar straits, Paris hoped for closer accord with London. Yet things never seemed to work out that way for very long. On close contact Great Britain usually shied away from Europe. There was no evidence of any English desire for an Anglo-French partnership of defiance toward the United States. In fact, Britain did not appear to be a strong advocate of continental points of view before its Washington auditors.

Forced to choose, the British time and again assigned first priority to harmony with the United States. After the French Assembly had buried the European Defense Community, it was Anthony Eden who came up with the formula to accomplish the American purpose of rearming the Germans. With victory at Suez in their hands, the British had capitulated to American frowns, breaking asunder the closest association of France and Great Britain since 1939. Worse, London and Washington had proceeded to work quickly to repair Anglo-Saxon ties within the Western alliance, leaving France, with a basketful of aspirations, standing outside the locked tradesmen's entrance.

Having had his own experiences with the English and Americans, De Gaulle could only regard the latest British approach to the continent as having promising possibilities, but ones on which it would be unwise to bet very much. In its second overture to the European Economic Community Great Britain had asked to discuss the conditions of membership. Presumably this meant belated acknowledgment that the Common Market could not be pulled apart by such devices as the Free Trade Area. With a decelerating growth rate relative to the Community, Britain faced the prospect of serious difficulties when the Six agreed on their external trade barriers. "If you can't lick 'em, join 'em," appeared to be Macmillan's policy (or was it, Gaullists might wonder, "if you can't lick 'em from a distance, lick 'em *by* joining 'em?").

As viewed from Paris, British military problems also appeared to be exerting pressure for closer association with the continent. Like De Gaulle, the Conservatives professed to be advocates of an independent, national nuclear deterrent, albeit one closely associated with American weapons systems. In response to Defense Secretary McNamara's criticism of such deterrents, Prime Minister Macmillan told the House of Commons that Great Britain had and would continue to maintain its own, independent force.[18] To Dutch criticism that the British nuclear system was "dangerous, expensive, threatened with obsolescence and lacking in capability as a deterrent force," Defense Minister Thorneycroft responded with a justification which might have been written by General Gallois. His country, he said, "could inflict today and for years to come such damage on any potential aggressor as to greatly outweigh anything he could conceivably hope to gain."[19]

Great Britain might covet its own deterrent, yet quite clearly it was having an increasingly hard time holding on to one. In 1956 Britain had started work on the *Blue Streak,* a missile designed to have a range of 2,000 miles. Four years later the project was abandoned with a loss of about $300 million, still short of completion by some billion and a half dollars.[20] In 1962 *Blue Water* was also cancelled, the government reluctantly deciding not to throw $150 million after the $70 million already expended on this short-range, surface-to-surface missile.[21] In the meantime, the Americans had come to the rescue when *Blue Streak* died. Not only could Great Britain purchase the Polaris missile, the United States declared, but the *Skybolt,* on which work was progressing, would be made available to prolong the life of Britain's V-bombers well into the 1960's. What Britain could not build independently for its inde-

[18] *New York Times,* June 27, 1962.

[19] Address to Assembly of the Western European Union, *Le Monde,* December 6, 1962.

[20] Thomas F. Field, "The Blue Streak Missile," *NATO's Fifteen Nations,* February–March 1962, pp. 33–41.

[21] *New York Times,* August 11, 1962.

pendent deterrent, the United States would magnanimously provide (no precedent, of course, for France).

Only two years later — in 1962 — a new administration seemed to have second thoughts. According to yet another set of American deterrence theories, allied nuclear forces were useless and dangerous. Defense Secretary McNamara told the NATO Council meeting in Athens what American leadership was now thinking, but he naturally provoked a greater international reaction when he said the same thing later in public.[22]

At the end of 1962 former Secretary of State Dean Acheson, advisor to President Kennedy on NATO policy, had some choice advice for Britain. That the words were almost an aside hardly made them ring more pleasantly in the ears of a government already disturbed at the disparity between military costs and security returns. "Great Britain has lost an empire and has not yet found a role. The attempt to play a separate role — that is, a role apart from Europe, a role based on a 'special relationship' with the United States, a role based on being the head of a 'commonwealth' which has no political structure, or unity, or strength and enjoys a fragile and precarious economic relationship by means of the sterling area and preferences in the British market — this role is about played out. Great Britain, attempting to work alone and to be a broker between the United States and Russia, has seemed to conduct policy as weak as its military power. H.M.G. is now attempting — wisely, in my opinion — to re-enter Europe."[23]

American actions appeared almost as harsh as American words. A very strong incentive for Britain to keep an independent nuclear deterrent was that presumably it would thereby enhance its influence with the United States; general as well as specifically atomic questions would be faced together. Then came Cuba. "France," pontificated the London *Times*, "observed the danger of war without being able to do anything about it." "Great Britain," responded *Le Monde*'s London correspondent[24] mildly, "wasn't much more active." Many Englishmen shared the

[22] At Ann Arbor, Michigan, in June.

[23] The statement was made at the United States Military Academy, to the Fourteenth Student Conference on United States Affairs, December 5, 1962.

[24] Henri Pierre, October 31, 1962.

French opinion. Said Liberal Party leader Grimond: "They told us that without it [the independent deterrent] we ran the risk of arriving naked at the conference table; but we have it, and we didn't even enter the conference room."[25]

How long would the British have any nuclear clothes left? *Skybolt,* the substitute for *Blue Streak,* the replacement for *Blue Water; Skybolt,* guarantor of the V-bombers' usefulness — *Skybolt,* American officials let it be known, would not be produced after all. The half-billion dollars which would have had to be added to an equal amount already spent was too much. It just can't be true, said London's *Financial Times.* Surely the rumors had been deliberately circulated; the "reaction would be so violent that there is no question now of abandoning this missile."[26]

Rejected by the United States, Great Britain's recourse, it appeared, lay in close military affiliation with France. Mutual cooperation had perhaps not become as intimate as the relations of either with West Germany, but it had made considerable progress. Periodic consultations were held on naval research projects under way in the two countries, and aircraft carriers of both nations bore planes from each indiscriminately. "Close and personal contacts thus created establish the basis for an atmosphere of common Franco-British thought," said Admiral Georges Cabanier, Chief of Staff of the French Navy.[27] Joint parachute exercises were held in Great Britain and France. They went smoothly, despite some nasty British remarks about Algerian practices of French paras and despite the French being asked to jump at a place called Frogs Hill.[28] Production of aircraft took a long, if wobbly, step forward when the two nations agreed to share expenses and build in both countries the supersonic commercial transport plane called the *Super-Caravelle.*[29]

A firm basis, the French could reason, existed for more intimate military collaboration, once Britain was inside Europe. Quite clearly both

---

[25] *Le Monde,* November 2, 1962.

[26] Quoted in *Le Monde,* December 13, 1962.

[27] *Le Monde,* July 21, 1962.

[28] *Le Monde,* February 27, October 31, November 1, December 2–3, 9–10, 1962; *Combat,* October 29, 1962.

[29] See above, p. 214. *Le Monde,* October 27, November 8, 10, 14, 30, December 1, 1962; *Combat,* October 23, 1962.

nations were searching for a way out of the nuclear-weapons dilemma. They wished to maintain or build an independent deterrent, yet climbing costs were endangering the one and lack of access to scientific knowledge, facilities, equipment, and matériel was delaying the other. In the Anglo-French partnership Great Britain could provide technological experience and, in the short range, much of the weaponry, while France contributed to the cost. The two could share the continental arms market, shutting out American competition. Although there would, of course, be no bi-national integrated nuclear deterrent, coordination of facilities and targeting, such as existed between Great Britain and the United States, could be arranged. British alignment with France might then force the United States to change its attitude toward the French nuclear deterrent. It would make no sense at all for Washington to persist in refusing to the Paris end of a London-Paris axis what had regularly been granted the other half. In time there might emerge a tri-partite nuclear force; if the strangely obsessed Americans wanted to attach their favorite labels "NATO" and "multilateral" to such a system, that too might be managed.

So hopeful were the French that Macmillan's visit in June 1962 inspired reports that the Prime Minister believed in "Europe" and accepted France's nuclear policy. Many in Britain, it was said, wanted to go further in military cooperation with France and regretted that Franco-British association in this field did not match that between France and Germany. Although British sources felt constrained to deny this interpretation of Macmillan's conversations,[30] Watkinson's replacement as Defense Minister by Thorneycroft in August was interpreted by the French press as another move toward Europe, this time in the name of economy.[31]

Then came the Anglo-American agreement at Nassau in December 1962. Great Britain gave way completely on *Skybolt*, up to then the "indispensable" ingredient of its independent deterrent. In fact, as the French interpreted the affair, the independent deterrent vanished altogether. Instead of *Skybolt*, the British were to be sold at bargain

[30] *Le Monde*, June 6, 1962.
[31] *Le Monde*, August 15, 1962.

prices Polaris missiles for compatible British submarines. The resultant force was then to be integrated with the American, Polaris-carrying subs. Although Great Britain reserved the right to regain control when "supreme national interests" were at stake, the complexity of the measures necessary for integration and British dependence on American supplies and facilities made the clause appear to be only a transparently thin, face-saving device.

De Gaulle, after some delay, delivered his *riposte*. He could only regard Great Britain's relations to Europe as now drastically and dramatically changed. Before going to Nassau, Macmillan had talked with De Gaulle in Paris. The Prime Minister had said nothing about surrendering *Skybolt* for Polaris. If the deal had actually been in the offing, such reticence indicated at the very least a peculiar reserve toward an ally with which closer economic and military relations were being sought. If the bargain had not yet been struck, then Britain had taken only a few hours to make again its same traditional choice.[32] "Great Britain, which was so slow, so demanding, so divided when asked to join Europe, was infinitely less so when asked to submit to American will."[33] Just as after Suez, Britain had collapsed with a sigh of relief on the capacious bosom of the daughter-protector.[34]

For De Gaulle there was no question of sparing Britain the corollary to its choice. If it were out of Europe, it could hardly pretend to be in. "Great Britain," De Gaulle told his press conference on January 14, 1963, "applied for membership in the Common Market. It did so after refusing earlier to participate in the community that was being built and ... after having put some pressure on the Six in order to prevent the application of the Common Market from really getting started. Thus, England in its turn asked to enter, but on its own terms ... It has in all its work very pronounced, very original customs and traditions. One must admit that the entry of Great Britain first and then of those [Free

[32] Paul Fabra in *Le Monde*, January 18, 1963. De Gaulle was reported to have told a group of deputies, "I remember Churchill said to me once, 'If England has some day to choose between Europe and the open sea, it will always choose the open sea.'" *Le Monde*, January 26, 1963.

[33] André Fontaine in *Le Monde*, January 30, 1963.

[34] Macmillan joined at Nassau in an "offer" to France, of which more below.

Trade Area] states, would change completely the structure of agreements, compensations, rules that have been already established among
the Six . . . In the end there would appear a colossal Atlantic Community
dependent upon and under the direction of the United States, which
would soon absorb the European Community."

Although Great Britain had made its choice, French friendship would
remain and French cooperation continue, particularly in science, technology, and industry. Some form of association with the Common Market could also be worked out, if the British wished. "Finally, it is very
possible that Great Britain's own evolution and the evolution of the
world will carry England toward the continent, whatever the delays
before that result. For my part, that is what I believe," said De Gaulle.

It only remained for French representatives to deliver the *coup de
grâce* to the Brussels negotiations between Great Britain and the Six.
These meetings had been going, off and on, for fifteen months and had
been all but stalemated since October. "No matter what anyone says or
writes," M. Lebel, spokesman for the French delegation, told the con-
ferees, "she [France] has interposed to Great Britain's entry into the
Common Market no veto. (Prolonged laughter) . . . It would suffice for
England to accept the clauses of the Treaty of Rome in order for her
adherence to cease to pose questions." But, declared Foreign Minister
Couve de Murville, "Great Britain is still not ready to accept the disciplines of the Treaty and notably those of agricultural policy . . . It is on
her, not on us, that the burden of proof falls . . . To criticism that rises on
all sides and according to which we French want a little Europe, I shall
say once more that we don't want to maintain a small or large Europe,
but to know whether this Europe that we are creating is a Europe that
will be European."[35]

The "criticism on all sides," of course, had no effect on De Gaulle.
He considered it partly irrelevant, partly misdirected, and he knew it
arose primarily from frustration at the lack of retaliatory possibilities,
at least in the short run. The French government did not, as Macmillan
charged, "have its eyes turned toward the past"; it did not believe that
"one nation could dominate Europe" or that "Europe could live alone,

[35] *Le Monde*, January 31, 1963.

without friends and without allies."[36] Whatever their annoyance at the manner and timing of his pronunciamento, France's five partners had, as they themselves recognized, no recourse but to accept the imposed break with Great Britain. Their interest, too, lay in standing on the Treaty of Rome. They had gone too far to turn back from the economic community that was being built. They could not easily abandon hope that the Common Market would inevitably lead to the political unification of Western Europe.

One is not justified in concluding, with the Socialist *Le Populaire,* that De Gaulle contemplated a lapse into "neutralism," still less to follow *L'Express* in the opinion the President was seeking a reversal of alliances. However, the Nassau agreement did lead De Gaulle to see American as well as British policy in a different and much less friendly light. The United States had professed to favor Great Britain's entry into the Common Market, yet there was little public evidence that the Americans had exerted any real effort to make the British see that true membership was attainable only through adherence to the provisions of the Treaty of Rome. On the contrary, when negotiations had reached an impasse, the United States offered Great Britain an escape from the military imperatives that were driving it toward full participation in continental affairs.

How real, indeed, was American support for the Common Market itself? American officials continually tried to negotiate modifications and exceptions to the Community's agricultural provisions in favor of United States farm products. The United States favored a tariff cut of 50 percent, opposing Common Market desires that higher duties be reduced more than lower ones and a general tariff level of 10 percent be reached. Moreover, the United States sought to exclude from any cutting at all some products it had previously protected by escape clauses. A basic aim of the Common Market was the advancement of European industry. However, although the United States pretended concern over an unfavorable balance of payments, it was doing nothing to check the deficit-producing invasion of Europe by American private investment. Studies showed that direct American investments in Europe

[36] *Ibid.*

increased from $6.7 to $7.7 billion between 1961 and 1962. Between 1957 and 1961 the value of production by European affiliates of American companies rose 70 percent, to $10.7 billion. While investments in Germany were almost double those in France ($2.3 billion as compared to $1.2 billion), about 500 American affiliates existed in France, employing some 100,000 persons. To make things worse, investments were concentrated in such industrial activities as oil, agricultural machinery, photographic equipment, food processing, and automobiles. The situation in the French automotive industry was highlighted by the announcement, early in 1963, that Chrysler Corporation had acquired a 63 percent interest in Simca.

Control of foreign concerns by United States interests could not be divorced from American economic philosophy. Aggressive investment policies raised the spectre of a capitalist-dominated Europe, one perhaps compatible with West German wishes, but most certainly not with those of De Gaulle. Politically irresponsible European "technocrats" might actually help to create a continental economy capable of being manipulated from abroad.[37] In January 1963 French representatives requested that the Six meet to consider the problem raised by United States investments. France's partners, however, derived some small pleasure from calling off the meeting to retaliate against De Gaulle's rupture of the Brussels negotiations with Great Britain.[38]

No doubt De Gaulle would have regarded American economic forays into Europe as less threatening had it not been for the long history of Franco-American conflict over the French nuclear deterrent. The issue was in effect a triple one, involving the *production* of nuclear weapons, the *possession* of those weapons, and the *deployment* of forces equipped with them. In all three respects, Gaullists viewed American policy as discriminatory, inconsistent, and irrational.

Despite the fact that French scientists had contributed to the original techniques for harnessing atomic energy, American cooperation with Canada and Great Britain had not been extended to France after World War II. Discrimination continued even after the Soviet Union had

[37] See Maurice Duverger, "Le grand dessein," *Le Monde*, January 10, 1963.
[38] *Le Monde*, January 20, 21, 30, 31, 1963.

demonstrated that it too possessed the ability to manufacture nuclear weapons. The French complained bitterly that Americans accepted with equanimity the spread of nuclear weapons technology across the Atlantic, while objecting to its movement across the English Channel. The United States signed agreements with such countries as Italy and Switzerland for cooperation in the peaceful development of atomic energy that were more favorable than the one finally negotiated with France. Yet all the while Americans admitted that French nuclear military capacity was a fact, that the process of acquiring this capacity antedated De Gaulle, and that production of weapons would in all likelihood continue, no matter who was his successor, or what evolution took place in the political institutions of the Fifth Republic.

With regard to the possession of nuclear weapons systems, continued the Gaullists, American policy revealed the same illogic. Again France was discriminated against in favor of Great Britain. At first the justification was that France had not demonstrated that it could produce an atomic bomb. When one was detonated, the criterion was changed to *substantial* nuclear capacity. Progress toward both the delivery system and the nuclear warheads for the *force de frappe*, however, still did not produce a change of American policy. Now Washington expressed alarm that a national striking force for France would provide a most dangerous precedent so far as West Germany was concerned. The French could find so little basis for this fear that they believed it must be either completely illogical or was presented as merely an excuse. West Germany was, after all, barred from the acquisition of atomic, biological, or chemical weapons by the Paris Accords of 1954, which had permitted a limited re-armament of Germany. While certain restrictions in the agreement had been relaxed, the power to do so rested with the Western European Union, in which both Great Britain and France were represented, and which was itself a subsidiary of the North Atlantic Treaty Organization, whose head was an American. Moreover, direct ties between the United States and West Germany were close (some Frenchmen would say too close). While there was some military thinking in Germany, notably by Defense Minister Strauss, that the army should be allowed to defend itself with nuclear weapons if necessary, official German opinion held that this desideratum could be effectively achieved with nuclear warheads remaining under American control until the crisis occurred.

The Americans themselves thus had the power to lay to rest any fears of Germany by maintaining firmly and publicly their opposition to outfitting the Federal Republic with nuclear weapons. They could also cease to press for more and more Germans in uniform, reversing policies which had whetted German appetites for more and more of the best possible equipment. Finally, the United States could change its practice, followed assiduously since World War II, of wooing the Germans. If West Germany was a potential menace, the United States had made it so. Instead of providing Germany with so much bargaining power, the United States could support the French end of the Franco-German combination. Insurance against German nuclear forces lay in support of, not opposition to, De Gaulle's military program and the form of European association he was seeking to promote. Conversely, American refusal to help France acquire nuclear weapons systems might force the Fifth Republic to bring West Germany into a production effort whose cost threatened to increase at an accelerating rate for an indefinite period of time.

Intermingled with American "irrational" opposition was just enough inconsistency to maintain French hopes that continued intransigence might ultimately cause the United States to give up its nuclear embargo effort altogether. President Kennedy had seemed quite firm when he told his press conference in March 1962, "We do not believe in a series of nuclear deterrents. First France, then another country, then another, until a very solid and, I think, effective defense alliance may be somewhat weakened." But a month later reports were circulating that "Pentagon officials" were supporting the release of both information and matériel to France. Behind the military position was said to be General Maxwell Taylor, the President's personal military advisor. Once a strong advocate of conventional forces for Europe, General Taylor was supposedly convinced by General Lauris Norstad, NATO's Supreme Allied Commander for Europe, that European countries, of which France of course was the most recalcitrant, would consent to a build-up of conventionally armed troops within the framework of the Atlantic alliance only after obtaining satisfaction on the question of a continental nuclear deterrent.[39] Believing that American concern over adverse balance of payments might also help change official policy, France included on a list of items it would be prepared to buy: atomic submarine blueprints, equipment for a gaseous diffusion plant for the manufacture of enriched uranium, guidance systems, missile parts, and propellants.[40]

Temporarily, the harsh face of American policy reappeared. Matériel related to nuclear weapons was marked "not for sale" on the old grounds that France had not as yet mustered an atomic capacity sufficiently advanced to qualify for aid under American law. Hardly had De Gaulle had time to wonder whether the Pentagon, the State Department, or the White House was making American policy, however, before the United States authorized Boeing Aircraft Corporation to sell France a dozen jet-propelled aircraft tankers, the KC-135.[41] Although non-atomic themselves, these tankers represented a substantial contribution at a critical moment to the French *force de frappe*. The delivery system for that force, it will be remembered, consisted of the *Mirage IV* bomber, which was capable of carrying nuclear bombs and, possibly in the future, air-to-surface missiles with nuclear warheads. The *Mirage* was not, however, able to go very far without refueling, and France did not have its own aerial jet tankers to repair that defect.

At one stroke the United States had increased the range of the *Mirage* and had lessened French dependence on precarious, out-of-the-way ground refueling stations in African states. More important, it helped to make the *force de frappe* believable to Frenchmen. A one-way or hedge-hopping delivery system was difficult to accept as a reliable guarantor of French security, but a system refueled by modern planes in the same manner as were American and British aircraft was convincing evidence that France indeed was en route to becoming a respectable, independent nuclear power. The United States was doing

39 *New York Times*, April 15, 1962; *Le Monde*, July 22, 1962.
40 *New York Times*, April 18, 1962.
41 *Le Monde*, June 15, 1962.

much more than admit grudgingly that a French nuclear capacity existed; it was actively assisting in converting a capacity into a force in being.

Under the circumstances, who could credit an explanation that the transaction had been consummated only to reduce the deficit in the American balance of payments? Who could believe the same motivation was behind subsequent plans to sell France a nuclear-powered submarine? Four years earlier Secretary of State John Foster Dulles, in one of the policy shifts for which he was notorious in Western Europe, had offered De Gaulle such a submarine. Unfortunately Dulles had neglected to gain the agreement of the powerful Joint Congressional Atomic Energy Committee, sceptical watchdog of the executive's programs for nuclear cooperation with foreign countries under existing statutes. The offer was tacitly withdrawn, and any American embarrassment soon vanished as officials gauged the full extent of De Gaulle's objections to "integration" of his army, conventional or atomic, under NATO. Now another overture was being made, "not necessarily a fulfillment of the four-year-old promise, but a new initiative under changed circumstances."[42] Alas for De Gaulle (and the *New York Times*), this deal also had not been cleared in advance with the Joint Congressional Atomic Energy Committee, difficult as it must have been for the French President to believe. A poll of the eighteen members of the Committee revealed that not one favored the sale.[43]

Additional apprehension and confusion in French minds concerning American policy was occasioned by the replacement during the summer of 1962 of the American Ambassador, General Gavin, and of SHAPE Commander, General Norstad. Although such was not always the case, both men when they were called home had become identified as advocates of broader nuclear cooperation. Each had served his tour of duty and was due to leave, but the French regretted the timing — just when United States policy seemed to be wavering.

[42] Jack Raymond in the *New York Times*, October 17, 1962. The *New York Times* immediately and enthusiastically supported the sale (October 19, 1962) as part of its recurrent effort to change American policy. See, for example, editorial of June 29, 1962 and column by C. L. Sulzberger, December 5, 1962.

[43] *New York Times*, October 22, 1962. Also Jack Raymond, October 18, 1962, in "follow-up" to original report.

In an interview granted immediately before he relinquished his post, General Gavin recalled that his Ambassadorial tenure had witnessed agreement to provide instruction for French troops in the use of nuclear weapons on the same basis as other NATO forces and an end to discrimination against France in the sale of aeronautical equipment. Gavin was then asked about "certain difficulties" between the two countries in the matter of the *force de frappe*. Under the circumstances, his answer, while diplomatically phrased, could hardly have been more encouraging to Gaullist aspirations. Gavin managed to imply: a) he favored nuclear assistance, b) so did President Kennedy, c) time would improve all things. "It is said that I have recommended to my government a line of conduct that will bring aid to France, and I think this is generally known. And I am fully in agreement with the line of conduct adopted by my government and with what it is trying to do. But it takes time to settle these problems — time and a little more comprehension concerning the road we are taking. I will say no more at the moment. In reality (smiling) I would not want to make the problem still more difficult by talking about it."[44]

Much more furore had been provoked by the announcement two months earlier that General Lyman Lemnitzer would replace Norstad, technically as senior American military officer assigned to SACEUR. "Everyone knows," wrote *Le Monde*'s diplomatic correspondent André Fontaine, "of the increasing conflict between himself [Norstad] and Pentagon leaders, which led him to refuse to participate in the April Ministerial Council of NATO at Athens." At that meeting, Fontaine recalled, American delegates proposed measures of consultation and exchanges of information on atomic matters which were "only a pale reflection of his suggestions."[45]

In the same issue of *Le Monde* appeared a "Portrait — A General Who Understood Europe." "His [Norstad's] departure from the head of SHAPE," concluded its author "J. N.," "will add a new chapter to the inexhaustible theme of relations between military chiefs and political power. For, like so many of his colleagues — the 'generals-who-have-

[44] Exclusive interview with *Le Monde*, September 27, 1962
[45] July 21, 1962. C. L. Sulzberger's column of August 13 in the *New York Times* was entitled, "When and How the Rug Was Pulled."

ideas' — he finally succumbed to the temptation which alone keeps all of them from weariness: that of defining himself the entire mission for which he has been charged with providing only the means, because the political authority which should be determining this mission has proved its inability to adapt its decisions to circumstances." American efforts to calm European flutterings were clumsy and somewhat ludicrous. NATO delegates solemnly accepted General Lemnitzer as Norstad's successor, beginning November 1, 1962. The arrival of the Cuban crisis then provided an opportunity for the United States to postpone the transition for two months, or to the exact date Norstad was originally supposed to leave.

In the climate of the Anglo-American agreement at Nassau and the successive disappearance of "offers" to France, one more incident assumes significance. Under Palm Beach datelines, several American and British newspapers reported at the turn of the year the contemporary attitude of "the highest authority" toward independent nuclear deterrents, NATO, and United States leadership of the Western alliance. "The highest authority" in Palm Beach was so obviously John F. Kennedy that within a few days the White House was moved to publish his "confidential" remarks. "All our policy," the President had said, "is opposed to the dispersion of resources for the creation of independent, national, deterrent forces . . . I think that it is one of the great problems of the alliance in 1963 to know if the alliance will begin to break up in national deterrent forces that will cost huge sums of money and cause political and strategic disequilibrium, or if it will be possible for us to conclude arrangements which will give Europe a greater feeling of security . . . I think that too often in the past we have conceived of our leadership rather as an attempt to be well liked in all countries. In fact it is impossible to carry out any policy at all without provoking some friction. I therefore think that we must be ready — more than we have admitted in the past — to accept a clearer opposition toward the United States on the part of the press or foreign governments in order to be able to do something. I don't expect that the United States will be more liked, but I hope we can do more things."[46]

[46] *Le Monde*, January 12, 1963; also January 3, 1963.

One may now see the Anglo-American proposal to France in the same light as did De Gaulle. Would the latest "offer" — that emanating from Nassau — help build a French nuclear striking force? De Gaulle concluded it would not. "A bladeless knife without a handle," he called it.[47] "France," he told his news conference less picturesquely, "has taken note of the Anglo-American accord of the Bahamas. As conceived, no one doubtless will be surprised that we cannot subscribe to it. It really would not be useful for us to buy Polaris missiles, when we have neither submarines to launch them nor thermonuclear warheads to arm them ... When we have these submarines and these warheads, what will Polaris missiles then be worth? At that time we shall probably have missiles of our own invention. In other words, for us, in terms of technology, this affair is not a question of the moment."

What the "affair" did do was re-confirm for France the existence of a certain equivocation in American opposition to French possession of nuclear weapons. Was it not a logical assumption that a struggle had been going on for some years within the executive and legislative branches of the United States, a struggle made more intense during 1962 by French advances toward a deterrent force composed of armament it had itself produced? Given the normally chaotic nature of American policy formation and implementation, an abnormal reliance on necessarily ill-informed "public" opinion, an obsession with moralistic phrase-making, might it not be possible to envisage an American declaratory policy quite distinct from action policy? Such a separation was not unknown, in, say, the days of Eisenhower and Dulles. The words might remain the same, but continued French intransigence might change the substance of American behavior.

Defense Minister Messmer used the most recent of the three American offers relating to submarines — that emanating from Nassau — to gain legislative support for De Gaulle's military program. "Now proof has been produced that the nuclear policy of General de Gaulle, far from alienating us from American cooperation as derogators of this policy had, with more passion than reason, prophesied, has on the contrary permitted us to receive the first proposition worthy of interest

[47] According to Claude Krief in L'Express, January 24, 1963.

ever made to our country in this domain."[48] Perhaps De Gaulle brushed aside the Nassau offer *in the manner he did* because, nothing much in itself, it could be the harbinger of better proposals. "If I had some ham, I'd have some ham and eggs, if I had some eggs"; so says the old adage.

Despite the words President Kennedy had carefully planted with Palm Beach correspondents, De Gaulle might also hope for a comparably favorable conclusion to American policy on the *organization* of nuclear forces. During the period that nuclear technology was restricted to the United States and Great Britain, deterrent forces were held apart from NATO, although there were soothing words about their dedication to the strategy of dissuading the Soviet Union from attacking Western Europe. Changing events brought a shuffling of American political feet. The development of the Russian nuclear capacity brought proposals that American-controlled intermediate range ballistic missiles be stationed in Europe. Their vulnerability, however, was obvious, and De Gaulle, pursuing his own (vulnerable) deterrent, rejected the idea of IRBM's on French soil. Came the Wunderkind of deterrence — the Polaris-missiled, atomic submarine. Some of these, the United States now suggested, could be assigned to the defense of the NATO area.

For De Gaulle, however, the problem was not just the positioning of deterrent forces. It was the firmness of American dedication to Western European defense. In solving this problem, it mattered not at all what Americans said their intentions were; what counted was the credibility of their resolve to the Soviets. How could the Russians really believe that the United States would commit its powerful nuclear arsenal to the protection of Europe, when any American government knew full well that the cost in American lives would be upward of fifty million? Conversely, how could Europeans completely trust the United States to show restraint and fortitude in the face of the first direct threat to its national existence, when sometime, somewhere, security might be bought at Europe's expense? On the political level the answer, to De Gaulle's mind, was his recurrent demand for a triumvirate atop the alliance. On the military level it lay in the possession of nuclear forces of a magnitude and type to provide both a French deterrent and a guarantee of United States involvement.

[48] *Le Monde,* January 25, 1963.

Even if they were called "NATO" forces, portions of the Anglo-American deterrent were not satisfactory so long as they lay beyond Europe geographically or in terms of control. For a realist, the operative question was, "Who's in charge?," not after conflict had broken out, but before and during the advent of a crisis. The purpose of deterrence was, after all, to deter. With the Kennedy Administration nuances appeared in the American interpretation of NATO's contribution to the general Western strategy of deterrence. As in the case of the actual use of nuclear weapons, the new team seemed to perceive more options. President Kennedy said in Ottawa on May 5, 1961 that the United States was looking forward "to the possibility of eventually establishing a NATO sea-borne missile force which would be truly multilateral in ownership and control, if this should be desired and found feasible by our allies, once NATO's non-nuclear goals have been achieved." The connection with conventional forces was unfortunate; "eventually" could mean a long time; who were these "allies" that were to desire and pass on feasibility? Nonetheless, "multilateral" sounded better to Gaullists than "integrated."

The variables introduced concerned the amount of initiative required from the continent, the nations that would be involved, and the extent of their participation in such a missile force. While McNamara inveighed against national nuclear forces, other prominent Americans appeared to be arguing that such weapons in French hands would be acceptable under certain conditions. Secretary of State Dean Rusk was reported to have asked French officials if American acceptance of a French nuclear force as irreversible could be traded for cooperation in NATO's European strategy. The French reply was that first there had to be settled the question of European, particularly French, participation in global thermonuclear strategy.

Then Henry Kissinger, mistakenly identified as "one of the principal military advisors to President Kennedy,"[49] appeared in print with another of his animadversions on the subject of European defense. American opposition to French possession of nuclear weapons was, he asserted, wrong. Moreover, said Kissinger, the United States could not

[49] Claude Valetti, *Revue de Défense Nationale*, August–September 1962, pp. 1413–1416.

expect European countries to integrate their conventional forces and place greater reliance upon them while the United States arrogated to itself both a monopoly of nuclear retaliation and decision on its use. Although French doctrine concerning small, independent deterrents was "erroneous," "support for a modest French nuclear force at this stage may also be the best means of bringing about the European force . . ."[50]

Hope no doubt produced the identification of Kissinger, but Mc-George Bundy *was* one of the principal advisors to President Kennedy. Bundy delivered a speech in September 1962 to the Atlantic Treaty Association, meeting in Stockholm. "If it should appear that a purely European system of multilateral deterrence — integrated with ours in NATO — is what is necessary and desired, it is not the veto of the American government which will make it impossible." After stating that the United States could not assist "separate, national" deterrent forces, Bundy continued: "It would be false to believe that the aversion we feel for individual, ineffective, and non-integrated forces, would be automatically extended to a European force really unified, multilateral, and effectively integrated with our own force, which is necessarily predominant in the nuclear defense possessed by the alliance."[51]

A spokesman for the State Department indicated that there was nothing new in Bundy's words, but France could not be blamed if it brushed aside the disclaimer and interpreted the speech in the context of co-incident American acts and of statements like Rusk's and Kissinger's. There was a perceptible difference between insistence on an American "monopoly" of nuclear deterrence and consideration of European requests for a multilateral force. There was an even greater difference between "eventual" consideration, after conventional forces had been increased, of some kind of European participation in the American deterrent system and "prompt" consideration of practically solicited requests for a European force closely tied to the deterrent structure of the Western alliance. As specific American policy indicated, the difference could involve dissemination of weapons, first, and then their

[50] Henry A. Kissinger, "The Unsolved Problems of European Defense," *Foreign Affairs*, July 1962, pp. 515–542, esp. 532–537.
[51] *Le Monde*, September 29, 1962.

re-collection under the alliance. Such a procedure would be an improvement, from the French point of view, over even General Norstad's long-standing proposal that NATO be made the "fourth nuclear power."

Again — Nassau. The trouble with the offer was not only its unsuitability so far as the nature of the weapons was concerned. It also presupposed that the re-collection process would be more complete than De Gaulle was prepared to accept. Whatever the British might pretend, the project involved "integration" pure and simple. Without doubt, Under-Secretary of State George Ball told the NATO Council, the "supreme national interests" of which the agreement spoke would practically never be invoked.[52]

President de Gaulle made clear at his January 1963 press conference his position on the organization of nuclear-provisioned forces, as on other related matters.

> It is obvious that a country, especially one like ours, could not conduct a large modern war all alone. To have allies goes without saying in the historic period we live in. But for a great people to have also freedom to commit themselves and the wherewithal to seek to protect that freedom is a clear necessity, for alliances are not absolute virtues, whatever may be the sentiments that founded them . . .
>
> Thus principles and realities combine to lead France to equip itself with an atomic force of its own. This does not at all exclude of course the combination of the action of its force with the action of the similar forces of its allies. But for us in this specific case integration is something which is unimaginable . . .
>
> [The Nassau offer] does not meet with the principle about which I just spoke and which consists of disposing in our own right of our deterrent force. To turn over our weapons to a multilateral force, under a foreign command, would be to act contrary to that principle of our defense and our policy. It is true that we too can theoretically retain the ability to take back in our hands, in the supreme hypothesis, our atomic weapons incorporated in the multilateral force. But how could we do it in practice during the unprecedented moments of atomic apocalypse?

As exasperated Americans pressed forward with maximum public ostentation to create a "multilateral NATO force," De Gaulle, encouraged

[52] So reported André Fontaine in Le Monde, January 30, 1963.

by two years of American internal argument and four years of rapid change within the alliance, continued to hold to his basic propositions. Integration of command was either a fiction or a dangerous weakening of military effectiveness. In either case, France saw no reason to accept it. On the other hand, if the United States wished to abandon the term or substitute for it "multilateral," properly defined, De Gaulle could meet the Americans part way. A "European" deterrent would mean in effect a French one. Great Britain had opted out of Europe, and if the Franco-German treaty worked, Germany would not stray down the dangerous, still legally barricaded, path to a nuclear capacity of its own.[53] If the Anglo-Saxons did not choose to aid France in either the production or the possession of nuclear weapons, France would continue to build its own. But if persistent French determination did change United States (and thereby British) policy, then France would certainly be happy to cooperate within the alliance on matters of nuclear strategy.

Should this become what "multilateral" meant, fine. Had not De Gaulle stated all along that the preservation of the alliance was essential to French as well as Western security? Had he not for over four years been arguing that there should be more equality of responsibility within the alliance, commensurate with alterations in the relative power of its members? To that end had he not repeatedly requested a political triumvirate to direct the global, including nuclear, statecraft of the alliance?

No more than any other statesman was De Gaulle able to construct a "grand design" for his country with elements exclusively of his own choosing. He worked with what he had at hand. The military power of France was circumscribed by refractory political and economic conditions. Reliance on conventionally armed forces alone would have impaired his critical effort to re-attach the army to himself. Continued maintenance under arms of the host of men who had enveloped Algeria would not only have strained the resources of the country, but would have

---

[53] This despite De Gaulle's off-hand comment at his press conference that the question of German possession of nuclear weapons was the Federal Republic's own business, and despite military cooperation between the two countries.

perpetuated organized civil-military alliances against himself and his Republic. On the other hand, subordination of a reduced French force to NATO command would wipe out long-standing vested interests of the military, without providing attractive substitute satisfactions in missions of great-power dimension. Since it was out of the question to build an army exclusively around nuclear weapons systems, the only course open was a force, primarily conventional, somewhat decreased in size, hitched like a long, heavy tail to the flimsy nuclear kite. The flimsiness of the nuclear kite was quite obviously the result of external as well as internal restraints.

Likewise, the "Europe" of Gaullist statecraft was not the Europe of Gaullist choice. "I prefer Europe to NATO," De Gaulle was supposed to have said in the Summer of 1962, "and of all the European systems it is the Six which appeals to me most."[54] Yet the President, events revealed, could not build Europe to his specifications nor bend it to his will. Said François Mitterand, inveterate opponent of France's "guide," "The positions ordained by General de Gaulle derive from premises which are perfectly acceptable," but, he added, Gaullist policy wound up making Germany the "arbiter and leader."[55] One-time premier René Pleven sided with Mitterand: De Gaulle's Europe is "more open to the East than to the West; . . . Europe dominated by the Franco-German couple is far from the true European ideal." Such criticism, responded Foreign Minister Couve de Murville, was tragically misdirected. "If the political entente is limited to these two countries, it is because we could not do otherwise, and the fault does not lie with France. If, in the Common Market, a political organization of Europe could not be undertaken, it is because two of the six countries [Belgium and the Netherlands] were opposed to it." M. Pleven, added the Minister, "knows the contradictions that characterize the positions of our partners: they are for Europe and for integrated Europe but at the same time for the entry of Great Britain into the Common Market, which everyone knows would substantially change the nature of the problem of integration and supranationality." Finally, the Foreign Minister concluded, France

[54] *Interavia,* August 1962, p. 965.
[55] *Le Monde,* January 26, 1963.

had no other choice regarding the Nassau offer. "I don't see how we could have taken account of words which were perhaps spoken off-stage but were never addressed to us . . . We could only reply to the American propositions in the form in which they were submitted to us."[56]

Only Chancellor Adenauer, committed to relinquish his hold on German power in the Fall of 1963, would play according to De Gaulle's rules. The other four of the Six would not subscribe to his "Europe of Fatherlands." Great Britain once more chose the United States. In the United States the " 'Hamlet of the White House' appears to have selected his route. Persuaded that the fate of the world is in the hands of the two Super-powers, he has decided to reinforce American leadership of the Western peoples."[57]

To persist in his own "grand design" Charles de Gaulle needed, and possessed, faith that he, not his opponents foreign and domestic, saw the evolving nature of the international environment most clearly. Even though he could not, with any conceivable statecraft, structure that environment, by conforming to basic realities his France could influence events, as a great power should. De Gaulle could await the day when the national interests to which its narrow margin of viability made it most sensitive brought Great Britain back to seek cooperation with the Six. In time the United States officially might well come to accept what many Americans already perceived — that the West would be more powerful *because* its power was more widely spread, the alliance more durable because relative positions within it were fully accepted by the members as satisfactory. The regime replacing Adenauer might logically be expected to be more nationalistic, but De Gaulle could hope that his and the Chancellor's policies had provided sufficient scope for *responsible* nationalism in a militarily powerful Franco-German partnership leading a tightly knit, increasingly prosperous Economic Community.

Was it chimerical to extend the vision even further? Might not Gaullist policies, working with emerging reality, ultimately help to create

[56] *Le Monde,* January 26, 1963.
[57] Maurice Duverger, *Le Monde,* February 9, 1963.

circumstances which, for the first time, would make possible the liquidation of war-created problems? Were the policies of Stalin's successors based on the fear of a Western Europe dominated by the United States, or by a vengeful West Germany, or by one unitary political construction of its own? The Western Europe sought by De Gaulle's statecraft had none of these attributes. If that statecraft succeeded, might not Soviet leadership come to permit Eastern European states, seeking, as had their Western neighbors earlier, to rediscover their identity, a role in a Europe — the only real Europe — of peaceful, cooperating nations?

"Come to," "in time," "ultimately" — these were words of the long-range future. For the septuagenarian President himself there was little time. But what of that? One who could discern so clearly for so many decades the direction of change in the world could conclude that he had founded his policy so firmly on domestic reality that those who followed him would by desire and by necessity pursue the same course toward a great nation's great destiny.

CHAPTER 10

CONCLUSION:

THE SPLIT VISION

All power with which civil authority has been invested is transferred completely to the military authority. Civil authority continues to exercise those functions which the military authority will not assume, under direct control of the latter. — Rebel "Radio Algiers," April 22, 1961

Behold the State mocked, the Nation defied, our power shaken, our international prestige debased, our place and role in Africa compromised. And by whom? Alas! Alas! Alas! By men whose duty, honor, reason for existence it was to serve and to obey . . . Beginning today I shall take as directly needed the measures that appear to me to be demanded by the circumstances. By the same token I reaffirm for today and tomorrow the French and republican legitimacy that the nation has conferred on me . . . — Charles de Gaulle, April 23, 1961

THE FRENCH army's argument with De Gaulle was not without an element of logic. At the core of the issue, in the opinion of many professional officers, was the best method of defending the nation's territorial possessions, particularly those North African areas officially classified as metropolitan departments. Moreover, behind the purely national interest of maintaining intact French territory lay the wider question of how to defend the West against forces which, both the army and De Gaulle agreed, were its deadly enemies. The army's experience in Indochina, Morocco, Tunisia, Suez, and Algeria led it to the conclusion that firm support by a strong government in Paris would make long-sought victory in North Africa and successful defense in Europe not just possible but inevitable. Had De Gaulle once shared this opinion? The army had reason to believe he had. Its subsequent bitterness was therefore readily understandable. The strong government made possible by military revolt did not advance causes believed to be held in common. Instead that government sought to force upon the army entirely different hypotheses concerning its own role and the nature of French interest.

The viewpoints of the French army on the need for strong civilian support of the military were similar to those advanced in other Western countries, pro-colonial and anti-colonial alike. Unfortunately for France, however, professional military contentions were also advanced to conceal highly illegitimate actions behind a sophisticated but shabby façade. For all its protests over lack of political support, for all its reflections about conflict, the army had been caught on the losing side of two revolutionary wars. Had it been able to win either quickly, a compromise between nationalism and colonialism might have been successfully imposed — for a time. But because the army, for whatever reasons, had failed to win quickly, its cadres had descended in Algeria to the use of abominable tactics against an enemy also willing to use any means to win recognition for an authority legitimatized in nationalist eyes by successful defiance of external control. Out of weakness both sides violated elementary principles of humanity, yet the shame and guilt of the French army was justifiably deeper than that of the FLN.

To expunge its dishonor the army had to find a transcendent goal. In creating such a goal, military leaders took flight from reality. They pretended that the army was not fighting for the special privileges of the "European" minority (as though a "French Algeria" could have any other practical meaning). They pretended that the Moslem majority hated and feared the FLN, loved France, and wished to side with France's army. Even as extremists were torturing, murdering, building concentration camps for over a million people, the army pretended that its schools, roads, hospitals, vaccines made it the agent of a Western civilization Algerians longed to embrace. Most indefensible of all, in a conflict polarized by its depth and duration, officers clung to the pretense that there was a middle ground. Because there was in fact no middle ground, they created one. Here was the transcendent goal at last — the militarized state: the state made to serve military objectives.

De Gaulle's crime then became the forcing of reality on the army. He said French possessions and French interests could not be defended in the old way any longer. He said the West needed France and France needed to be strong, but that strength could not be found in the permanent envelopment of Algeria. He said the war was in fact a two-sided war, that the army, instead of defending anachronistic European privileges, should prepare conditions for an honest consultation of the Algerian people. He surprised the army by defining the Moslems as adults, sensate beings possessed of intelligence, able and therefore having the right to make choices about their future, even though Europeans and France itself might be temporarily hurt.

With fierce tenacity professional cadres defended their dream against intruding facts. Obsessed with the loved-hated Algeria, they had no wish to leave behind their fantasies, however atavistic, however brutish the form they had come to assume. In North Africa and in the Metropole they fought French civilian authority and its self-styled symbol, Charles de Gaulle. Phantasmagoria followed phantasmagoria: the eternal State, the eternal Nation, the noble virtues of the Christian warrior. The most vicious of means, the lowest of social outcasts, became sanctified by the exalted goal: a militarized French Algeria within a militarized France.

In their revolt against the Fifth Republic, military activists were not alone. By involving the army, however, they provided the indispensable ingredient. Without the army there would have been no dream, no myth, no façade, only a European minority trying desperately, even gallantly to hold on to tangible gifts from a colonial past. Without the army there would have been no organized, politicized insurrection in Algeria, no Secret Army in search of a new political directorate in the Metropole. Even though only a small minority had committed itself irrevocably to the destruction of De Gaulle, the army as a whole was for all too long a surprisingly docile captive of this hard core of military extremists. "Unity of the army," a myth designed to make command in combat possible, became a device to defend desperadoes, to secrete them, to question openly the legitimacy of the government which plotters were seeking clandestinely to destroy. The French army did not accept, let alone respect, civilian leadership because it was civilian and had been legalized by election and by constitutional referendum; instead the army was merely prepared to grant power to those authorities who were ready to make militarily approved decisions.

As an organization the army eventually became separated from its military activists as a result of the failure of the Algerian revolts, the strength and determination of De Gaulle, and the eroding effects of time. The barricaders might have succeeded in January 1960, but the army was not ready. In April 1961 it was too late. With the demise of French Algeria, the situation of the military services was altered. The navy and air force, previously adjuncts to the French ground forces, found acceptance of other missions possible, even pleasant. The ground forces, however, were forced to undergo a series of revisions: in geographic location, in military matériel, and in definition of organizational purpose. All three helped to increase the distance between the ground forces and the rebellious activists, now perforce transplanted to metropolitan France.

Also at work was De Gaulle's great tenacity. This dedicated leader, certain that *his* vision was clear, was resolved to persevere and win the army back to formal acceptance of his authority, using the same skills that had brought him his initial success in Algeria.

And time does pass. Lost causes cannot remain causes forever; they become foundations for new causes, fade to ritualistic ceremony, or disappear entirely. Causes are people with a purpose. People of one stamp in Algeria assumed, however reluctantly, however slowly, at least some of the metropolitan imprint. Fanatics of French Algeria passed from positions of power in various organizations inside and outside the army; others, for whom Algeria was a story and not an experience, took their places. There was no more French Algeria, hardly any France in Algeria. "What do you want me to do?" Defense Minister Messmer asked in effect, when Moslem violations of the Evian agreements were brought to his attention. "Do you want France to re-invade Algeria?" A shocking change had come about, but it was real.

De Gaulle's statecraft presented a dilemma for his opponents, scattered along the political spectrum. United, they could muster a majority, as deputies demonstrated with the "European Manifesto" in June 1962. But, as the Manifesto also revealed, their unity was essentially negative, transitory, and passive. Except for the Communists, a group of Socialists, and a few Radicals, they had originally welcomed De Gaulle's bid for power; at least they had not defended the Fourth Republic. They knew at the time, or should have known, that the man for whom they were garroting the old regime had a highly developed preference for personal rule and a profound distaste for the democratic procedures developed under both the Third and Fourth Republics. Leftists had to choose between De Gaulle's objective – peace in Algeria – of which they approved, and his means of attaining that goal – rule by decree, sanctioned by referenda, of which they did not. Conservatives were faced with an equally distasteful mixture: drastically reduced legislative power, for which they had long argued, and abandonment of Algeria, a policy which they thought they had installed De Gaulle to prevent. Guy Mollet, perennial Secretary of the Socialist Party, symbolizes the former; Jacques Soustelle, prominent participant in the events of May 1958, the latter. De Gaulle's new parliamentary supporters were an agglomeration of clashing political hues, which the maneuvering of the President left with no program, no credo but himself alone.

Events at times obscured the personal, authoritarian nature of the emergent Fifth Republic. Its old-fashioned tolerance of "respectable" dissent gave it a democratic appearance, even to some Frenchmen. De Gaulle could afford to allow dissenters a degree of latitude because they were impotent to change national policy by constitutional means.

Farmers could block roads and conduct "manifestations," but the "power" ignored the absolute majority of deputies seeking to convene the National Assembly for discussion of agricultural issues. Liberal journals continually assailed the President, but found no political organization able to translate their wails into a program capable of competing with *le grand Charles* for the allegiance of the electorate. The clearest road from articulated dissent to altered policy led through the miasma of subversion. Plots to assassinate the President helped to immobilize adherents to the rules of democratic opposition, at the same time that they justified further moves toward authoritarian rule. While it might be an exaggeration to conclude, as did one journal, that De Gaulle actually needed the OAS, the interaction between the two would certainly present unhappy France with yet another test of the viability of its political institutions. The country had witnessed failures in the past; whether there was enduring flexibility in its latest constitutionally prescribed, formal system, as distinguished from its personal, contemporary manipulation, was problematical. American officialdom, whose foreign preferences for strong, centralized leadership have been most apparent in relations with France, might contemplate the instability which authoritarian control frequently brings in its wake and also the reduced scope for policies of persuasion while that control remains.

Since the OAS operated clandestinely, the continuing seriousness of its threat is difficult to evaluate. Just when things seemed to be calming down, another plot against the President would be revealed, more arrests made, another round of trials begun. In a personalized regime which was so vulnerable, Gaullist efforts to win back the army were vital. Whatever their success in practical terms, however, it is doubtful that the result was a depoliticalized army. Just as it had been the individual, Charles de Gaulle, whom the army had placed in power, so was it his individual authority which the army subsequently challenged over Algeria. De Gaulle carried the day over a specific policy, not because the professional corps accepted either the desirability of that policy or the right of executive authority to make decisions binding on the military, but because the army could not and would not mobilize sufficient force to topple De Gaulle as it had toppled the Fourth Republic. Officers tried persuasion, blackmail, defiance, and intimidation on various parts of the decision-making system; they encouraged, actively and passively, some of their cohorts and many civilians to go further in the application of pressure. But they drew back from open, full-scale commitment to a revolution.[1]

The confrontation, then, was a highly specific one. In itself De Gaulle's triumph provided no necessary precedent for his successor, particularly if executive power became diffuse and feeble. Military adherence to civilian decisions might come to depend on a lack of issues about which army leadership felt deeply. A lack of issues might in turn be caused by limitations on national statecraft voluntarily accepted by civilian government, without the army being forced to state them openly. Such restrictions might be even more severe than those imposed by military establishments of greater intrinsic strength in other Western countries.

Impersonal organizational relations between the military and civilian hierarchies provided no effective buffer to the army–De Gaulle confrontation. They were centered in the Government, one-half of the bifurcated executive branch, which was proving to be just as frail as the Fourth Republic's Council of Ministers. Members came and went; portfolios were shuffled back and forth; even the Premier was changed, just as in the bad old days. The Government lived in the long shadow cast by President de Gaulle. De Gaulle named the Government ministers; they held office at his pleasure. As the fates of Defense Minister Guillaumat and Jacques Soustelle demonstrated, there was no place in Gaullist councils for those who feared or wished to appease revolting groups. Also eliminated were those who possessed potentially independent sources of power, as, for instance, Premier Antoine Pinay and Premier Debré. Debré left, even though he enjoyed the confidence of the National Assembly (or at least the lack of an absolute majority in opposition). On the other hand, Premier Pompidou was able to stay without parliamentary support.

The organization of military relations, moreover, was new. Ever since

[1] Revolting groups produced a succession of "rivals" to De Gaulle, none of whom had any popular appeal, all of whom were regarded as far worse alternatives by the President's legal opposition. After General Challe, advanced as a national military leader, there was General Salan, the revolutionist. Salan in turn was succeeded by the civilian political type: Georges Bidault.

World War II political leaders had been experimenting with various forms, giving none a real chance to work. The Fifth Republic was initially constrained by the Algerian war to focus substantial, formal authority within the office of the Premier. That office was itself a fairly recent development in French political institutions, and it could serve far better as an instrument for policy implementation than as one of the sources of policy determination. With the establishment of peace in Algeria, there was no longer the same need for centralization, and structural lines were redrawn to give individual ministers more executory responsibility, while freeing the Premier for general administrative supervision. Under the best of circumstances it would take time to judge whether the re-allocation of roles, logical in itself, would produce either greater efficiency in the carrying out of military policy or greater congruence between decisions as to action and action itself. Time would likewise be needed to determine whether the new structures would be more effective in bringing military ideas and counsel to the process of policy-formulation.

In the interaction between office and office-holder, problems existed as much on the military as on the civilian side. The French professional army corps tended to take a negative view of what were called "political" officers, meaning those who were helping civilian authority formulate and execute national policy irrespective of military objections. The traditional "professional" attitude was more than deliberate aloofness from particular governments; it also included suspicion, fear, and active hostility. The paradoxical result was that the army became substantially politicalized. When De Gaulle sought loyal officers to execute "his" Algerian policy, the shuffling of positions and the recurrent rebellion of the supposedly trustworthy demonstrated the narrow margin of control he held over the thoroughly politicalized military hierarchy. The few officers who proved themselves strong-minded, dedicated followers of De Gaulle's government were not enough to operate indefinitely the necessarily complex military organization and civil-military councils. Succeeding senior officers had to be trained in outlook and behavior for which there was no deeply rooted tradition in France. Habits of mind and action had to be inculcated under the great pressure of accelerating military technology, which civilian leadership had deliberately chosen to embrace.

The substantive, as distinguished from the organizational, responsibilities of the army also pointed to its continued politicalization. The concept of the Nation in the Army's service was one of the most significant features of the political army. While combatting the poison of such military ideas, Gaullist policy failed to transform the army-nation relationship. Military curricula, which had become vehicles for indoctrination by activist officers with their ideas of revolutionary warfare, were not systematically replaced by rigorous study of social, political, and international relations. Gaullist leadership continued to go out of its way to espouse the myth of compulsory military service, despite the isolated criticism which was advanced, largely on economic grounds. For all the debasing military activities in Algeria, for all the specific outrages in the training of men and officers, an enforced period in the army was still presented as a "good," civilizing experience for young Frenchmen. Moreover, the decision to maintain a large standing army would inevitably mean that French forces must be largely foot soldiers, the very status so strenuously opposed as an imputed American objective.

Ironically, while the military's contribution to youth was being applauded, while the concept of "equality" of service was being specifically endorsed, the recruitment of officers was proceeding under quite a different code. No great attention was paid to broadening the social and economic base from which officer candidates were drawn or to changing the nature of the professional corps by substantial promotions from within the ranks.

There still remained the possibility that the post-Algerian ground forces might prove to be transitional in size and therefore in character. Increasing costs of the military establishment could force a reappraisal. The easiest expenses to cut, for a number of reasons, might well be those of recruitment, processing, and maintenance of manpower. As some commentators on military affairs were beginning to point out, the end of the Algerian war had also brought the end of a period when manpower was a relatively cheap way of obtaining military effectiveness. Its maintenance might become ruinously expensive when added to a modernization program designed for the new, largely European army.

Discontent on the part of those destined to provide the anonymous manpower might reinforce financial pressures. Would De Gaulle's authoritarian regime inspire sufficient dedication by the nation's youth so that it would embrace the judgment that military service was an enriching privilege? Would the utility of large ground forces for national and European defense remain uncontested, particularly in the absence of an overt threat by the Soviet Union? If, to maintain its hold over French youth, the army began to use a large number of draftees for a wide variety of non-military jobs, from teaching to harvesting, some might question the need, or even propriety, of a military overseer standing between a man and his job. Moreover, professional officers themselves might become dissatisfied with the role of parent-teacher-nursemaid-employer. A body of military opinion had always existed that the best army was a specialized one comprising a highly trained, career elite. This view might attract considerable support if it became apparent that neither prestige in society nor standing in professional military circles came from peace-time command over resentful draftees.

A final factor inviting reconsideration of the size and character of the Europe-based army was, once again, time, which was fading memories of the hundreds of thousands conscripted to fight in Algeria and retiring officers raised in the tradition of massed manpower.

Because official statements concerning military missions assayed so high in propagandistic content, they provide few clues to the future place of the military ingredient in national statecraft. De Gaulle had come to power saying that only the absence of strong government in Paris prevented the army from successfully meeting its responsibility to defend all of France's interests. Presumably he was re-educated by Algeria, but the omnibus nature of military missions was not changed. All he did was reverse the Fourth Republic's military-enforced priority on colonial combat, with continental security a distant second.[2] The primary mission was now to be the defense of France by nationally directed forces within the Western alliance. The overseas mission was not, however, abandoned. In fact, it was formally described as

[2] The mission of internal defense is discussed below.

broadened to include all states of the African Community, all French possessions anywhere, all French interests anywhere, and even compatible interests of France's allies. Most of this was sheer bombast. If the days of colonialism were over in North Africa and sub-Saharan Africa, the days of what native nationalism was prone to call "neo-colonialism" were fast ending. African affairs, including defense or the lack of it, were coming fully into the hands of African leaders. The Fifth Republic in practice paid scant attention to its own declarations about overseas missions, releasing foreign bases and assigning minimal forces to discharge remaining overseas responsibilities. The behavior of Tunisian, Moroccan, Algerian executives and the evolution of the Community gave no indication that any African state, except possibly Mauritania and the Malagasy Republic, would voluntarily invite French "forces of intervention" to defend them. The prospect of employment of these forces outside Africa, whether independently or in conjunction with units of France's allies, appeared equally remote. One must conclude that De Gaulle postulated a vast overseas military mission only to ease the army's shock at the loss of Algeria; it was a smoke-screen of sorts to cover the narrowing of French horizons to the continental hexagon.

Another mission — "operational defense of territory" — was also largely propagandistic. However, it reinforced, rather unpleasantly, the potential role of the army as instrument for social control. Meticulously prepared exercises provided opportunities for officers to become acquainted with each other, with France, and with new equipment. That the exercises were remote from any conceivable circumstances under which internal defense would become necessary might be temporarily irrelevant, but sooner or later a mission so isolated from reality would arouse a certain scepticism, even among professional officers enjoying fun in the open air. Reserve cadres and aging equipment would not improve on repeated inspection.

No more than its predecessor did the Fifth Republic take the steps necessary to create the type of militia capable of confronting a real occupying enemy with guerrilla resistance that was organized, pervasive, and persistent. Militarily directed guerrilla action might keep alive

— as World War II had so significantly failed to do — popular support
and trust in professional units. Such a definition of internal defense,
however, ran directly counter to historically imbedded views the army
had of itself. It also contradicted De Gaulle's aspirations for his France.
Therefore, while the relationship between the army and De Gaulle required the positing of multiple military missions, in paramount position
was necessarily the one concerned with the external defense of the
country.

Contrary to some American predictions, De Gaulle did not bring Algerian troops back and place them in NATO's European shield. Four
of the six divisions were ostentatiously kept outside the Organization,
although the President magnanimously said NATO could count them
for planning purposes. The responsibility of all six was to defend France
first, help its allies second. Was this conception of the army's role any
more realistic than the others? Where on the scale of probabilities stood
a Russian assault with conventional forces? Could one conceive of a
conventional war in the heart of Europe? If such a war were possible,
did not the true defense of France begin with the defense of West
Germany? Did not effective defense of Germany require in turn a
highly centralized, allied command? Should not France in its own interest, therefore, insist on integrating all conventional forces, including its
own, under the North Atlantic Treaty Organization? If the primary
purpose of conventional shield forces was to prevent a swift Russian in-
cursion, raise the stakes of invasion, provide the "pause for reflection"
that NATO planners talked so much about — if, in other words, the
value of the shield was its contribution to the over-all structure of deterrence, then the conclusion seemed obvious: the credibility of deterrence
would be enhanced by unified command and weakened by France's insistence on holding most of its forces aloof from the Organization,
whatever the Gaullist professions of loyalty to the alliance.

The apparently aberrant assignment for French conventionally armed
forces in Europe is explained by De Gaulle's domestic and international
objectives. A large standing army was needed to provide employment
and diversion for officers. The devil makes mischief for idle hands. Deprived of its Algerian occupation, undergoing a reduction in size, the

army might otherwise have far too many officers for available jobs. French industry could not suddenly absorb all the surplus, especially those officers who lacked modern technical training. For unemployed officers an alternative "career" beckoned, one dramatically spotlighted by Antoine Argoud's tour of French camps in Germany. Under-employed, dissatisfied officers could scheme and plot revenge on the man held responsible for their fall from favor.

And so De Gaulle undertook to convince officers in a series of speeches, particularly the one made at Strasbourg, that France had never had "so great a need of her soldiers." They were to be responsi-ble for the defense of France itself, not a North African territory. They and they alone were to have this assignment; they would not, as "the sirens of decadence" would have it, slough it off onto allies far and near. De Gaulle purposely devoted a third of his Strasbourg speech to recounting the tale of the city's defense during World War II. The lesson was plain. He sought another personal contract with the profes-sionals. He would refurbish them, exalt their missions, equate their prestige inside and outside France with his own. In return they would do their duty, for "outside these regulations, there can only be, there are only lost soldiers."

A second political consideration could hardly be voiced aloud. Whom were the French forces watching on the Rhine — the Russians, or . . . the Germans? West Germany was building a large and powerful army, one not possessing (yet) atomic weapons, but one with an increasing array of conventional and dual-purpose equipment. Its abnegation in abiding by formal prohibitions actually enabled Germany to concentrate on conventional power, as Gaullist nuclear ambitions prevented France from doing. Already, even as Germany was still bisected, the West German army was too big for its geographic trousers and was acquiring bases in other countries. French cooperation with this latest edition of the Wehrmacht was intimate; unified training, facilities, and arms pro-duction were capped by Adenauer–De Gaulle understandings, solem-nized in a Franco-German Treaty.

Merely to hold its own, let alone lead and channel the military rela-tionship, France needed to maintain conventional forces of considerable size and effectiveness. Would the six divisions, even when re-organized and re-armed, be enough to assure a continuing balance? Possibly, if German forces were committed to NATO and most of France's were not; if the right under Western European Union to place a ceiling on conventional forces were maintained; if the place of conventional forces in Western defense strategy remained secondary; if France and not Germany possessed the most prestigious weapons of all; if there were diplomatic recognition of which country led Europe, by the elevation of France to a position alongside Great Britain and the United States in a political directorate for the Western alliance.

A final objective to be supported by French conventional forces was increased influence with the United States. The Americans wanted a strong NATO; De Gaulle wanted a strong France in a world-encompassing alliance. The French President had taken no pains to conceal from his ally either his wishes for a reconstructed alliance or the "anti-integration" actions he was prepared to take to get his way. So far as De Gaulle was concerned, his evaluation of NATO's "integration" depended on who was doing the integrating. A NATO dominated by the Anglo-Saxons would remain unacceptable to the Fifth Republic. However, were the Organization to be revised to accord with France's continental position and global responsibilities, then a multi-national system of command over closely cooperating conventional forces might be acceptable. With Great Britain withdrawing militarily from the continent — "the Botch on the Rhine" — with West Germany (hopefully) bound to France, the prospects of eventual American compromise were not unpromising.

Obviously more bargaining power was required than four conventional divisions held aloof from NATO's shield (while officially committed to allied defense). The *force de frappe*, both in anticipation and in being, offered far larger possibilities at the conference table. Now emerges a second partially legitimate argument: this one between De Gaulle and the United States. In its diplomacy, by its statutes, the United States had defined a great state as one having atomic weapons. In France it had been a Premier of the Fourth Republic, Félix Gaillard, not the President of the Fifth, who had first pointed out the influence

American policy had had on France's decision. In a choice between great power or nothing, between relative independence or satellite status, France must perforce become an atomic nation. How France reached that inexorable end depended entirely on the United States, which held the weapons, the technological skills, the industrial resources, and, since Nassau, the reins to British policy as well. In confronting their mutual potential enemy, was it correct treatment of an ally, was it even rational policy, for the United States to compel France to duplicate at great expense all the steps toward an atomic military capacity?

Assistance in developing a modest French nuclear force, on the other hand, would contribute in several ways to American statecraft. A more powerful France would become, as it most anxiously desired, a greater participant in affairs of the alliance. If made truly multi-national, the credibility of the Western deterrence system with the Russians would be considerably strengthened. The United States would find that, with the removal of this long-standing irritant, France stood forth as a major, dependable partner. Finally, De Gaulle might add, *sotto voce*, there are my problem children to deal with. American officials should appreciate what soldiers are like; they also had learned the hard way here and there around the globe. Soldiers need a firm hand, but they need tangible rewards for good behavior, too. It was not easy to bring the politicalized army back to obedience; without the prospects of a *force de frappe* it might have been impossible. Now French military spokesmen were criticizing the projected national deterrent both as too weak and as destructive of ties with their counterparts in other countries, especially Great Britain and the United States. If there were substance to such complaints, the cure was to be found, De Gaulle might conclude, in Washington, not in Paris.

"Of course," President de Gaulle told his fourth press conference on April 11, 1961, "it is understandable that the powers which possess atomic weapons, that is the United States, the Soviet Union, and Great Britain, do not wish France to acquire them." Not at all understandable to the French President or in fact to any observer were the confusion and contradictions in American policy toward the French *force de*

frappe. Even before France produced an atomic bomb, American statecraft had shown itself as inconsistent and vacillating on this subject as it
was on the larger, related issues of deterrence and arms control. Public
debate *followed* instead of preceded each official pronouncement.
Declarations were repeatedly "interpreted," until they lost any meaning
or even assumed the opposite of that originally intended. Outbursts
against independent nuclear weapons systems were succeeded by warn-
ings of the inevitable spread of such systems. Proposals to "satisfy"
France and "solve" the "problems" of NATO were a dime a dozen; not
infrequently they sought to do one at the expense of the other. Expressions of outright hostility to the French force were accompanied
by those of "understanding" for the French viewpoint and of a desire
for improved Franco-American relations.

Studying American declaratory policy over a decade and placing it
against concrete actions, French leaders concluded that continued intransigence might bring the United States around. Whether it did so or
not, unwavering determination to pursue a national nuclear force remained necessary, for how could a country which had such difficulty in
deciding what it thought of Western defense, nuclear proliferation, and
the *force de frappe* be counted on to commit its people indefinitely to
the protection of Europe?

Nonetheless, in spite of all the French arguments — and many are
not without logic — measured evaluation of postwar French politics, of
the nature of the Fifth Republic, of De Gaulle's statecraft, of the nature
and potentialities of the French deterrent force, points to the conclusion that no aid or encouragement should be volunteered to France's
nuclear pretensions. No sharp dividing line, of course, exists between
"ordinary" weapons and those indirectly contributing to a nuclear striking force. A policy of "no aid or encouragement" could therefore be
construed to mean little if any military cooperation. On the other hand,
a limited interpretation of what constitutes positive support could find
the United States providing everything — missiles, planes, carriers, submarines — except nuclear warheads. Relatedness of weapons systems,
their overlap in destructive potential, the multi-purpose nature of many
military items have frequently been used by Americans, in their deal-

ings with many countries in the world, as justification for a policy of "let them have what they want if they really want it and can pay for it or will promise someday to pay something for it in some kind of currency." The reasoning is as spurious as the conclusion is dangerous. The result is non-statecraft, since statecraft consists in drawing essentially arbitrary, *ad hoc* distinctions among shadings that are often scarcely perceptible. No one selection could, perhaps, be completely defended in isolation, but no one selection must stand alone. With others, it contributes to a pattern: splotchy, discontinuous, but recognizable.

Let the American approach to France's nuclear striking force then be: as little aid and comfort as possible, beginning with none at all. Why? For years scientific prognostications that national nuclear weapons systems would rapidly proliferate were accepted without much questioning in the United States, possibly because Americans had been twice shocked by the speed with which the Soviet Union had demonstrated an atomic, then a thermonuclear, capacity. Yet there were several things wrong with these predictions. They under-estimated or disregarded altogether the variety of serious constraints, in addition to technical ones, which discouraged states from developing their own nuclear weapons. If effective nuclear systems did spread, it would be largely the result of assistance rendered by "established" nuclear nations.[3] "Proliferation" achieved by purely national effort might well be more apparent than real. As the United States government could testify, the precise moment a country possessed a "substantial" nuclear capacity was very difficult to determine. Of course, the spread might actually occur eventually, but even so the United States would be wrong to assume that what would some day be, would necessarily be good. Deterrence "theorists" might derive fun and profit by constructing "games" which posited the existence of several nuclear powers, but "benefits" accruing to American statecraft from pushing the presumed inevitable along a bit faster are as illusory as notions of "defending" Western Europe through limited atomic warfare. The United States, like the Soviet Union, has a literally vital stake in retarding to the utmost the diffusion of atomic armament. France suspects the United States of

[3] See Beaton, Maddox, *op. cit.*, esp. pp. 35–65, 185–210.

desiring a nuclear arms control pact with the Soviet Union, containing as a cardinal provision restrictions on the transfer of such weapons. It must be hoped that France's suspicions are justified.

France would no doubt continue its own efforts to develop an atomic capacity despite expressed opposition and positive discouragement from the United States. American interest, to put it bluntly, would nevertheless continue to be best served if the French *force* were as slow as possible in emerging and as weak as possible when it did emerge. So far, two characteristics of the French deterrent are certainly slowness and weakness. In matters of nuclear technology there is an understandable but regrettable tendency for thought to take an anticipatory leap from blueprint to mass production. Mistakes have been made in predicting operational date, numbers, even the existence of Soviet, British, and American nuclear weapons systems. These mistakes should not be duplicated in the case of France. Painfully France has crept up on a nuclear capacity, in the only way it could, testing large, obsolete bombs, wrestling them down to size and up in power, scrapping one obsolete delivery system for one-way or hedge-hopping aircraft. The French contention that "everything" has been on schedule is in itself eloquent testimony to the problem of building a deterrent force from scratch, with insignificant resources compared to those of the United States. For, if all went according to plan, what would exist by the end of 1963 would certainly not be a *deterrent;* it would hardly be a *force* at all. Available would be a bare handful of bombers, a small pile of bombs. A beginning, perhaps, enough to do some suicidal mischief if placed in the hands of a maniac, but still, even by the minimal standards of rationalizing generals and politicians, an ineffective military instrument.[4] Still ahead lay any form of "production in series" of either weapon or delivery system.

All the while France, instead of "catching up" with the United States or the Soviet Union, has been falling further and further behind, as De Gaulle's dismissal of the Anglo-American Nassau offer indicated. Loom-

---

[4] It was a "nuclear striking force" of this limited measure which the United States aided so materially and psychologically by selling jet tankers at a strategic juncture.

ing on the horizon for every nuclear power is the awesome problem of the "second generation," the substitution of missiles and submarines for manned aircraft. Notwithstanding American assistance and the experience of its own scientists, Great Britain was forced to re-examine the value of an independent deterrent in light of the cost required to make that transition. Even the United States decided that, for all its wealth, the nation should not try to produce everything military considerations alone might make desirable. Painful cut-backs were ordered, whole weapons systems deferred or scrapped, the panoply of nuclear protection trimmed.

France's ambitions were more limited. It opted for restrictions from the very beginning of the development process. Still the cost climbed, and at an accelerating rate. Impoverish its conventional arsenal as it will, France cannot succeed in evading the issue of transition. The credibility of a deterrent is linked to the inexorable advance of military technology. The credibility of a few planes and bombs is low; that of *older*, though more numerous, planes would be still lower.

"You might not frighten the enemy," Wellington is supposed to have told his troops during the campaign in Spain, "but by God, gentlemen, you certainly frighten me." The spectre of an operational national nuclear force frightens many Frenchmen. This outlook, plus the number and prominence of those who hold it, constitutes another compelling argument against American assistance. Most Western peoples still believe that American power is committed to their defense, that American leadership, regardless of party, will continue to accept the responsibilities derived from the commitment. This applies to Frenchmen, as to Canadians, Englishmen, and Germans.[5] Does Gaullist France really seek an independent nuclear force because it doubts the stability, sincerity, or capacity for execution of the American commitment? Or does Gaullist France voice such doubts because it has already decided to pursue the nuclear will-o'-the-wisp and needs must use every justification it can scrape together? To gain acceptance by the French of a national all-out nuclear effort has been a difficult, indeed an impossible,

[5] Unfortunately for American policy makers, this trust in the United States is one reason why Europeans do not rush to build up their conventional forces.

job. Both the National Assembly and the Senate turned down the original program in 1960; it passed only because an absolute majority could not be mustered to censure the government. The "European majority" of 1962 made a unified Western defense, organized along the lines of the Common Market, a part of its Manifesto. A month later the French parliament was again rejecting credits for the nuclear force.

Such determined opposition is remarkable, especially when one considers the grave weaknesses of established parties, the dominating power of De Gaulle, and the vacillations of American policy. Might not resistance follow the cost curve upward as more public attention is devoted to the question of missiles and submarines? Is it not possible to envisage today's divided, passive, impotent majority becoming tomorrow's policy makers? The military nuclear transition is not the only one in the offing. The United States would compound past misjudgments if it ignored the inevitable devolution of political power in France. "We live in our time," declares De Gaulle. True, but enlightened statecraft plans for future contingencies.

De Gaulle's Eurovision has provoked from the United States a reaction as dubious as that to the *force de frappe*. The French President's diagnosis of the developing nature of the international environment seems substantially correct. Shifts in the power and policy of the Soviet Union, recovery of Western Europe, threats in Asia to the security of the non-Communist world have all produced pressure for evolution away from the hierarchical North Atlantic Treaty *Organization* toward the North Atlantic *alliance*. Other countries, not just France, actively seek a greater sense of participation in Western affairs than can be provided by an exclusively military, predominantly Americanized, Organization. So far American responses have been contradictory and unimaginative. The system of political consultation has improved, but comparable development in political control over military decision has not taken place.

Instead, the United States pursues the worst of both possible worlds by producing plans for what is labelled a multi-national nuclear defense force. If that force remains in actuality under United States control — and this provides the only guarantee of responsibility *plus* effectiveness — nothing has been enhanced except European frustration, French intransigence, and German appetite. If the force is in actuality subject to direction by participating European states, the United States has pushed the cart well to the front of the horse. As De Gaulle stated in his memorandum of September 1958, what is needed is more European involvement in the process of making decisions affecting the alliance. Many of America's allies are more than satisfied with a practical United States monopoly of nuclear weapons; they, like the United States, fear the possible consequences of diffused national control over their use. It is not the firmness of the American commitment to defend Western Europe which is questioned, but rather events which, by weakening the credibility of deterrence, might make that commitment ineffective.

In attempting to reconcile military imperatives with European desires, American statecraft should seek to restrict and loosen the Organization, broaden and strengthen the alliance. The function of the former should be to serve the alliance by supervising conventional aspects of Western deterrence under a representative, politically satisfactory system of command. Like the Organization, the alliance should rest on recognition of several levels of authority and responsibility. One of its primary purposes should be to widen the avenues toward understanding the process of American policy-formulation, particularly aspects of atomic strategy, for which the United States should continue to bear ultimate responsibility. There is no need to define an acceptable Atlantic Community as a supranational political system or NATO as fifteen (or some fewer) fingers on the atomic trigger. What is long overdue is adaptation to the reality of rediscovered national identities in an alliance whose military justification rests on successful deterrence in Europe and avoidance of nuclear war anywhere in the world.

De Gaulle's analysis of Britain's position toward the continent was more realistic and more frankly expressed than that publicly offered by the American or even by the British government. Abandoning the policy of centuries, Great Britain seeks to enter Europe — so ran the American-English theme. As propaganda it might have had some value. As description it lacked verisimilitude. Recurrently throughout its history and unremittingly since the first decade of the twentieth century Great Britain has been involved in European affairs, much as a man caught in a revolving door. Britain was *always* entering or leaving Europe, for reasons as obvious in 1963 as in 1923. Great Britain could not tolerate a Europe which might be militarily, politically, or economically combined against it — in other words, *united*. Since 1947 it had been presenting to Europeans definitions of unity which, if they did not mean disunity, certainly meant limited international cooperation. Or, as in the case of the European Defense Community, the British suggestion was essentially "let's you and him unite." Great Britain's approach to the Economic Community merged the elements of previous advances. Entry of Britain and the countries of the Free Trade Area, to which Britain was formally committed, would, as De Gaulle suggested, have loosened the bonds of the Common Market. Simultaneously, exceptions sought by Britain would have created two types of integration — one applying to the Inner Six, the other to the Outer Seven (or less).

There is no villain in the piece. The problem stems from the continuing nature of Britain's historic ambivalence. Before De Gaulle caused the rupture of stalemated negotiations, some familiar questions, previously submerged by Anglo-American officialdom, were again attracting attention. Why should Great Britain turn its back on the Commonwealth, which, for all its lack of definition, represented Britain's primary claim to being a world power? Why should Great Britain give up its special ties with the United States, which, for all their fragility, represented Britain's secondary claim to being a world power? Whether defined economically and militarily by De Gaulle or politically by the Benelux nations, the "Europe" Great Britain sought to "enter" entailed a reduction in British status. With American support, Britain might remain for a long time a leading participant in the three overlapping groupings of Commonwealth, Europe, and Anglo-American alliance. Although French governments have aspired to make a triumvirate of the duality, they have also referred continually to the "Anglo-Saxons," recognizing facts of international life which might require France to be satisfied with something less.

For the organization of Western Europe does indeed present the three-pronged problem De Gaulle so clearly perceives. West Germany is the key. Without German participation there can be no lasting economic progress, political stability, or military security on the continent. It would be chimerical to expect the regime succeeding Adenauer's to have either *Der Alte's* grasp on German political life or his dedication to the proposition that Germany's future must rest only on responsible commitment to Western Europe and the Western alliance. Thanks to the speed with which the United States transformed occupation into restored nationhood, it is too late to anchor West Germany's position by submerging its sovereignty in a supranational political system. But the prospects would be extremely grim if the time had also passed to make more durable the ties binding Germany to its Western neighbors. Recognizing the challenge, French statecraft for almost a decade has been directed toward a Franco-German partnership within an organized Western European framework.

De Gaulle also perceived, albeit in somewhat tendentious terms, that successful cooperation required that the directorates of the three Communities be made responsible to political authority. The need was exactly the same as existed in the North Atlantic Treaty Organization and arose because of, not in spite of, the importance of the Communities. Decisions, as commission presidents proudly maintained, had inevitable political consequences, since they required congruent state behavior in an ever-widening area. There could be no "purely" technical, economic actions in such matters as agricultural price-supports, mobility of labor, international cartels.

The alternatives were equally clear. Without explicitly defined political authority, the commissions would themselves become that authority. Unanswerable to any electorate, they would construct a new Europe. Given the great economic power of the United States, the Europe they built might well, Gaullists feared, be more Anglo-Saxon than European, more privately capitalistic than state-directed. Whatever the logic of their fear, Gaullists found the only other source of responsible direction was in the states themselves. The Six had come together to build the Communities. When the cooperating countries were still relatively weak, they had agreed to place aspects of supranational power in the High Authority of the Coal-Steel Community. In its operations, however, the Authority depended on building a consensus among participating private as well as public groups within the Six. Political unification was the goal written into the treaties, but national leadership was the contemporary, operational reality.

There was no third alternative between national and supranational responsibility. There was no "Europe" in the sense of political unification of the Six. How, when, even why such unification might come about was hotly debated. When World War II left them helpless, their independence threatened, their right to separate existence questioned, it had appeared possible — because it seemed necessary — to submerge national sovereignties voluntarily. The fate of the Council of Europe and the European Political Community proved otherwise. Whence now would come the will; what force would now be the federator? Several types of Europeans emerged. Some expressed what through repetition had become an article of faith; true believers had their value, but not as policy makers. Some sought to enhance their own importance, or that of their party, or that of their country; they saw in the slogan "political unification" an alternate extra-national route to power, just as West German leadership had when the defeated country was occupied. Some criers after "Europe" sought freedom for themselves through constraints on others. And finally there were those who had concluded that unification was not only desirable, but inevitable.

De Gaulle had answers for each group. The present ingredient with which statesmen perforce must work was the Western European state system. It was conceivable that unification might someday come, but it was a long way off. Imminent or delayed, however, the desirability of unification was open to serious question. Therefore, what national benefit could be derived from speeding up the tempo?

Far from encouraging the French policy of developing German responsibility through durable connections with Western Europe — a policy perfectly attuned to American interests — the United States, whether intentionally or not, played a dangerous balance-of-power game. After World War II Americans found defeated Germany more amenable to direction than a France they sometimes felt did not act defeated enough. After West Germany had recovered its sovereignty under American sponsorship, the United States continued to act as though bilateral connections would bring maximum advantages. Military preferences in this regard were particularly noticeable because they were so openly expressed. But civilian diplomacy also seemed to seek out Germany when relations with France were difficult (as they almost always were). American policy thereby invited mockery of its professed belief in the unification of Europe. Irresponsible, unnecessary risks were assumed in its optimistic presumptions about the behavior of a post-Adenauer Germany. And all for naught. There was no balance struck. No moderation was forced upon French policy. France's choice was to move even closer to West Germany. Surely the United States cannot view with pleasure or equanimity the prospect of a weak France in a multi-national Western Europe dominated by an increasingly nationalistic West Germany.

De Gaulle and the French military leaders might legitimately argue over how best to defend the nation's interests; France and the United States might legitimately argue over the French national nuclear force; but Franco-American divergence over the organization of Europe seemed to arise mainly out of individual conflicts. So long were Americans bemused by the myth that their own miraculous unity could guide Europe toward the cure of its own ills that they sometimes persisted in prescribing "unity" as a placebo, without either defining it or bothering to notice that many of Europe's postwar distresses were vanishing without it. Not the formal attributes of the continental system, but the satisfaction of peoples' wants within responsible political institutions must be the common goal of both Gaullist and a realistic American diplomacy. One can endow these rather vague phrases with concrete meaning. A European system should be an evolving one, not closed and discriminatory. Since the Economic Community is inherently discriminatory and, at least in the short run, closed, the United States can only use its influence to reduce to a minimum its undesirable effects. Such has, indeed, been one of several American policies adopted toward the Community. Necessary periodic bargaining over the Community's provisions, the failure of the British application, leveling off of economic advance by the Six, the continuing question of Africa's relation to the Community should all make it possible for the United States to seek more consistently than in the past liberal trading principles applied as broadly and in as wide a multilateral context as possible.

Another aspect of a European system compatible with both French and American statecraft is suggested by De Gaulle's quite obvious preference for a "European" Europe. To the extent that this implies a system without vested interests in East-West tensions, it could materially aid a United States trying to improve the chances for human survival. The ability of the United States to manipulate the international environment *is* declining. The break-up of the frozen bi-polar world *is* far progressed. Yet the individual conflicts begun during the cold war all remain. Multi-faceted approaches to their solution are urgently needed.

In this post-postwar world a "European" Europe of closely cooperating states can have a crucial part to play — the very part De Gaulle has envisioned. The United States did not spend billions of dollars and commit thousands of men in order that Western Europe might remain indefinitely a subservient dependent. The United States has always sought to reduce, and eventually to eliminate, the danger arising from Soviet-American military confrontations on the body of Europe. In the larger perspective there is no necessary clash between the "grand design" of Charles de Gaulle in Europe and an equally far-sighted American statecraft.

BIBLIOGRAPHICAL NOTE

INVALUABLE for any study of the French army's opposition to De Gaulle's Algerian policy are the accounts of the trials of military and civilian figures. Transcripts of the proceedings against Generals Challe and Zeller (Paris, Nouvelles Editions Latines, 1961), Salan, and Jouhaud (separate volumes published by Editions Albin Michel, 1962, Paris) are available, but for other trials of OAS-CNR activists the author relied on the full reports, with lengthy quotations, by Le Monde's J.-M. Théolleyre. Jacques Isorni, who defended wholeheartedly some of the accused, has written a general defense of the French Algeria viewpoint, Lui qui les juge, Paris, Flammarion, 1962. A special record of disillusionment is Jacques Soustelle's L'Espérance trahie, Paris, Editions de l'Alma, 1962. Leaping from the trial records and ex parte pleading is the depth of feeling concerning the place which the army should occupy in the nation. Equally conspicuous is the view of political institutions as temporary, suspect — hence challengeable — embodiments of national virtues to which the officer corps should be dedicated. Both complexes of attitudes are also revealed in military writings. Among the most reasoned is General Jean Valluy, "Le nouveau duo, Armée-Nation," Revue des Deux Mondes, October 15, 1962, pp. 481–499; "Réflexions sur l'armée de demain," same journal, July 15, 1962, pp. 161–172.

Secondary accounts of the Algerian uprisings help to document the types of political action undertaken by army officers. Merry and Serge Bromberger followed their Secrets of Suez, London, Sidgwick and Jackson, 1957, and Les 13 complots du 13 mai, Paris, Fayard, 1959, with Barricades et colonels, Paris, Fayard, 1960, which concerns the Algiers civilian uprising of January 1960 and to which Georgette Elgey and J.-F. Chavel also contributed. Although well known for their skill as political commentators, Jacques Fauvet and Jean Planchais have limited themselves almost entirely to chronological exposition of the April 1961 military revolt in La Fronde des généraux, Paris, Arthaud, 1961. Henri Azeau's Révolte militaire, Paris, Plon, 1961, includes sketches of the prime participants, along with a chapter on "revolutionary war." In The Fall of the Republic, Ann Arbor, University of Michigan Press, 1962, James H. Meisel is concerned with more than the events of May 1958. He also seeks to reconstruct the patterns of military thought and relate them to major strains in European political philosophy. The conspiratorial atmosphere which characterized Algeria from 1956 to 1962 led to an abundance of "inside" stories. Besides the Brombergers' effort to disentangle the *complots*, there is J.-R. Tournoux, *Secrets d'état*, Paris, Plon, 1960, and Claude Paillat, *Dossier secret de l'Algérie*, Paris, Le Livre Contemporain, 1961. Among the best accounts of the role played by draftees in the April 1961 revolt is Christian Hébert, "Quatre journées en Algérie," *La Nef*, No. 7, July-September 1961, pp. 112–123.

General studies of the French army are primarily historical exegeses. Paul-Marie de la Gorce, whose reports on military maneuvers were used in the preparation of Chapter 7, has written *The French Army*, translation by Kenneth Douglas, New York, George Braziller, 1963. An earlier study, more concerned with French military thought, is Raoul Girardet, *La société militaire dans la France contemporaine*, Paris, Plon, 1953. Richard Challener, *The French Theory of the Nation in Arms, 1866–1939*, New York, Columbia University Press, 1955, is a most adept analysis of the interaction of abstract formulations, political interests, and military experience. More far-ranging than its title implies is Philip C. F. Bankwitz, "Maxime Weygand and the Army-Nation Concept in the Modern French Army," *French Historical Studies*, Vol. II, No. 2, Fall 1961, pp. 157–189. Three journals devoted one issue to analyzing the "problem" of the French army. *Guerre-Armée-Société*, *Revue Française de Sociologie*, April-June 1961, focussed primarily on the latter two variables. Appearing over a decade earlier, *Esprit's Armée française?* (May 1950) was unusually reflective, perhaps because the anticipated crisis was not yet at hand. *Les Cahiers de la République*, No. 28, November-December 1960, presented in *A la recherche d'une Armée perdue* a brief analysis by François Gromier, followed by a wide-ranging debate on its validity.

There is, of course, no dearth of soul-searching by and for the French army, in addition to the items previously cited. Three authors and one journal (*Revue de Défense Nationale*) are especially prominent: Jean Planchais (*Le malaise de l'Armée*, Paris, Plon, 1958), Tony Albord ("La pensée militaire française," *Revue de Défense Nationale*, October 1960, pp. 1577–1588), Vincent Monteil (*Les officiers*, Paris, Editions du Seuil, 1958). Nor should one neglect Gilles Perrault, *Les parachutistes*, Paris, Editions du Seuil, 1961, or René Deslisle, "La crise interne du corps des officiers," *La Nef*, No. 7, July-September 1961, pp. 39–51. As mentioned in the text, the pages of the *Revue de Défense Nationale* were filled between 1956 and 1960 with (sometimes fairly oblique) expositions of "revolutionary war." Particularly noteworthy contributors were General Zeller ("Armée et politique," April 1957, pp. 499–518), General Marchand ("Stratégie et psychologie en Afrique Nord," February 1956, pp. 190–200), General Gazin ("Réplique ou représailles," October 1958, pp. 1488–1496), General Chassin

("Du rôle historique de l'Armée," October 1956, pp. 1182–1200), Colonel Nemo ("La guerre dans le milieu social," May 1956, pp. 605–624), Lt. Colonel Rousset ("A propos de subversion et d'insurrection," March 1960, pp. 498–507), and Thierry Maulnier ("L'Armée, l'Algérie et la Nation," March 1960, pp. 393–400). Maurice Megret's *La guerre psychologique,* Paris, Presses Universitaires de France, 1956, is indicative of the many expositions of the French-fabricated phenomenon which pay inadequate attention to the motivational link between ideas developed to combat an external enemy and ideas applied to the destruction of the nation's government.

The most uncompromising indictment of French behavior in Algeria is that by Pierre Vidal-Naquet, *La raison d'état,* Paris, Editions de Minuit, 1962, although both Henri Alleg, *The Question,* New York, George Braziller, 1958, and *The Gangrene,* New York, Lyle Stuart, 1960, attracted more attention. The contrast between assertedly lofty motives and actually base means was one theme in Jean Lartéguy's novel, *The Centurions,* New York, E. P. Dutton, 1962, and in Jean-Jacques Servan-Schreiber's personal account of a *Lieutenant in Algeria,* New York, Knopf, 1957. Four treatments of the complex of military attitudes are Xavier Grall, *La génération du djebel,* Paris, Editions du CERF, 1962; Lieutenant X, "Pourquoi nous avons 'perdu' la guerre d'Algérie," *La Nef,* No. 7, July-September 1961, pp. 19–37; Yves Bertherat, "Lettre d'ancien combattant," *Esprit,* October 1962, pp. 382–386; and Edgard Pisani, "Un officier parle," *Revue de Paris,* November 1960, pp. 118–127. Commentary on the Algerian war continues to appear. Among those which best illuminate the non-military aspects of the confrontation are Jules Roy, *The War in Algeria,* New York, Grove Press, 1961, Germaine Tillion, *France and Algeria,* New York, Knopf, 1961, and Joseph Kraft, *The Struggle for Algeria,* Garden City, Doubleday, 1961.

Americans acquainted with the manifold, detailed studies of national policy-making will be surprised at the relative lack of attention to political and administrative relations between the military and civilian hierarchies in France. Political affairs are treated by Raoul Girardet, "Pouvoir civil et pouvoir militaire dans la France contemporaine," *Revue Française de Science Politique,* March 1960, pp. 5–39; Georges Lescuyer, "Les militaires et la politique," I, II, *Revue Politique et Parlementaire,* May 1962, pp. 101–106, June 1962, pp. 76–81; Edward Behr, "The French Army as a Political and Social Factor," *International Affairs,* October 1959, pp. 438–447; and Guy Chapman, "France, the French Army and Politics," in Michael Howard, ed., *Soldiers and Governments,* London, Eyre and Spottiswoode, 1957, pp. 51–73. Exceptional in its addition of sociological-ideological factors to political and administrative considerations is Louis Dullin's, "L'Armée de nos enfants," I, II, *Revue Politique et Parlementaire,* October 1962, pp. 98–102,

November 1962, pp. 79–86. More recent interpretations of national defense organization include Michel de Lombares, "L'Organisation de la défense: questions préalables," *Revue de Défense Nationale*, August-September 1962, pp. 1307–1316; J. Dours, J. Duboc, "La nouvelle organisation générale de la défense," same journal, February 1959, pp. 219–227. Some viewers of the kaleidoscopic nature of the Fourth Republic's military administration were Edgard Pisani, "L'Organisation de la défense nationale," *Revue Politique et Parlementaire*, February 1956, pp. 158–169; Michel Morin, "Les vicissitudes de l'organisation de la défense nationale," *Revue de Défense Nationale*, April 1951, pp. 458–468; and André Monteil, "L'Organisation de la défense nationale," *Revue Politique et Parlementaire*, May 1948, pp. 117–124. Primary sources of data and analysis remain the military commentators for such newspapers as *Le Monde, Figaro,* and *Combat.*

The best commentator on Gaullism is, of course, Charles de Gaulle. His important speeches and press conferences have been rendered into English and made available to Americans by the Service de Presse et d'Information of the Ambassade de France, New York. André Passeron has included many of De Gaulle's statements when touring the provinces or Algeria in his collection *De Gaulle parle*, Paris, Plon, 1962, although his choice of a substantive rather than chronological division sometimes causes confusion. For those unacquainted with De Gaulle's recent career (if such there be) Edmond Michelet has written a uniformly laudatory primer: *Le Gaullisme: passionnante aventure*, Paris, Fayard, 1962.

It is perhaps too early to expect analysis of changing concepts of justice under the Fifth Republic, apart from brief commentary in newspapers and in a few journals. *Esprit*, chronicler of the strains of dementia spewed forth by OAS-CNR groups and sympathizers, has published two articles: Paul Thibaud, "Les atteintes à la sûreté des Français," March 1961, pp. 353–381; and Casamayor, "La justice vivante," October 1962, pp. 399–430. Military recruitment and training has received more, but not adequate, attention. Under NATO auspices a handbook on *Military Education Systems* was prepared for a conference in 1962, with each member supplying minimal data on its own program. The April-June 1961 issue of the *Revue Française de Sociologie*, mentioned above, contained a report on "Attitudes et motivations des candidats aux grandes écoles militaires," pp. 133–152; and Viviane Isambert-Jamat's brief "Remarques sur le service militaire," pp. 100–106. *La Revue Libérale*, No. 37, 1 Trimestre, 1962, pp. 69–76, contains Lothar Hilbert's useful "L'Officier français à notre époque." General Jean Malgré had earlier written of "La crise de Saint-Cyr et ses remèdes" for *Revue Politique et Parlementaire*, April 1956, pp. 21–30, in an article whose primary title was "Recrutement des officiers et structure sociale."

Details of France's military modernization program must be gleaned
with care from as large a variety of sources as possible. As with other armies,
the emphasis tends to be on what is planned, rather than on what has
actually been produced in quantity. *Revue de Défense Nationale's* monthly
"Chronique militaire" helps to bridge this gap, as do two articles by Perret-
Gentil in *Revue Militaire Suisse:* "Armée française: faits d'actualité," October
1961, and "Vers la force de frappe," June 1962, pp. 277–287. Defense
Minister Pierre Messmer sets forth official plans for the Gaullist army in "The
French Military Establishment of Tomorrow," *Orbis,* Summer 1962, pp. 205–
217 (a translation of an article appearing February 15, 1962 in *Revue des
Deux Mondes*). As the text indicates, *Interavia* and *Flight and the Aircraft
Engineer* have devoted continuing attention to France's air force program. In
addition, Georges Hereil, aircraft company executive, has summarized
France's record and hopes: "L'Aviation, son présent, son avenir," I, II,
Revue Politique et Parlementaire, January 1962, pp. 50–56, February 1962,
pp. 53–59.

The history of France's search for an independent nuclear deterrent has
received considerable attention. Among the best accounts are the government's own White Paper; its pamphlet entitled *France and the Atom;* French
scientist Bertrand Goldschmidt's "The French Atomic Energy Program,"
Bulletin of the Atomic Scientists, September 1962, pp. 39–42; and Leonard
Beaton, John Maddox, *The Spread of Nuclear Weapons,* London, Chatto and
Windus, 1962, pp. 81–98. The most thorough and unalloyed case against the
nuclear program is Daniel Dollfus, *La force de frappe,* Paris, Julliard, 1960.
Raymond Aron has followed the twists and turns of official policy with some
of his own — cf. articles in *Le Figaro* and "De Gaulle and Kennedy: the
Nuclear Debate," *Atlantic,* August 1962, pp. 33–39. In the forefront of
analysts of the international political repercussions of France's effort is
Jacques Vernant, whose articles appear regularly in *Politique Etrangère,*
published under the auspices of his Centre d'Etudes de Politique Etrangère,
and in *Revue de Défense Nationale.* In the latter journal presentations have
been made by such authorities as General Ailleret, General Chassin, and
Claude Delmas (see, particularly, Delmas' timely "La 'force de frappe'
nationale: les données du problème," October 1960, pp. 1549–1566). Contre-
Amiral Lepotier argues for a French version of the Polaris in "La force de
'dissuasion' sous-marine," November 1962, pp. 1666–1683. One of the tire-
less General Gallois' longer explanations of just how the French atomic
arsenal would contribute to Western strength and safety is *Balance of Terror,*
Boston, Houghton Mifflin, 1961. (This volume also contains a vigorous
defense of Dulles' "massive retaliation" dogmas.)

A brambled thicket of exegesis has sprung up around the subject of

France's relations with the West. Claude Delmas propounded his country's point of view in "Quel est l'avenir du pacte atlantique?" and "L'Europe et l'Atlantique," July 1958, pp. 1103–1116, January 1960, pp. 51–67 of *Revue de Défense Nationale*. Delmas, Carpentier, Gallois, and Faure also collaborated in a discussion of *L'Avenir de l'alliance atlantique*, Paris, Berger-Levrault, 1961. Aspects of Gaullist European statecraft are considered by Maurice Schumann, "France and Germany in the New Europe," *Foreign Affairs*, October 1962, pp. 66–78; André Fontaine, "De Gaulle's View of Europe and the Nuclear Debate," *Reporter*, July 19, 1962, pp. 33–35; Stanley Hoffmann, "Les rapports franco-américains," *Esprit*, October 1962, pp. 528–540. Some early sceptics of the alliance were Pierre Billotte, *Le temps du choix*, Paris, Robert Laffont, 1950; and Marshal Juin, Henri Massis, *The Choice Before Europe*, London, Eyre and Spottiswoode, 1958.

Americans concerned with European defense fall easily into several types of confusion, taking exhortation for analysis, prescription for probability. Henry Kissinger has given his current opinions in two articles in *Foreign Affairs*: "The Unsolved Problems of European Defense," July 1962, pp. 515–542 and "Strains on the Alliance," January 1963, pp. 261–286. Sandwiched between, McGeorge Bundy writes of "Friends and Allies," October 1962, pp. 14–24, and Dean Acheson provides some thoughts on "The Practice of Partnership," January 1963, pp. 247–261. Walter Lippmann sketches with a very broad brush in *Western Unity and the Common Market*, Boston, Little, Brown and Company, 1962. Of particular interest is U.S. Senate Document 132, 87th Congress, Second Session, "Problems and Trends in Atlantic Partnership I, Some Comments on the European Economic Community and NATO," Government Printing Office, September 14, 1962.

Alastair Buchan (*NATO in the 1960's*, London, Wiedenfeld and Nicolson, 1960) was an early advocate of nuclear cooperation. (See also his "Reform of NATO," *Foreign Affairs*, January 1962, pp. 165–183.) Robert E. Osgood has written perhaps the best extensive treatment of NATO: *NATO, the Entangling Alliance*, Chicago, University of Chicago Press, 1962. Stewart Alsop attempts to explain the Kennedy Administration's nuclear hypotheses in "Our New Strategy: the Alternatives to Total War," *Saturday Evening Post*, December 4, 1962, pp. 14–19. A thoughtful attack on the same hypotheses is launched by Michael Bower, "Nuclear Strategy of the Kennedy Administration," *Bulletin of the Atomic Scientists*, October 1962, pp. 34–42. Amidst the welter of American suggestions for how to "deal" with Gaullist ambitions, the present author has not concealed his preference for the line taken by, among a few, Malcolm Hoag. His "Nuclear Policy and French Intransigeance" appeared in *Foreign Affairs*, January 1963, pp. 286–299.

INDEX

A

Acheson, Dean, 264
Adenauer, Konrad, 309; and De Gaulle, 258, 284; and EEC, 258; on Franco-German relations, 259; on NATO, 258
Africa, 238, 239, 242; *see also individual countries*
Agate (missile), 194
Agricultural clubs in armed forces, 170
Agricultural machinery industry, 270
Ailleret, General Charles, 106, 134, 208, 216
Air, Ministerial Committee for, 214
Air Base Officers School, 176n.
Air defense, 233
Air force: budget, 187, 191; maneuvers, 231; missiles, 192, 194; political action, 121; role, 290; strength, 163, 164, 188
Air School, 175, 176n.
Air units in internal defense, 225
Aircraft carriers, 265
Aircraft industry, 213–15; planes and missiles, 192–94
Aircraft research budget, 187
Albord, Tony, 135, 174
Algeria, 53, 104, 291, 297; army behavior, 28–29, 212, 288; army mission, 26, 28–30, 46–48, 50, 87, 115, 222, 236, 288–90; army strength, 22, 46, 74–75, 87, 163; atomic testing, 196, 238–39; bases, 186, 237; concentration camps, 25, 158, 289; and De Gaulle, 1–2, 28, 33, 53, 73–75, 79, 82, 85, 91, 108, 177, 289, 292; and EEC, 312; focus of crisis, 1, 5, 79–80, 148; French civilians in, 26; French government and (general), 33, 76–77, 85, 94, 96, 289–91; independence, 74, 96; and OAS, 27, 96, 317–18; police, 80, 97; Provisional Government of, 27, 31–32, 57, 59, 96, 223, 237; referendum, 60, 126, 142, 156; refugees, 31, 39; *see also* Barricades Revolt; Evian-les-Bains agreement; Generals' Revolt; Moslems

Algerian Problem—French Solution, The, 57
Algerian War, 19; army aims, 3, 24, 29, 51, 68–69, 115; costs, 183, 185; end, 4, 31; importance, 53, 68–69, 115; nature, 23–24, 42–44, 46–48, 117, 288; tactics, 46–48; vested interests, 49–50
Algiers, 57, 75
Allard, General Jacques-Marie-Paul, 47, 53, 81
"Alliance vs. Organization," 249, 250–51, 307
Alouette (helicopter), 260
American investments in Europe, 269–70
Amnesties, 92, 100, 108–109, 119, 158
Anouil, Colonel Gilles, 213
Anti-tank weapons, 260
Appeals from special courts, lack of, 158
April 1961 Revolt, *see* Generals' Revolt
Arab League, 53
Argoud, Colonel Antoine, 30n., 85, 87, 159, 299
Armaments, Ministerial Committee for, 214
Armed forces, 295–96; agricultural clubs, 170; civilian relations, 67, 95 (*see also* Civil-military relations); foreign policy views, 7; modernization, 132, 213, 241; and police and gendarmerie, 226; strength, 120–21, 164, 165, 188; *see also* Conscription; Military schools; Officers
Armed Forces, Chief of Staff of the, 131, 134
Armed Forces, Minister of the, 131, 133, 167, 170
Armée (periodical), 189
Armée-Nation concept, 13–14, 29–30, 33
Armies (general), 65–66
Armored units, 188
Army: aims, 1–3; chain of command, 110–11, 115–16; failures, 2–3, 29–30, 69, 120, 288; missions, 2–3, 40, 190, 212, 221–25, 236–37, 240–43, 245, 250, 297; modernization, 135, 144, 185–86, 188, 190, 221; role, 162–63, 177, 213, 218, 241, 290, 296, 298; self view, 100, 108, 241, 288, 298; World War II effects, 14, 16–17, 44–45; *see also* Armed forces
Army–Youth Committee, 170, 172

Index 325

Grall, Xavier, 26n.
Grenoble speech (De Gaulle), 246
Grimond, 265
Gromier, François, 118
Gross national product, estimated, 186
Guadaloupe, 236
Guerrilla warfare, *see* Revolutionary war
Guiana, French, 236
Guillaumat, Pierre, 35, 84, 87, 88, 293; and nuclear force, 208; quoted, 184, 185, 222
Guillaume, Lieutenant Pierre-Jean-Marie, 107
Guillebon, General Jacques de, 84
Guinea, 239

H

Harkis, 31–32, 122, 150
Hawk (missile), 193–94
Héreil, Georges, 214
Héritier, Georges, 54n.
Herzog, Maurice, 167
Higher Council of Algeria, 100
Hirsch, Etienne, 255
Ho Chi-Minh, 116
Hogard, Commander, 48
Housing, 142
Hugo, General, 107

I

Illiteracy, 171
Immigration, 255
In-Amguel base, 236
Independent Party, 90, 126, 130, 136, 140; Algerian credits vote, 91; and Bidault, 95; censure votes, 92, 137; factions, 93; "OAS amendment," 92
Indochina War: and defense of France, 228; Dien Bien Phu, 23, 46, 182; effect on army, 19, 22–23, 45, 73, 79; as revolutionary war, 47, 116, 117, 288
Indonesia, 45
In-Ekker base, 237
Infantry strength, 188
"Inner Six," *see* European Economic Community
Institute of Advanced Studies of National Defense, 132
Interior, Ministry of the, 167, 230
IRBM (missile), 278

Isorni, Jacques, 70, 71–72, 99, 108; courtroom tactics, 153, 154
Israel, 54
Italy: European relations, 255, 261; military strength, 165, 194; United States relations, 271
Ivory Coast, 240

J

Jacquelot, Colonel, 85
Joint Congressional Atomic Energy Committee, 274
Jouhaud, General Edmond, 25, 74, 81, 107; Algerian future, 73, 81; assignments and duties, 25n., 88, 121; and De Gaulle, 84, 229; OAS role, 55–56, 78, 100, 119; trial and sentence, 56–57, 59, 70, 100, 155
Jourdain, 41
Joxe, Louis, 114
"Joy through strength," 3
Judiciary, 152, 154, 157, 160–61; *see also* Courts
Juin, Marshal Alphonse, 34, 35, 84, 99
Juries, 151–52
Justice, concepts of, 160

K

Kabylia, 75
Katanga, 148
Katz, General, 96
KC-135 (aircraft tanker), 273
Kennan, George, 228n.
Kennedy, President John F., 54, 276; on NATO forces, 279; nuclear proliferation views, 272, 275, 276
Kenya, 45
Khemisti, Mohammed, 238
Kissinger, Henry, 279, 280
Korea, 45
Krief, Claude, 234

L

Lacheroy, Colonel Charles, 48
Lacoste, Robert, 46, 77, 81
Lacoste Lareymondie, Alain de, 92–93, 191
Lagaillarde, Pierre, 85, 90, 98, 106, 109, 148; communications, 99, 121
La Gorce, Paul-Marie de, 156, 161